HISPANICISM AND EARLY US LITERATURE

HISPANICISM AND EARLY US LITERATURE

Spain, Mexico, Cuba, and the Origins of US National Identity

John C. Havard

The University of Alabama Press
Tuscaloosa

The University of Alabama Press
Tuscaloosa, Alabama 35487-0380
uapress.ua.edu

Typeface: Minion

Cover image: *The Cuban Melodrama* by Charles J. Taylor, chromolithograph, Keppler & Schwarzmann, 1896; Library of Congress, LC-DIG-ppmsca-28912
Cover design: David Nees

Library of Congress Cataloging-in-Publication Data

Names: Havard, John C., author.
Title: Hispanicism and early US literature : Spain, Mexico, Cuba, and the origins of US national identity / John C. Havard.
Description: Tuscaloosa : The University of Alabama Press, [2018] | Includes bibliographical references and index.
Identifiers: LCCN 2017038246| ISBN 9780817319779 (cloth) | ISBN 9780817391744 (e book)
Subjects: LCSH: American literature—Latin American influences. | American literature—Spanish influences. | National characteristics, American, in literature. | American literature—19th century—History and criticism. | American literature—18th century—History and criticism. | Latin America—In literature. | Spain—In literature.
Classification: LCC PS159.L38 H38 2018 | DDC 809/.897—dc23
LC record available at https://lccn.loc.gov/2017038246

Contents

Acknowledgments

I could not have completed this project without intellectual support from relatives, friends, and colleagues. Many teachers, first of all, deserve acknowledgment. During my time as a graduate student at the University of Rochester, John Michael, Ezra Tawil, Stephanie Li, Jeffrey Tucker, and the late and missed Frank Shuffelton played important roles in shaping my thinking. Jorge Camacho, Leon Jackson, and Paul Allen Miller at the University of South Carolina and Robert Coleman and Moira Amado-McCoy at the University of South Alabama also greatly influenced me.

My thinking has also benefited from conversations with friends and fellow scholars. Especially notable are Justin Coyne, Russell Sbriglia, Steve Lownes, Jennie Lightweis-Goff, Peter Zogas, Melanie Hernandez, Thomas Hallock, Donald E. Pease, Molly Winter, Bryce Condit, and Hilarie Lloyd.

My work was supported by a New Faculty Grant-in-Aid awarded by Auburn University at Montgomery. This grant enabled me to conduct archival research at the American Antiquarian Society, the Massachusetts Historical Society, and Antioch College's Antiochiana special collections. I am grateful for Auburn University at Montgomery's support, and to the repositories' staffs. Antiochiana's Scott Sanders was particularly helpful.

Earlier versions of chapters 3 and 4 were respectively published as "Ironizing Identity: Cosmopolitanism and Herman Melville's 'Benito Cereno' as Critique of Hispanicist Exceptionalism," *Literature Interpretation Theory* 25, no. 2 (2014): 128–50, and "Mary Peabody Mann's *Juanita*: US National Identity and Cuba," *Studies in the Novel* 44, no. 2 (2012): 144–63. I appreciate these journals' editorial staffs and reviewers for their constructive feedback. I shared parts of each chapter at conferences, and I am indebted to the informative comments I received. The University of Alabama Press's Wendi Schnaufer, the anonymous reviewers who evaluated the book manuscript, and copyeditor Dawn Hall played invaluable roles in shaping the project's final stages.

I lastly thank my family. My parents, Johnnie and Susan, encouraged me to pursue my passion for the advanced study of literature and history; I could not have achieved what I have in my career without their support. My wife, Katie, has had many engaging conversations with me about the book's subject matter, and her thoughtfulness has been a major source of inspiration during the arduous journey to bringing the book to fruition. My sons, Oliver and Theo, inspire me every day to do what I can as a scholar to make the world a better place.

HISPANICISM AND EARLY US LITERATURE

Introduction

In his posthumously published autobiography, the Harvard-based paleontologist, geologist, and slavery apologist Nathaniel Southgate Shaler reminiscences that one morning in the spring of 1861, he found his teacher, Louis Agassiz, weeping on Cambridge's Divinity Avenue. One of the world's foremost natural scientists, Agassiz was a faculty member in Harvard's Lawrence Scientific School, where Shaler was conducting studies. Shaler describes Agassiz as "greatly disturbed" and "almost raving in his misery." When Shaler asked what was wrong, Agassiz bawled, "They will Mexicanize the country" (Shaler 1909, 170). Agassiz had just learned that South Carolina had fired on Fort Sumter, and Shaler writes that Agassiz continued to be distraught for some time. At the root of his dismay were the forces he believed had sparked the Civil War: abolitionism and arguments for social equality between the races. Given his belief in immutable racial hierarchies, Agassiz held that emancipation and equality deviated from a naturally stratified order. Such deviation would result in racial intermixture. Consistent with the era's pseudoscientific, polygeneticist views (Johnson 1993, 210), Agassiz believed miscegenation resulted in degradation (Agassiz and Agassiz 1868, 139, 298). Emancipation thus portended dire biological and social ills—indeed, the end of what made the United States great. Encapsulating this failure for Agassiz was the fearful idea of a mestizo, "Mexicanized" United States (Menand 2000, 101–12).

This moment speaks to issues familiar to scholars of US literature,[1] culture, and history, such as antebellum Anglo-Saxonism and prejudice against African Americans. The story attests to how race and national identity were thought of interrelatedly in the period. For Agassiz, the concept of race was necessary to understand not only the races themselves but also the natures and destinies of nations.

However, the moment suggests aspects of this story of nationality that scholarly accounts have underemphasized. Scholars of race and nation in US culture have tended to focus on a white (Anglo-American), black (African American), and red (Native American) triad, but Agassiz is preoccupied by relations between Anglo-Americans and Mexicans. Second of all, it is easy to associate brash confidence with Anglo-Saxonist racialism. According to racialist myth, the Anglo-Saxon race "follows the sun" toward progress, displacing all in its wake. However, doubt pervades Shaler's account; Agassiz agonizes over whether the United States is immutably its Anglo-Saxon self or whether it can be "Mexicanized." Agassiz was chauvinistic, but his words bespeak fear more than arrogance. In exclaiming that abolition "will Mexicanize the country," Agassiz expresses worry that the United States will lose its distinctiveness by devolving into Mexico, a racial and national Other.

My book takes this moment as a point of departure. Reading the set of issues broached by the Agassiz episode against eighteenth- and nineteenth-century US literature set in, representing, or focusing on Spain and Spanish America, I ask a series of questions: Why, when confronted with the prospect of a racially mixed United States, did Agassiz resort to Mexico as his explanatory metaphor? How did US literary representations of Spain, Spanishness, Spanish America, and Spanish American-ness construct US national identity and imperial ideology? Why did these issues provoke uncertainty and fear in many US Americans?[2]

My study builds on work that suggests the salience of Spain and Spanish America to US culture and that thus argues for a transnational frame for US literature (e.g., Boggs 2007; Gruesz 2002; Jakšić 2007; Rodríguez 2010; Streeby 2002). I maintain that representations of Spain, Spanish America, Spanish-ness, and Spanish American-ness are integral to early US literature's evolution. Spain and Spanish America play a major role in all the era's literary genres, genres ranging from epic poems with multiple chapters focusing on the Spanish conquest of the Aztec and Incan civilizations, travelogues about Cuba, novellas about slave mutinies on Spanish slave ships off the South American coast, and antislavery novels criticizing Cuban slavery. These themes encompass both canonical and noncanonical traditions. I highlight both understudied texts that deserve greater attention and use discussion of such texts to reframe more familiar works. Our understanding of US literature is immeasurably enhanced when we recognize the formal and conceptual uses to which writers put representations of Hispanophone peoples. Abolitionist novelists, for instance, could enhance their oft-noted elicitation of sentimental engagement with the slave's plight by connecting slavery to Cuba and the Hispanophone world's association with gothic horror. Cuba was thus a natural choice of setting or point of reference for such novelists. Romantic historians were drawn to Spanish American histories in their effort to identify the United States' nation-defining historical moments.

These histories allowed them to consider both New World difference from Europe and the United States' difference from its New World neighbors.

In addition to exploring such aesthetic relationships, I also historicize the texts I analyze by pointing to how they reflected and shaped significant social and ideological concerns. Literature tells us much about such concerns. Benedict Anderson influentially suggested that in the eighteenth and nineteenth centuries, print culture—including literary print—not only reflected the content of the lived experience of many people but also shaped their "imagined communities." Consistent with this account, early US Americans consumed print culture that modeled ways to imagine their world. Literature figured in this print along with periodical, historical, scientific, and other writing. Whereas today the lines demarcating literary, historical, and scientific discourses may seem precise, this was not the case for early US readers (Horsman 1981, 159; Tawil 2006, 14). US Americans' fascination with Hispanophone peoples figured largely in this print culture.[3] Like other genres in which this fascination is observed, literature exploring the Hispanophone world contributed to public sphere debates and shaped US attitudes.

Hispanicism: Prehistory

These literary texts construct, reflect on, express uncertainty over, and contend with what I refer to as Hispanicism, a literary tradition that displays a US interest in producing knowledge about Hispanophone peoples. Ed White coined this usage of the term "Hispanicism" to refer to an antebellum literary interest in exotic Latin American locales that is analogous to Orientalism (White 2004, 77–78). "Hispanicism" is more conventionally used to refer to words borrowed from the Spanish language, much like "Gallicism" is used to refer to terms borrowed from French. My rationale for adopting White's usage despite the potential for misunderstanding inherent in repurposing the term will be explained when appropriate.

Hispanicism construes Hispanophone peoples as different from Anglo-Americans. Moreover, whereas Hispanicism reflects distinctions in Anglo-American attitudes toward peoples from different parts of the Hispanophone world, it also elides the geographical, ethnic, and racial heterogeneity of the peoples of Spain and Spanish America by focusing on purportedly shared characteristics. It constructs a static, simplistic narrative regarding the nature of Hispanophone peoples.[4]

Literary Hispanicism took many forms that depended on time period, author, and text. Some works exhibit a taste for Hispanic exoticness. Examples include Washington Irving's interest in Spain's Islamic heritage in *Tales of the Alhambra* and William H. Prescott's depiction of Aztec and Incan antiquity in his histories of the Mexican and Peruvian conquests. Such texts figure Hispanic difference as fascinatingly quaint.

Other Hispanicist texts are more explicitly Hispanophobic and focus on Hispanic moral failings. Such narratives owe a debt to the Black Legend of Spanish depravity. The term "Black Legend" was coined by Spanish journalist Julián Juderías, who in the early twentieth century used the term pejoratively to refer to what he criticized as questionable northern European historiographical attitudes toward Spain common since the early modern period. Popularized in the Anglophone world by the translation of Bartolomé de las Casas's *Brevísima relación de la destrución de las Indias* (1552, *A Brief Relation of the Destruction of the Indies*; translated for Anglophone audiences in 1583 as *The Spanish Colonie, or a Brief Chronicle of the Actes and Gestes of the Spaniards in the West Indies*), the Black Legend painted a picture of Spaniards as a violent, vengeful, morally "black" people. It emphasizes the conquistadors' violent colonization of the West Indies, Mexico, and Peru and Catholic religious authoritarianism, especially the Inquisition.[5]

These stock narratives were central to early US literature. However, they now took particular forms that spoke to the period's sociohistorical concerns. The colonial-era Black Legend focused on the Spanish empire's cruelty and avarice. De las Casas's history spawned accounts of Spanish brutality against Amerindians. The gothic tales of the Inquisition tend to linger, similarly, on Spanish delight in torture and on how Catholicism is a duplicitous religious hierarchy that uses a spectacular, form-based faith as a smoke screen for bloodthirsty authoritarianism. These narratives performed an ideological function in the Anglophone colonial world. Early modern Spain and England vied for colonial preeminence in the Western Hemisphere. For Anglophone peoples working for this superiority, the Black Legend provided moral legitimacy. By representing colonial cruelty and avarice as special characteristics of Spanish colonialism, the English convinced themselves of the contrasting innocence of English colonialism. Relatedly, in this era of religious reform, the Black Legend provided a means for glorifying the Protestant Reformation flourishing in northern Europe.

Hispanicism: Race and Lethargy

How did the US version of the Black Legend compare to the original? In a study regarding interest in Spain among antebellum US intellectuals, Iván Jakšić explains that early US Americans continued to perceive Spain in terms of martial temperament and religious fanaticism (Jakšić 2007, 2). Yet there were two key differences. First of all, race became more important, especially in the antebellum period. Although colonial US Americans operated with a conception of cultural difference, they only had a rudimentary understanding of that difference as racially and biologically determined. Even when race played a role in their writing, the understanding of race they worked with was foggy. This remained true in the early United States. In the late eighteenth century, Anglo-Americans perceived a hierarchy among the world's peoples, but these Anglo-Americans generally ascribed that hierarchy to environmental, historical, and cultural factors. They thought all peoples shared a common human ability to improve morally and intellectually through education (Horsman 1981, 46).

By the antebellum years, though, a new pseudoscientific racialism that "proved" that innate racial differences were traceable to phenotype had attained support. Anglo-Americans discarded monogenetic, environmentalist conceptions of race (that is, everyone descended from Adam and difference is a product of environment) and adopted polygenism (the races had distinct origins). These Anglo-Americans viewed their "power, progress, governmental stability, and freedom"—their success in establishing liberal governmental institutions and achieving economic prosperity—as unique racial endowments, with less fortunate peoples with undesirable characteristics doomed to destruction or servitude (Horsman 1981, 43). US Americans, Reginald Horsman explains, "had long believed they were a chosen people, but by the mid-nineteenth century they also believed that they were a chosen people with an impeccable ancestry" (5). In adopting such beliefs, antebellum Anglo-Americans grafted previously existing discourses about the Germanic love for liberty onto emerging pseudoscientific theories about innate differences among peoples (185).

US American attitudes toward Hispanophone peoples reflect this trajectory not only in the case of indigenous, African, or mixed-race but also Caucasian Hispanophone peoples. Early national US Americans believed that tropical and semitropical Hispanophone climates negatively affected local populations. However, Hispanicist prejudices among these US Americans were often balanced by hope that Hispanophone peoples could improve. In the antebellum period, this hope waned. Although antebellum Anglo-Americans viewed Caucasian Spaniards as white like themselves, that identification persisted only to a point.[6] During this time, Anglo-American observers became more concerned with Spain's large Celtic and Jewish populations, its history of Muslim rule, and its frequent commerce with Africa. US Americans began to view this population as only ambivalently white and racially inferior despite its European origins (Bradley 2010, 25; DeGuzmán 2005, esp. xxiv, xxvii). They moreover became increasingly appalled by perceived creole intermixture with the Native American and African inhabitants of the Americas (e.g., Horsman 1981, 212, 216). Their writings foreground physical, phenotypic descriptions of Hispanic difference.

This pattern can be observed in many textual traditions, such as the geography textbooks that were instrumental in popularizing US attitudes toward race and ethnicity.[7] Jedidiah Morse's 1789 staple *American Geography* exemplifies the eighteenth-century view. This work contains long, condescending descriptions of national cultures that are typical of the era's geography texts. Yet although Morse sought "to impress the minds of American Youth with an idea of the superior importance of their own country, as well as to attach them to its interests" (Morse 1789, vii), his hierarchies are not racial. For instance, whereas a description of Native American phenotypical characteristics (17) reflects nascent racialism, Morse concludes this discussion with the environmentalist claim that perceived native inferiority "is not to be ascribed to any defect in their natural genius, but to their state of society, which affords few objects for the display either of their literary or political abilities" (18). Morse's statement that "religion, although its tendency is to unite people in those things that are essential to happiness, occasions wide differences as to manners, customs, and even character" (291–92) is similarly environmentalist. Morse's depiction of Spain follows suit. Morse appraises Spain negatively, but he ascribes Spanish religious intolerance and aversion to commerce not to race but to an oppressive religious and political climate, especially pervasive clerical interference in governance (495–96).

Thomas Smiley's 1839 *Encyclopædia of Geography*, a classroom adaptation of Murray's popular geography, exhibits racialist views. Smiley opens with a section (Smiley 1839, 36–37) explaining the "wealth, political union, social, intellectual, and moral condition" (6) of the world's peoples via phenotype. Although "the Caucasian race has given birth to the most civilized nations, both in ancient and modern times, and every age witnesses a progressive and surprising advance in all those qualities which indicate intellectual endowment," other races are less developed (36). Like environmentalists, he states that "the *religion* professed by any people is also an important feature in their social condition" (40). Race, though, is his chief determinant, with other differences such as religion being a product of race. In his depiction of Spain, Smiley expresses the Anglo fascination with Spain as exotic, but continues, "In respect to industry and wealth, with every opportunity [given natural resources] of becoming the foremost nation in Europe, Spain is the poorest and most uncultivated" (162). Given Smiley's insistence on race's influence, that Spaniards are not sufficiently industrious to live up to European standards owes to their being ambivalently Caucasian.

Not all early national depictions reflect nonracialist attitudes toward Spaniards, nor do all antebellum texts reflect racialist ones. For instance, the nations-of-the-world chapbook *Peep at the Various Nations of the World* exhibits a preantebellum sensibility (Anonymous 1831). During the antebellum period racialism became more common, environmentalism less.

Before consensus on race emerged, US Americans were less likely to see immutable differences between themselves and other peoples. Many took pride in US American accomplishments, but many also hoped other peoples would achieve similar successes (Horsman 1981, 85, 300). This was true of attitudes toward Hispanophone peoples. During the Napoleonic wars, US Americans often sympathized with besieged Spain. At an 1809 Boston banquet honoring Spanish patriotism that was attended by luminaries such as Paul Revere, the speakers praised the republican self-sacrifice of noble Spaniards who sought to preserve their national culture against French influence. Although US Americans often felt Spain's martial history exhibited Spanish bloodthirst, here that history represents will to liberty. Resistance to Napoleon replayed the medieval wars with Muslim occupiers. The banquet celebrated Spaniards as fellow travelers of the US Americans who a generation prior had liberated themselves from European empire (Anonymous 1809). Facilitating the era's fraternal demonstrations were historical coincidences, including not only perceived similarities between US and Spanish resistance to empire but also Anglo-American admiration of the Cádiz Cortes's 1812 experimentation with a liberal constitution. The absence of more rigid understandings of racial difference also made friendly sentiment possible. The racialization of Hispanophone peoples in ensuing decades would make similar sentiments less likely.

Moreover, despite racialist pseudoscience's push to categorize peoples, antebellum US Americans increasingly homogenized Hispanophone peoples—a profoundly diverse population—into a single type. For instance, although they knew of Mexico's racial diversity (Smiley 1839, 118), US Americans frequently used the term "Mexican" to refer to people with peculiarly Hispanic racial characteristics, thus leveling differences within the nation. John A. Perry's popular 1853 account of his travels through Mexico, which spread nativist views (Larkin 2013), collapses distinctions in this sense. Perry observes that Mexicans "vary much in their color, from a very dark to almost white. This is owing to the amalgamation of the Castilian with the native Mexican" (Perry 1853, 28). Perry recognizes Mexican racial variety but not human diversity. For Perry, Mexico is not a nation of many peoples; rather, a "Mexican" is a representative of a nation defined by degrading intermixture. Perry presents "Hispanic" weaknesses such as susceptibility to "priestcraft" and "kingcraft" and physical and intellectual sloth in this racial light (38, 40).

Anglo-Americans did acknowledge differences, including racial ones, among Hispanophone peoples. They ascribed peninsular Spanish racial inferiority to the corruption of Germanic elements by intermixture with Celtic, Jewish, and North African elements. Creoles, they commonly believed, exhibited exaggerated manifestations of Hispanic deficiency due to reasons that depended on context. Given proximity, the Spanish American regions of most interest to Anglo-Americans were the Caribbean, Mexico, and Central America (Johnson 1993, 27). The Mexican and Central American population, they believed, had been degraded by a long history of intermixture between Spaniards, Native American, and, to a lesser extent, Africans, such that a pure-blooded Castilian Mexican was perceived as rare by the nineteenth century (Horsman 1981, 210, 212, 216; Pike 1992, 147–48). The products of racial amalgamations, according to prevailing views, exhibited intensifications of the constituent parts' worst aspects but displayed none of those parts' best traits (Johnson 1993, 10, 14–15, 210; Pike 1992, 144–45). Indian bravery and eloquence and Spanish chivalry were lost, whereas Indian improvidence, cruelty, and stupidity and Spanish decadence, cruelty, and superstition synergistically combined. Due to their own history of removing rather than assimilating the North American Indians, Anglo-Americans found it difficult to fathom Spain's much different experience in Mexico and Central America. During the conflicts with Mexico in the 1830s–1840s, US Americans were so preoccupied with defining themselves as an unadulterated race by contrast to Mexicans that they began using the term "Anglo-American" in the racial sense we know today to signify their difference (Horsman 1981, 208–9).

Anglo-Americans viewed the slaveholding Caribbean and especially Cuba as somewhat more racially stratified. However, many, especially nonslaveholding Northerners who condemned similarities between the US South and the Hispanophone slaveholding world (e.g., Abbott 1860, 320, 340), viewed Cuba suspiciously because of its many Afro-Hispanics. Moreover, they thought that reliance on slave labor enervated the creoles, making them even more lazy and passionate than might be expected of peninsular Spaniards (Pike 1992, 141, 150). They thought that amalgamation was less common here than in Mexico, and they found incorporation of Africans somewhat easier to understand than that of Native Americans given the presence of blacks in the United States. There remained, though, all too many mulattoes who, like mestizos, exhibited the two races' worst rather than the best. In the Caribbean, Mexico, and Central America, creoles exhibited a prevailing tendency toward miscegenation, which corrupted Spanish America as a whole (Pike 1992, 147, 149). I will have occasion often in this book to refer to differences in US American attitudes toward specific Hispanophone peoples such as those I have identified here in views about Cuba, Mexico, and Central America. These views reflect important elements of US racialist attitudes toward Hispanophone peoples, elements that found *mestizaje* unfathomable and that upheld hierarchical distinctions.

Although US Americans frequently noted such differences, it remains true that Hispanicism exhibited overarching features: Hispanophone peoples exhibit peculiarly Hispanic deficiencies rooted in the Spanish character as it was illustrated by the Black Legend, and those deficiencies are products in varying ways of racial inferiority. Why did US Americans inconsistently focus on overarching type but sometimes acknowledge variance? Emphasizing sameness rather than difference in construing Hispanic deficiency made it easier for Anglo-Americans to understand Hispanophone peoples in terms of new, peculiarly nineteenth-century value systems.

These systems become apparent when, upon leaving, Perry "cheerfully bid adieu to Mexico, with her bigotry, superstition, priestcraft and degradation, hoping the Americans will pity them and take the country and civilize and moralize the people" (Perry 1853, 69). As this passage illustrates, a second key difference between the early modern Black Legend and US Hispanicism resides in what US Americans understood the negative qualities of Hispanophone peoples to be. Late eighteenth- and nineteenth-century US Americans continued to claim that Spaniards and Spanish Americans exhibited tendencies toward immorality, but these US Americans did not so much emphasize wanton cruelty and avarice as laziness, inefficiency, and deceitfulness. Moreover, they focused on Hispanophone peoples' place outside history and modernity. When one reads US literary works set in Hispanophone locales or browses through articles about Spain and Spanish America published in US periodicals, one is not so much confronted with images of gothic, irrepressible evil as with evolutionary rejects. Weighed down by an inherited torpor, one bred, for instance, from long-standing religious superstition and reliance on slave labor in the New World, Hispanophone peoples are unable to compete with the powerful forces of a quickly progressing world.

This shift in focus reflects, to an extent, US Americans' perceptions of shifting geopolitical power relations. Whereas for the colonial Anglophone observer Spain was a force to reckon with, for the United States the case was different. By 1776 Spain was thought to have begun a decline in geopolitical influence, a decline that would be epitomized in US Americans' minds by Spain's loss of most of its colonies by the antebellum period. Those former colonies, moreover, were now understood as highly unstable nations, frequently written off as unproductive anarchies and "banana republics." (Like "Black Legend," "banana republic" is of recent coinage even though the idea has a long history. Its first usage occurs in O. Henry's *Cabbages and Kings*, and its origins are tied to complications resultant from US banana companies' activities in Latin America.) The Black Legend's evolving character speaks to these responses to relations between nations. Yet those responses do not tell the whole story.

Hispanicism and US National Identity

Anglo-Americans' consistent fixation on racially inherited lethargy among Hispanic types must be seen in terms of US national identity construction. When confronting a widespread interest in a cultural Other, one is dealing with something ingrained in a collective consciousness, something that says as much about the observer as it does about the observed. When referring to Hispanophobic aversion or to romanticization, I use the term "Hispanicism" to connote self-reflexivity. "Hispanicism" invokes two more familiar terms, Edward Said's "Orientalism" and Toni Morrison's "Africanism." Said's *Orientalism* revealed the role European studies of the Orient played in the construction of Western modernity. These purportedly objective studies provided an Oriental counterimage against which Europeans defined themselves, an image that in turn offered a rationale for European imperialism in the Middle and Far East. Morrison's "Unspeakable Things Unspoken" and *Playing in the Dark* explored how US literature's white, male canonical authors differentially understood US national identity against an abject Africanist presence that haunts US literature. In her view, Africanist figures signified for these canonical writers everything US identity was not. This line of inquiry has also been taken up in many studies exploring US representations of Native Americans, such as Roy Harvey Pearce's *Savagism and Civilization*.

The analogy between what I am describing and Morrison's Africanist presence and especially Said's Orientalism explains why I chose the term "Hispanicism." Using "Hispanicism" as I am risks misunderstanding given that the term conventionally refers to words borrowed from Spanish. It is also phonetically similar to and thus easy to confuse with "Hispanism," which refers to studying Hispanic culture in an organic framework and to that framework's conservative tendencies. That said, the analogy between Hispanicism as a literary and intellectual tradition of commenting upon differences between Anglo-Americans and Hispanophone peoples and Orientalism as a tradition of analyzing differences between Europe and the Middle East illustrates a crucial aspect of my study: the idea that Hispanicism is a way for Anglo-Americans to homogenize a diverse group of people as the Other to elaborate an opposition between themselves and those people that illustrates cherished self-conceptions. "Hispanicism" captures this analogy even better than "Hispanicist presence," which would more clearly echo Morrison. Although I make important analogies between Hispanicism and what

Morrison describes, she is focused on elaborating an unspoken, haunting presence in US literature. Said discusses a conventional, institutionalized European literary and scholarly discourse that is closer in form to what I am analyzing.

Said and Morrison point toward the evidence literature provides for the role difference plays in the construction of nationality. Providing a theoretical underpinning for such views, Anne Norton argues that narratives of national identity rely on the representation of peoples whose place within the nation is ambiguous (Norton 1988, 57). Such representations stage the limits between national inclusion, exclusion, and self-definition (4). Norton not only confirms but also gestures toward a blind spot in much race-nation scholarship. Whereas Norton calls for looking broadly at the boundaries of and outside the nation for the Others against which the nation defines itself, scholars interested in US race-nation issues have tended to fixate on relations among Anglo-, African, and Native Americans. Even studies that treat this red-black dyad in innovative ways typically follow this assumption (e.g., Tawil 2006, 5). This focus follows from the fact that scholars traditionally viewed US literature in terms of what occurred within the nation's borders. The academic discipline of American studies has thus historically devalued literary works that treat extranational concerns. When the discipline has focused on such works, it has subsumed these concerns under more national ones. For instance, scholarship construing the pre–Louisiana Purchase and pre–Mexican Cession western frontier as a national space obscures how that territory was not inevitably destined to be part of the United States. This tendency is reflected in the claim that the expropriation of Native lands is a form of "internal colonialism" rather than the invasion of an extranational space (Streeby 2002, 9–10). As I discuss in chapter 3, this phenomenon is also observed in studies of Herman Melville's "Benito Cereno." Melville's classic takes seriously the slave trade's international dimensions and the United States' relationship with Spain and Spanish America. However, scholars traditionally reduced its treatment of such matters to internal concerns such as US debates regarding slavery.

In recent decades, scholars have taken the tendency to ignore extranational contexts to task. Such scholars have provided various explanations for American studies' national focus, among them area studies' disciplinary tunnel vision. More fundamentally, these scholars have argued that the national focus involves a willful blindness to the nation's long-standing involvement in nationalist chauvinism and imperialism, an involvement that must be acknowledged, studied, and understood to be undermined (e.g., Fishkin 2005, 21). These critics have asked us to resist conventional habits of thought by taking seriously US literature's transnational dimensions. We can do this, they argue, by studying how that literature engages with or was produced on the nation's margins and thus expanding our understanding of what should be considered significant "American" literature (e.g., Saldívar 2000). The transnational turn inspired by this work may be the discipline's most significant recent paradigm shift.

This shift need not mean the end of the nation as a topic of inquiry, though. The nation remains a primary concern of the texts, cultures, and historical periods we investigate. The transnational turn may even facilitate a dynamic reconsideration of the nation (Levander and Levine 2008, 9). What does nationality mean, once we recognize that the concept is a discursive construct that obfuscates relationships and connections that exceed the nation-state's boundaries? This question has yet to be answered satisfactorily, perhaps because Americanists drawn to the conventional question of how writers have conceptualized the United States as a national entity have been left unprepared by the inadequate language training required in most English doctoral programs to pursue transnational work in multiple linguistic traditions. There are, of course, Americanists with unique language skills who are prepared to do such work. Many of them have focused on the necessary work of excavating forgotten, marginalized literary communities and thus expanding our definition of US literature by revealing that it is transnational in character (e.g., Coronado 2013; Gruesz 2002). Such efforts have left relatively brief space for illustrating how our new understandings of this transnational character can lead to novel insights regarding how US writers have conceptualized the nation.

Ed White provides a model for doing such work, one that coheres with Norton's position on difference and the relationship between the extranational and the national. White revised the work of Benedict Anderson, whose concept of "imagined community" remains the urtext for understanding the construction of nation. Americanists have found very attractive Anderson's "creole pioneers" thesis that nationalism was inspired by creole functionaries who developed identification with their colonial administrative circuits rather than the metropole and creole printers who propagated the functionaries' understanding of community to the general populace (Anderson 1991, 47–48, 51, 55–57, 61); the thesis places nationalism's origins in the Americas. White points out, though, that despite Anderson's ubiquity in discussions of nation in US literature and culture, the field has not rigorously scrutinized his claims. White claims that Anderson's theories, and especially the "creole pioneers" thesis, contain many flaws. In particular, the functionary as Anderson describes him only existed in Latin but not North America, and the printer was more present in North than Latin America and is based on a misleading caricature of Benjamin Franklin (White 2004,

57, 59). Despite these errors, White demonstrates that Anderson's emphasis on the experiential, phenomenological, and textual aspects of imagining the nation still compel attention. White suggests that it may be possible to retain this emphasis while addressing the flaws in Anderson's argument. His revision focuses on Anderson's point that the concepts of bound and unbound seriality determine one's relationship to nationality. Bound seriality, Anderson argues, refers to a sense of belonging to a particular part of a series. "There is a second, *unbound* seriality," though, "whereby it is imagined that certain categories are universal and applicable to zones outside of the bound totality" (61). Unbound seriality refers, in other words, to a mode of understanding one's nation as part of a series of nations—that is, to recognizing the universality of community.

White confirms this Andersonian premise. However, having dismissed the "creole pioneers" thesis, he claims that the historical rise of bound seriality in the United States did not occur as Anderson describes. Rather, in revising Anderson's thesis, White claims that "in reconstructing the origins of the national series, we need to locate the dominant and influential forms of seriality. . . . We then need to determine which of these series have a crucial link with the emergence of the nation and with the nation concept itself. . . . [To do so,] we must examine other [i.e., external] collectives at work in the construction of the national series" (White 2004, 63–64). For White, the "creole pioneers" thesis—among its other failings—relies on an organic conception of nation that overfocuses on what appears internal to the nation. White suggests that understanding the nation requires considering its place within external contexts, as he asks that we look to the imperial ethnographies of Native America and schemes for land speculation—texts White refers to as imperiographies—of writers such as Cadwallader Colden (64, 67, 69). White argues that the sensibility expressed in these prerevolutionary documents persists in the early national period. This sensibility of an only rudimentarily national imagined community resembles not a particular, self-contained entity but, rather, a fluid empire consisting of thirteen states bordering numerous Indian nations. Such texts do exhibit an emergent fixation on national difference, often articulated to protoracial understandings of identity. White claims that by the 1820s, though, a markedly greater sense of bound nationhood had begun to appear in US culture, a sense of the United States as unique vis-à-vis external peoples. To understand this shift, White asks that we "map [this] transition from the imperial imagined community of unbound serial 'nations' to the insistence upon the bound unified and singular nation, with some appreciation of the stages of this process" (76). Such work can be done, he argues, by remembering Anderson's equation between print culture and ways of imagining community, an equation that posits that the proliferation of print made new understandings of community possible by the 1820s and 1830s.

An increasing fascination with Spanish-ness—the Hispanicism I am discussing—is a key element in this story, as White hints in his closing remarks (White 2004, 77–78). The literary record indicates an increasing such fascination during the period White identifies as pivotal to the rise of national identity. Anglo-American concern with Spain and Spanish-ness goes back to the nation's very roots, indeed predating the revolutionary period, but it became increasingly significant as the nineteenth century progressed. This is an extranational fascination; although increased immigration in recent decades has made US American interest in Hispanics an increasingly domestic concern, such interest has only been figured in domestic terms in a few of the nation's regions for most of US history. This extranational fixation occurred concurrently with the emergence, mentioned before, of racial science and essentialist conceptions of race, which replaced less blood-based Enlightenment views. Taken together, increased focus on Spanish-ness and race constitute the emergence of Hispanicism. Read according to the terms provided by Norton and White, Hispanicism provided US Americans with the reflexive grounds necessary to constitute nationality. Jakšić argues that antebellum scholarly fascination with Spain exhibits a concern with defining US nationality by learning national lessons from Spain's failure (Jakšić 2007, 1–3, 6).[8] I am claiming, even more fundamentally, that US nationality is unthinkable without reference to literary Hispanicism.

US National Identity and Liberalism

What did US Americans get out of their self-reflexive fixation on the Hispanophone world? Whereas Hispanicism worked hand in hand with other racial discourses to contribute to national identity formation, its conjoined focus on race and lethargy did so in a particular manner. Providing an entryway into understanding this manner is María DeGuzmán's work on the Black Legend in US culture. DeGuzmán charts the representation of Spanish figures in a series of canonical works of US literature and visual arts, positing that in the Anglo-American cultural imaginary, Spain served as an "off-white" figure against which Anglo-Americans reflexively understood themselves (DeGuzmán 2005, xxvii). Nineteenth-century Anglo-Americans inherited the Black Legend, racialized it, and put it to work to abet the construction of an Aryan discourse conflating American-ness with Anglo-American racial identity (xxiv, xxviii). This discourse was deployed by imperialists, DeGuzmán writes, through the "construction of Anglo-American empire as an antiempire, innocent of the barbarities of the Spanish Empire" (xxv). Through contrast to a Spanish foil figure, Anglo-American expansionists presented their territorial projects as something more acceptable to their liberal sensibilities than the matter of self-interest they might just as easily have been taken to be.

The political dimensions of Hispanicism must be emphasized here. US American liberals who wished to open constrained Spanish American economies particularly found Hispanicism appealing and deployed it to argue for their aims. I do not use the term "liberal," here, in reference to its contemporary association with the welfare state, unionization, and identity politics. Rather, I use it in the classical sense, in reference to opposition to aristocracy, support for understanding government as being based on a social contract, faith in the rational subject, defense of natural rights, defense of private property and market values, and support of other concepts of Lockean political economy. Hispanicism's rise in prominence occurred concurrently with the growing hegemony of liberal ideas regarding politics, representation, and economics in the United States. This hegemony informed emergent conceptions of national identity. The terms of US political culture over the late eighteenth and, increasingly, the early nineteenth century shifted from centering on republicanism and its insular devotion to communitarian virtues to liberalism and its expansive, individualistic, and market-based ideals (Coronado 2013, 114; Pocock 2003, 523). The shift from viewing the Spanish and Spanish Americans as a bloodthirsty, violent people to one that was lethargic, inefficient, authoritarian, and incapable of rational self-government should be seen in light of these increasingly liberal views. Representing Hispanophone peoples as being averse to the enterprising, acquisitive spirit thought to be essential to the liberal state's success provided the perfect manner through which US Americans could think of themselves as a people especially devoted to liberalism's possibilities.

Hispanicism, in this sense, is a racial discourse especially invested in imagining the United States' political orientation as an ideal and in construing that foundational orientation as a unique racial capacity of the nation's Anglo-Saxon people. This political dimension differentiates Hispanicism from Africanism and other US racial discourses. A major aspect of US Anglo-Saxonism was the idea that Anglo-Americans were racially fitted for liberal-democratic self-government. Hispanicism had a special role in this discourse. Africanism, by contrast, was less invested in constructing whiteness as underpinning the capacity to establish liberal institutions than it was in constructing whiteness as a prerequisite for freedom and agency (Morrison 1993, 44). When Africanist discourses represented black figures as lacking reason, individuality, as without voice, and, thus, as peculiarly fitted for servitude, it construed the Anglo-American observer as a rational individual with voice who was prepared for mastery (Doyle 2008, 3, 6; Morrison 1993, 5, 38, 55, 57). Hispanicism functions to similar effect; certainly, exhibiting

Anglo-Americans as possessing a great capacity for agency is a basic aspect of the discourse. However, Hispanicism has a more political import. Hispanicism focuses on Hispanic lethargy and devotion to autarkical economic forms to construct US Americans as an entrepreneurial people whose devotion to individual acquisition fits them for success in a market-based society. Moreover, Hispanicism represents a Hispanic tendency toward authoritarian political forms to demonstrate a contrasting US devotion to procedural (that is, nonarbitrary), representative government. What Anglo-Americans got out of Africanism can be thought of as groundwork for the more particularly political cultural work done by Hispanicism, as certainly agency and freedom are prerequisites for individualism, entrepreneurialism, and market rationality. Hispanicism specifically, though, points up the ideal character of US liberal institutions and US Americans' peculiar capacity to thrive under them. In sum, Africanism constructed Anglo-Americans as capable of political self-organization, whereas Hispanicism constructed Anglo-Americans as capable of liberal political self-organization.

DeGuzmán's description of US Americans' understanding of the Spanish as an "off-white" people is useful here, as this description highlights the racial aspect of the ambivalent role Spaniards and Spanish Americans played in the Anglo-American imaginary. This ambivalence is central to the discursive function such peoples played vis-à-vis US Americans' perception that the United States is a liberal nation. Although the African served as an absolute Other in early national and especially antebellum US American culture, the Spaniard or Spanish American played a more liminal role: Hispanophone peoples were both western and nonwestern, white and nonwhite, civilized and antipathetic toward modernity. Dominant stereotypes of Africans suggested they are not western, not white, and are incapable of civilization. Africanism's absolute differentiation points toward its role in discourses that posit a diffuse sense of Anglo-American agency and freedom; by contrast, I argue, Hispanicism's suggestion of liminality facilitated a more specific yet similarly fundamental and significant cultural work, that of producing a conception of the United States as a particularly liberal nation. US national identity formation required a national Other that posed a sufficient likeness in terms of governmental organization to serve as a proving ground against which to illustrate the defining qualities of US dedication to liberal values. Whereas the Africanist Other could only go so far because Anglo-Americans viewed blacks as incapable of maintaining complex governmental institutions, histories and narratives of Spanish and Spanish American imperial and national mismanagement broached governmental and institutional questions. Hispanicist representations of all sorts focus on such issues, and their most special significance must be viewed in this light.

Norton is again helpful here. She argues that identity construction requires liminal or border figures, representations that are both like and unlike the self (Norton 1988, 53). "Liminars" (Norton's term for border figures) take shape via representation and narrative. When confronted with difference between itself and its Other, the self resorts to a third term, the representation of the limit figure. By reflecting on likeness and difference while comparing itself to this figure, the self abstracts a self-idealization. The process requires that the self determine the limits of likeness by considering where exclusion begins (54). Norton emphasizes that these practices occur not only on interpersonal but also on communal levels. Liminars constitute collective narratives of identity and difference that are repeated via narrative formation. As writers such as Homi Bhabha (2004) have illustrated, these narratives provide models through which collective identity—nationality, significantly—is constituted and institutionalized. The Hispanic Other is such a border figure, and the narratives analyzed in this study are a communally sanctioned collection of stories that constitute a discourse of national identity.

In this respect, liberalism in US culture is not simply a doctrine of universal rights and political goods. Rather, liberalism is a historically conditioned discourse with a deep relationship to identity. This may not be immediately clear due to current perceptions of the significance of the term "liberalism" and historical distance from the early national and antebellum periods. Because we inherit the liberal revolutions of the various progressive agendas of the nineteenth and twentieth centuries, such as the abolition of slavery and labor and civil rights reform, it is customary to think of liberalism as being opposed to reactionary appeals to deny rights according to national, racial, class, or gender identity. These appeals, one might say, comprise failures to fulfill the Enlightenment's promise by neglecting to acknowledge the Rights of Man. Such claims offer transformative rhetorical power in contemporary sociopolitical contexts. In the early United States, liberalism was frequently articulated to identity discourses. Racialism may conflict with contemporary understandings of the Rights of Man, but in the antebellum period the question of who belonged in the category "man" was fiercely debated (Riss 2006, 2). Failure to acknowledge this point entails a presentist fallacy, as doing so applies our contemporary consensus that liberalism promises liberty to all identities to a context for which that conception usually did not hold. For many early national and antebellum whites, it seemed obvious that the capacity to establish liberal institutions was a specifically Anglo-American faculty. Liberalism and racialism were not at odds for these US Americans. They were related part and parcel, and this book explores the Hispanicist dimensions of this relation.

US liberal national identity construction has a material context I explore:

US imperialism. It is no coincidence that US representations of Hispanic difference focus on what is construed as the metaphysical aversion to liberty of the Spanish and their New World descendants in a period in which US expansionists turned their eyes toward Spanish Louisiana, Mexico, the Caribbean, and Central America (Horsman 1981, 5, 300; Nelson 1993, 7). Granted, it is easy to overstress the popularity of imperial ventures into Spanish America in the early national and antebellum periods. Constituencies within the nation variously worried that imperialism portended the addition of slave states, the normalization of corruptive despotic policies that contradicted the nation's origins, the incorporation of racially impure peoples who were incapable of acclimating to the United States' free institutions, and diversion of valuable resources for purposes of conquering and maintaining foreign territories that could be better used in other ways (Streeby 2002, 9; Jakšić 2007, 2–3). As seen in the US-Mexican War, for instance, many were prepared to explain away such concerns. Their explanations would flower as the century progressed. They attained their greatest appeal in 1898 and its aftermath, when imperialist theories such as Theodore Roosevelt's corollary to the Monroe Doctrine posited that the United States had the duty to interfere in Latin American activities that undermined US interests. This doctrine resulted in more active US imperialism in the form of involvement in Cuban affairs after the Spanish-American War, US intervention in Panamanian-Columbian conflict to ensure a propitious Panama Canal agreement, and other military ventures in Latin America. These pursuits came complete with cultural defenses such as formalized depictions of Latin American republics as either dependent women or unruly children. These representations were intended to support the idea that these nations needed US chivalric protection and paternal guidance (Johnson 1993, 73, 116–19). Earlier manifestations of Hispanicism abetted these ventures by providing a rudimentary ideological rationale for imperialism. Hispanicism's cultural work was necessary in a nation with conflicting commitments to both liberalism and imperialism. To deny to imperial targets the self-determination that US Americans valorized in their national mythologies, imperialists had to racialize liberty. They did so by denying the capacity for self-determination to Spaniards and Spanish Americans and suggesting that capacity to have reached its peak potential in Anglo-Americans. Only then could those championing imperialism in the Hispanophone Americas imagine their projects' ethical viability, doing so by arguing that those regions needed the United States' protection to establish the liberal-democratic institutions necessary for their peoples' moral and material progress.

The liminal view of Hispanic identity played a key role in Hispanicism's imperialist dimensions. Ambivalently white, the progenitor of a once strong but now dilapidated empire, the Hispanic Other functioned as a foil for early US imperialists. Against this foil, they construed their exceptional capacity to establish progressive, liberal-democratic institutions that would improve upon Spain's despotic example. Expansionists became intent on constructing a benevolent empire that would prove better than the Spanish empire that had deteriorated into the unstable Spanish American republics.

The concept of race facilitated framing Hispanophone peoples in Hispanicist terms by enabling the argument that all such peoples exhibited essential Hispanic racial deficiencies, with those deficiencies being modulated in different ways depending on particular nations' racial compositions. Eighteenth-century US expansionists had deployed anti-Spanish prejudices in arguments for US expansion into Spanish Louisiana. As imperialists eyed Cuba, Mexico, and other Hispanophone locales during the age of Manifest Destiny, they found it expedient to argue that dispossessed peoples were racially incapacitated for self-government and would benefit from US direction.

The central role Hispanicist narratives played in the cultures of early US imperialism has been underappreciated. Although recent interventions by Shelley Streeby (2002) and Jaime Javier Rodríguez (2010) and an older one by Robert W. Johanssen (1985) have challenged this state of affairs, scholarship on antebellum expansionist culture has traditionally fixated on the depiction and dispossession of Native Americans despite the obvious example of the US-Mexican War. This fixation reflects how, as Rodríguez observes, "the U.S.-Mexican War remains largely, and infamously, unknown by most citizens of the United States" (Rodríguez 2010, 1). Scholarship repeats Anglo-American popular culture's denial of the presence of another nation's legitimate claims to sovereignty on the southwestern frontier. Motivating this failure of recognition is the fact that the war gives the lie to cherished self-perceptions of the United States as an unequivocally benevolent agent in hemispheric history (129). Given the United States' questionable means and motivations for entering the war, historical amnesia conveniently massages the national conscience (Van Wagenen 2012, 6). Instead of acknowledging this dubious moment and other, even less discussed, earlier examples of expansionism such as early national interest in Spanish Louisiana (which I discuss in chapter 1), most US discussion of imperialism in the Hispanophone world begins and sometimes even ends with 1898. This is certainly a key moment, but we must be careful not to neglect earlier instances, as doing so perpetuates the blindness endemic to exceptionalist views. My work continues that of recent pioneers in this field of scholarship in further linking Hispanicism to early national and antebellum imperialism.

This is not to say that 1898 was insignificant in terms of how Anglo-

Saxonists deployed racialism to legitimate imperial projects in the Hispanophone world. The year 1898 witnessed US Americans' newfound confidence in the possibility of managing foreign peoples, a challenge that had stayed some of the more excited antebellum imperialist notions. Along with racialism more generally, the sense of immutable Hispanic difference indeed peaked during the Spanish-American War (Horsman 1981, 302). For example, in a war commemorative, Trumbull White praises US intervention in the Cuban revolution against Spain on the grounds of Spain's exploitation of Cuba. He explains that "the signal fact that will present itself to the student of Spanish history is that from the earliest times the country has been in a continual state of conflict, internal, with its colonies, and with other nations; and seldom has it been a war of defense.... The Spaniard has ever been perfidious, avaricious, and ferocious. In his veins still flows the blood of Ferdinand, of Torquemada, and of Phillip II" (White 1898, 73). White frames Spanish iniquity transhistorically: Spain has always been a violent, oppressive nation. Later in the passage he speculates on the possibility of Spanish reform, but he implies that change is unlikely (73). Spanish iniquity manifests Spanish blood flowing from one generation to the next. That iniquity is immutable; John J. Johnson emphasizes that the Black Legend held that the Spanish character had not changed since early modernity (Johnson 1993, 10), and that notion is bolstered by the language of race in White's account. A heroes-villains depiction of US-Spanish conflict is thus an easy leap for White, as is the claim that the United States must intervene in Spanish affairs for humanity's welfare.

Although 1898 is thus an important flashpoint in the history of Hispanicism, I insist here that 1898 had deep roots. Just as late-century imperialists would figure Hispanophone peoples as incapable of self-government in the build-up toward the Spanish-American War, so did, for instance, late eighteenth-century US Americans who sought to undermine Spanish government in Louisiana under the premise that Spanish autarky was wasting the region's resources. The difference between 1898 imperialism and prior ventures is of degree not kind, and my project explores the relatively uncharted realms of 1898's prehistory.

National Uncertainty and Hispanicism as Cultural Battleground

Reflecting New Americanist critiques of classic US literature as overdetermined by rather than purposefully engaging with pernicious ideologies, DeGuzmán describes works written by Anglo-Americans about Spaniards as being complicit in Hispanophobic racialism regardless of the works' particularities. Although she powerfully illustrates previously unrecognized ways in which US literature voices racialist attitudes toward Spain, I emphasize that early national and antebellum authors often viewed issues of nation, race, and Hispanicism with different levels of uncertainty. In doing so, I have been spurred by Robert S. Levine's contention that "recent historicist criticism . . . has too confidently imposed fixed narratives on the past." Applying such narratives "risks diminishing the otherness or alterity of the past and thus closing off, rather than opening up, the complexities, problematics, and specifics of debates on race and action both of an earlier age and our own" (Levine 2008, 2). Reflecting this tendency, DeGuzmán's argument construing antebellum literature regarding the Hispanophone world as being defined by a broader, fixed Hispanophobic narrative minimizes the alterity of the past and historical actors' perplexed attitudes. The argument overdetermines the past in terms of the present, belying how authors could not have known, to the extent we do, the relationship between their positions and later eras. Such interpretations are tempting because early US authors may at times tell stories about the Hispanophone world that seemingly prefigure the obviously Hispanophobic rhetoric used to defend policies such as the Spanish-American War and pro-fascist intervention against Latin American leftism. When viewed on their own terms, these authors oftentimes agonized over and questioned predominant views of race, nation, and expansion. These questions challenged the writers' ability to tell coherent stories about their nation, which prompted them to use literary methods purposively to put their individual stamp on the debates (Levine 2008, 5). Levine consequently engages a recent scholarly trend to emphasize how exceptionalist rhetoric often belies uncertainties regarding national identity (Streeby 2002, 39, 57; Rodríguez 2010, 7, 13, 127–29) by arguing that a responsible historicist criticism attends to "the *unknowingness* that writers convey in their writings, an unknowingness that often takes expression as a resistance to cultural certainties and what I would term a wise bafflement about the meanings, trajectories, and plots of the unfolding narratives of history" (Levine 2008, 2). The writers who most reward study resist being easily conflated and demand nuanced close reading and historicization. Hispanicism is ripe for the approach Levine advocates, as is the broader field of transnational studies.

Understanding Hispanicism requires recognizing not only this perplexity but also rejecting the Foucauldian notion that resistance to discursive power is impossible. Although much early US literature written by Anglo-Americans voices the era's broader racialist attitudes toward Hispanophone peoples, many authors used their writing to stage powerful critiques of such pernicious ideologies. This is even true of authors who were to some extent writing from positions of privilege. These authors struggled to think outside their culture's confines, but their work all the same forms part of a cultural battleground made up of unique manners of addressing Hispanicism. For instance, in composing a perspectival narration that captures how Hispanicism conditions Amasa Delano's misinterpretation of events aboard the *San Dominick*, in "Benito Cereno" Melville provides a powerful warning against the dangers of Hispanicism. DeGuzmán argues that Melville's suggestion that Delano is mistaken in his self-satisfied assumption of superiority to Cereno is frustratingly unresolved at the point of irony and thus guilty of not escaping the view it questions (DeGuzmán 2005, 47–67). This reading risks losing sight of the clear differences between, on the one hand, Melville's recognition that Hispanicism blinded Anglo-Americans and, on the other, more naively Hispanophobic views such as that of Joel Barlow, who I discuss in chapter 1. Surely readers should differentiate between these approaches, in doing so recognizing Hispanicism as the richly contested cultural terrain it was.

In engaging in a responsible mode of ideology critique that is sensitive to how individual authors address Hispanicism, I work from a conception of literature that shares much with what Marjorie Levinson refers to as "New Formalism," particularly the movement's "activist" camp. Far from doing so to evade questions of power, I focus on form and the literary qualities of how creative writers address Hispanicism to reveal literature's agency against power. As Levinson describes this approach, "That complexity . . . which is attributed to the artwork and recoverable only through a learned submission to its myriad textual prompts, explains the deep challenge that the artwork poses to ideology, or to the flattening, routinizing, absorptive effects associated with ideological regimes" (Levinson 2007, 560). Literature, at its best, draws attention to the complexities of human relationships. It highlights the subtleties of social setting by examining the subtexts informing human interaction. It suggests how our lives are shaped by communally sanctioned narratives, such as those concerning race.[9] Illustrating how attention to the ways narrative takes shape can inform powerful critiques of exceptionalist discourses such as Hispanicism, Joseph Darda explains that "maintaining a belief in American exceptionalism . . . relies on selectively remembering and construing the past, by negating the state-sanctioned violences that directly contradict the nation's alleged exemplarity. It is no coincidence, then, that many of exceptionalism's leading critics . . . were trained as literary scholars and write with a sensitivity to the ways in which narratives are constructed within and contribute to, even structure, a national political culture. Exceptionalism is a psychosocial logic, a way of differentiating and absolving the state, and a rationale for warmaking. But it is also a narrative framework" (Darda 2014, 80–81). I attend to how authors who certainly possessed insights into narrative form that compare favorably to those of contemporary scholars put those insights to work to interrogate Hispanicism.

Another crucial aspect of how I describe the particularities of individual texts' approaches to Hispanicism is my emphasis on ideological dissent between liberals and antiliberal conservatives. This emphasis further illustrates how my goal in pushing back against the way ideology critique has been practiced in recent decades is not to avoid questions of ideology but rather to achieve a more sophisticated understanding of the relationship between early national and antebellum culture and ideology. Hispanicist liberalism inspired both liberal and conservative critics. Although it was conventional for Anglo-Americans to associate racial identity and potential for the supposedly universal right for self-determination that liberalism assured individual subjects, some liberal writers such as John Rollin Ridge recognized the incoherence inherent in proclaiming US liberalism via the imperialist demonization of supposedly less capable national Others such as Mexico. Ridge and others contrarily argued for the protection of Hispanophone peoples' natural rights (Havard 2015, 333–43).

Hispanicism also provoked antiliberal, conservative critics. Following Russell Sbriglia, I use "conservative" here not to refer to the politics of the Republican Party, whose rhetoric of laissez-faire and commitment to interventionist foreign policy represent classical liberalism with a vengeance. The antiliberal conservatism of the early nineteenth century is unlike both contemporary liberalism and conservatism in that it was a countertradition to classical liberalism. Its defining philosophical features were organicism, traditionalism, and skepticism. These three tenets formed the basis for communitarian impulses; suspicion of excessive commitment to the "free" market; and celebrations of culture that might, as counterintuitive as it might seem, be appealing to many of today's progressives if they were not frequently conjoined to outdated racial views (Sbriglia 2013, esp. 7, 9, 16–17). By highlighting how Hispanicism divided conservatives and liberals, I illuminate the contested nature of the Hispanicist discursive terrain. For instance, Hispanicist liberals bemoaned Hispanic traditionalism as an impediment to the successful participation of Hispanophone peoples within cosmopolitan markets and public spheres, an impediment that might be rooted out through imperial tutelage. Conservatives, though, recognized Hispanic and Anglo-American cultures as distinct, organically constituted communal entities, entities that would not be easily leveled via imperial management. Similarly, whereas Hispanicist liberals aggressively touted the superiority of an intrinsically liberal United States via contrast to despotic, inefficient Spain, conservatives argued for restraint, skeptically questioning American exceptionalism's faith-based rationales.

Highlighting such ideological conflict is only possible by historicizing each author's relation to Hispanicism. One of the most characteristic examples of scholars imposing fixed narratives on the past is how many have viewed liberalism as the United States' ineluctable political philosophy. According to this perspective, although much US liberal intellectual production reveals symptoms of an exploitative, "conservative" core at the heart of US liberalism, US political culture remains, categorically, liberal (Sbriglia 2013, 4–5, 17). I focalize a more diverse portrait of the early US political landscape via discussion of Hispanicism, thus not only enabling better understanding of Hispanicism but also continuing the work of Sbriglia and others in resuscitating nuances in early US political cultures.

Hispanicist Moments

Each chapter is devoted to analyzing a specific author. The chapters are divided into two parts. In part I, "The Black Legend, Hispanicism, and the Emergence of National Identity in the Early United States," chapters 1 through 3 focus on Joel Barlow, James Fenimore Cooper, and Herman Melville. This section explores how the US interpretation of the Black Legend emerged during the early national period and was later debated and challenged in the antebellum period. My arguments regarding national identity, liberalism, and conservatism emerge in these chapters. For instance, Barlow exemplifies how liberals used Hispanicism to argue for US intervention into unproductive Hispanophone economies, and Cooper illustrates how conservatives used Hispanicism to argue against expansionism's excesses. In part II, "Hispanicism and the Case of Cuba," the last two chapters discuss Mary Peabody Mann and José Antonio Saco. Part II contrasts US and Cuban views on Hispanicism and Cuban annexationism. It explores nationality and ideology by examining nuances such as differences between US and Hispanophone liberalism.

The book is organized this way for a few reasons. Part I illustrates my historical argument that the emergence of liberal US nationalism was heavily informed by Hispanicism. Although my chapter progression roughly follows chronological order, I do not intend to yoke the evolution of Hispanicism to the era's evolution of literary genres from gothic to romance to realism. I comment on how authors used these modes to engage Hispanicism, but I hold that Hispanicism does not itself change along with them but rather informs and oscillates between each. However, I do make a historical argument. The chapter trajectory demonstrates that whereas Hispanicism buttressed early conceptions of nation, that articulation was increasingly questioned in the antebellum period in light of divisive social conflicts over expansion and slavery. These questions were raised by both traditionally canonical authors and authors from the transnational margins and both by concerned liberals and skeptical conservatives. Part I focuses on a specific US debate over Hispanicism between liberal, radically cosmopolitan, and conservative views. Part II on Cuba continues to highlight the liberal-conservative divide, but this time with the added feature of discussion of differences between US liberalism and a creole Cuban version that incorporates elements of the more anti-individualist Hispanic liberal tradition. Lastly, I devote special attention to Cuba because, along with Mexico (which I address in chapter 2), Cuba has had a more lasting hold upon the Anglo-American imagination and has spurred more US nationalist fantasy than most of the Hispanophone world (Johnson 1993, 27). The United States has likewise figured largely for Cubans. This special relationship has a long history. As Louis A. Pérez Jr. explains, in the nineteenth century "North Americans considered Cuba essential to the politico-military security of the United States; Cubans looked upon the United States as vital to the socio-economic well-being of the island" (Pérez 1990, xiv), whereas in recent decades "North American resolve to control Cuba and Cuban determination to resist control have become part of the national character of each and something of an obsession for both" (xvii). Somewhat occluded by this general proclivity among US Americans to emphasize difference and hierarchies between the United States and Cuba is an antebellum tendency among US southerners and Cuban creoles to perceive shared interests in establishing racially stratified slave-based economies. Such contradictions in attitudes inform an intense anxiety apparent in US attitudes toward Cuba. This level of anxiety was perhaps not even present in attitudes toward Mexico until immigration from Mexico and Central America increased. After a brief lull in US media attention toward Cuba, the recent reestablishment of diplomatic relations between the two nations has spurred polemics regarding their intertwined histories. This renewed interest illustrates that old attitudes die hard. For instance, right-wing criticisms of Barack Obama's conciliatory tone toward Cuba regarding historical US imperialism on the island (e.g., Bonicelli 2016) demonstrate the persistence of US obsession with assuming power over Cuba. Part II on Cuba illustrates the history of these concerns, a history that exemplifies broader Hispanicist trends. I also note peculiarities of US American attitudes toward the Spanish, Mexicans, and Cubans as appropriate.

These concerns inform my choices of focal points in each chapter. This study could have addressed other authors. It also could have discussed other historical phenomena, such as US responses to early nineteenth-century European wars in which Spain was a crucial participant, US responses to the Spanish American revolutions, or the debates regarding a Central American canal that resulted in the Panama Canal. Space limitations made it impossible for me to discuss everything at great length. My focus on Spain, Mexico, and Cuba reflects how these are the Hispanophone nations of greatest interest to US Americans. Moreover, although Washington Irving's stature in early national US literature and his obsession with Spain might make him seem a likely choice for an example of early national Hispanicism, I discuss Joel Barlow instead because he wrote during the nation's earliest years, and his work highlights the connection between liberalism, imperialism, and Hispanicism. He provides a window into the emergence of understandings of a peculiarly US national identity as liberal and imperial in relation to the Hispanophone world. James Fenimore Cooper proves useful because his turn to realism as a way to engage the US-Mexican War enables me to focalize literary form while addressing that consequential moment in the history of Hispanicism. Moreover, Cooper's stringent conservatism makes him useful for illustrating the ideological contours of debates regarding Hispanicism. Herman Melville, as an author whose interest in Hispanicism inspired literary experimentation with free-indirect narration, also proves valuable for highlighting formal issues. In the Cuba subsection, I discuss Mary Peabody Mann's *Juanita* instead of Martin Delany's *Blake* because *Juanita*'s liberal, ambivalently pro-annexationist argument contrasts so well to José Antonio Saco's conservative skepticism regarding annexation.[10] I chose to focus on the early national and antebellum periods rather than the later nineteenth century because 1898 is the year most conventionally associated with the rise of US Hispanophobia. It has received greater attention. I connect my work to this period by concluding with a coda that explains how early US literature reveals a prehistory of 1898. William Graham Sumner proves useful in this coda because his work powerfully distills the Hispanicist rhetorical strategies established by the earlier authors my study addresses.[11]

Chapter 1 examines Joel Barlow's nationalist epics *The Vision of Columbus* (1787) and its revision *The Columbiad* (1807). These poems construct a progressive narrative that culminates in the American Revolution. For Barlow, the Revolution represents an end to humanity's enslavement to violence and exploitation. The poems establish many Hispanicist conventions. Spain is depicted as a tradition-bound foe of innovation that the United States must displace to undertake its redemptive role. Spanish recalcitrance and iniquity provide the self-reflexive mirror by which US Americans can conceptualize themselves as citizens of a liberal nation. This chapter drives my historical argument that the early national emergence of US identity and literary nationalism was propelled concurrently by Hispanicism and a nascent sense of the United States' liberal mission. Barlow was an early proponent of American exceptionalism; I contend we cannot understand his role as such without recognizing how he deploys Hispanicism. Barlow's exceptionalism is particularly evident when the earlier poem is compared to the revision's more epic scope. An antinationalist Enlightenment cosmopolitanism pervades Barlow's works. However, the increased prominence of epic convention in the later poem articulates a more nationalist tone. *The Columbiad* thus reflects the new conception of national identity as particular and different that was emerging at the end of the early national period, a point I tether to Hispanicism's presence in the poems. In the background of these revisions is Barlow's involvement in expansionist projects to foment revolution in Spanish Louisiana. Reading his poems beside archival evidence of these projects, I establish Hispanicism's relationship to imperialism.

Chapter 2 begins probing conservative responses to Barlow's model for liberal Hispanicism by turning to James Fenimore Cooper. Although Cooper is known for his frontier romances and their commentary on westward expansion and Indian removal, *Mercedes of Castile* (1840) and *Jack Tier* (1848), respectively, focus on Columbus's first voyage and the US-Mexican War. The novels reveal the interest Cooper took later in his life in US expansion to the south. Cooper was not an enemy of expansion per se, but he took issue with jingoistic rhetoric that masked the horrors of expansionist corruption and violence. In the two novels, Cooper interrogates Hispanicism via a historically responsible, realist style that does not romanticize US interests or uncharitably stereotype proud Hispanophone cultures. His work demonstrates that Hispanicism was not a totalizing discourse that co-opted all texts that addressed it. In *Mercedes of Castile* Cooper suggests that the Black Legend account of Columbus's voyages, an account seen in Barlow, makes it difficult to recognize the fact that these aspects of Spanish history should be regarded as consistent with the times rather than as evidence of eternal Spanish depravity. In *Jack Tier* Cooper questions Hispanicism by contrasting the novel's villain Stephen Spike with the Mexican patriot Don Juan Montefalderon, with whom the treasonous Spike seeks to trade gunpowder during the US-Mexican War. Whereas Cooper represents Montefalderon as a devoted patriot rather than relying on the stereotype of the degraded Mexican found in the pro-war press, Spike is a venal trader who masks corrupt self-interest with appeals to a popular jingoistic philosophy of free trade. Cooper's insistence on the ambiguous moral reality underlying relations between the United States and the Hispanophone world represents his conservative insistence on prudence and restraint in the face of liberal abstractions regarding the United States' providential role in world affairs. He moreover uses Montefalderon as a mouthpiece for the idea that excessive expansion into Mexico's heavily populated portions would prove futile because intrinsic differences between the Mexican and Anglo-American populations would make these parts of the nation inassimilable to the United States.

Picking up on chapter 2's points regarding realism, chapter 3 continues to develop my argument regarding how interest in literary form powerfully enabled engaging the ideological battlefield of Hispanicism. Whereas many scholars (e.g., DeGuzmán 2005, 47–67; Nelson 1993, esp. 112–14) read Herman Melville's attempt in "Benito Cereno" to interrogate racism and slavery as being overdetermined by racialist ideologies, I contend that he offers a critique of Hispanicism through his ironic depiction of his protagonist Captain Amasa Delano. Melville's representation of Delano's understanding of the creole Spanish captain Benito Cereno, which Melville focalizes through the tale's perspectival, free-indirect narration, ventriloquizes Hispanicist arguments about Cuba, Spanish America, and US national identity. Melville thus uses the narrative frame to render what it is like to perceive the world through Hispanicism. I explore how the arguments structuring Delano's viewpoint were articulated in, among other venues, the pages of *Putnam's Monthly*, which first published Melville's tale. "Benito Cereno" highlights how the conception of US liberal identity found in this publication obscures the savagery shared by Delano and the Spaniard from whom Delano self-confidently distances himself. Instead of acknowledging this commonality, Delano differentiates his brutality from that of Cereno, recasting it as cosmopolitan fellow feeling. Melville likens Delano's assumptions to the ideological mystification by which the United States conceived of its imperialism as the beneficent spread of liberalism. Melville thus emphasizes moments in which Delano's actions belie his self-understanding's incoherence. In contrast to the difference-motivated form of cosmopolitanism Delano assumes in contrast to Cereno, Melville suggests that Delano would be better served by a cosmopolitanism premised on skeptically questioning self-certainties. Melville thus emerges as a unique author among those I discuss in that he does not use Hispanicism to argue for or against liberal expansionism but rather questions Hispanicism per se. Whereas Cooper takes a step in this direction by challenging Hispanicist simplification and Hispanophobia, he does not go as far as Melville because he retains emphasis on national differences. In addition to explaining how the text interrogates Hispanicism, this chapter also explains how Delano's attitude toward Cereno works hand in hand with Delano's more often-noted view of Africans. I explain that whereas Delano views both as Other, the African and the Spaniard play particular roles in Delano's process of identity construction.

Next is part II: "Hispanicism and the Case of Cuba" on Cuban annexationism. Chapter 4 focuses on Mary Peabody Mann's *Juanita*, which illustrates both US obsession with controlling and anxiety over Cuba. The book is a recovered abolitionist novel written mostly between the 1830s and 1850s but not published until the 1880s after a final set of revisions. The dual temporality produced by the novel's prolonged composition offers insights regarding how Hispanicist attitudes toward Cuba developed during the nineteenth century and then coalesced around the Spanish-American War's territorial stakes. *Juanita* hews to the Hispanicist conventions identified in Barlow by presenting US identity as liberal in contrast to that of despotic, slaveholding Cuba. Mann particularly fixates on how the need to silence slavery's horrors conflicts with the transparent public discourse idealized by liberalism. Mann celebrates US devotion to liberalism via her protagonist, New Englander Helen Wentworth. Especially as governess to her hosts' younger children and her friendship with the oldest one, Helen antagonizes the closed Cuban society by drawing attention to slavery's horrors. She thus shocks Cubans out of their acculturated indifference to the institution. In Helen, readers observe an early representation of the tutelary role many Anglo-Americans believed the United States occupied in relation to Cuba, one later popularized, for instance, in cartoons depicting Cuba as a child (Johnson 1993, 116–19; Pérez 2008). Mann deploys this contrast between the United States and Cuba by portraying discussions suggesting that annexation would allow the United States to educate Cuba in liberalism. I historicize these conversations in terms of antebellum debates over Cuban annexation and in terms of postbellum US military intervention in Spanish-Cuban affairs. What most concerns me is how Mann finds that illiberal US slavery troubles her dichotomy. She muses on the possibility that its history of slaveholding makes the US South more like Cuba, a Hispanophone nation that many US Americans have peculiarly fixated upon as Other, than like her ideal vision of the United States. The discourse of national identity that Mann's novel develops thus runs aground against the realities of US history. The US South, for Mann, is an Other within the nation, an anxiously regarded sign of national fragmentation. The chapter thus illustrates that Hispanicism serves not only to glorify US liberal national identity but also as a topos that provokes concern that the nation is not what it seems to be.

Chapter 5 provides a Cuban viewpoint as a contrast to Mann's perspective. Discussing José Antonio Saco's critique of Hispanicist imperialism's contradictions, I read Saco as a representative of Cuban resistance to the United States. From the point of view of US and northern European political tradition, Saco's critique is conservative like Cooper's; however, it is more appropriately described as consistent with Spanish Enlightenment traditions that influenced how liberalism was understood in the Hispanophone world. Saco's position takes shape in attacks on Cuba's radical liberal annexationist movement. This movement argued that Cuba was most likely to succeed in establishing beneficial liberal-democratic institutions if it was annexed by the United States. Saco claims that this argument unwittingly capitulates to

Hispanicism's view of Hispanophone peoples as incapable of attaining liberal identities without an Anglo-Saxon education in liberal democracy. Such an education, Saco points out, entails not only the construction of liberal institutions but also the eradication of Cuban cultural identity. Saco concedes that the development of liberal institutions might benefit Cuba. He claims such a prospect is dim in the case of annexation due to the unlikelihood that despite its claims to benevolence and stated support of liberty, the United States would ever grant Cuba statehood. Even were it more likely, it would come at too great a cost. Although it may surprise liberal Cubans who view agency in terms of institutional structures, Saco claims that adopting abstract, liberal-democratic political forms through incorporation into an imperial nation will obliterate Cuban self-determination. Agency, rather, can only be protected if Cubans preserve uniquely Cuban (here meaning Spanish) sociocultural traditions. Saco's "conservatism" is apparent in his resistance to giving up Cuba's cultural identity and historical inheritance. His view resonates with the Spanish Enlightenment position that although intellectual, political, and economic modernization is desirable, reform must not come at the price of failure to maintain the integrity of the *pueblo* (people) as an organic unit. Insofar as Saco concedes radical Cuban difference from the United States, his critique of US rapacity seemingly relies on Hispanicism. Whereas Hispanicism posits that Hispanophone peoples are unable to self-determine, Saco contends that maintaining Cuban difference is the only way for Cubans to retain self-determination. The chapter thus further illustrates that Hispanicism and national discourses comprised a multivocal, contested terrain. I read Saco's Hispanicist "conservatism" not as internalized hegemony but, rather, as incisive critique of Hispanicism.

I conclude with a coda on 1898, when the United States undertook widespread imperialism in the Hispanophone world via the Spanish-American War, whose conventional name belies the fact that the war was begun not by the United States but, rather, by anti-Spanish forces in Cuba and the Philippines. Although many studies cede the existence of US imperialism and anti-Hispanic feeling before 1898, this year is frequently viewed as exceptional. I show that 1898 should be considered as a maturation of Hispanicism, significant but not unique. I focus on Yale sociologist William Graham Sumner's anti-imperialist claim in "The Conquest of the United States by Spain" (1898) that in becoming imperial, the United States was becoming Spain. Sumner contends that this transformation portends the loss of the moral certainty and the material prosperity that the United States has enjoyed. It should not surprise us that Sumner uses Spain as his central metaphor when evoking the loss of national significance. The fact that Spain was the United States' enemy during the conflict was not the only reason the metaphor was powerful; Spanish-ness had always been a primary site of national meaning-making. Sumner's audience would have thus possessed a variety of cultural vocabularies related to Hispanic difference, and his essay's rhetorical efficacy lies in how it conjures and plays off these meanings to present imperialism as a portentous prospect. I argue that Sumner reflects a larger historical accumulation of Hispanicist significance in 1898. I construe the period, finally, as a moment in which Hispanicism, which had always been a powerful strain in US culture, took on explosive significance in the context of debates about imperialism, national identity, and the nation's future at the turn of the twentieth century.

Hispanicism: Then and Now

Although I focus on the literature of the early United States, Hispanicism does not end with either the Civil War or 1898. In the era of neoliberal globalization, interactions between the United States and the Hispanophone nations are as significant and intimate as ever. Old habits die hard, too. In US cultural and political discourse, this interaction is often imagined as a dangerous threat to national identity. In recent years Hispanicism has been most evident in anxiety over Mexican and Central American immigration (Rodríguez 2010, 114). The discourse remains evident in other discussions, too, often with the old tendencies to racialize Hispanophone peoples in ways that obscure differences among this heterogeneous population.

In one example that illustrates the place of Hispanophone peoples in US cultural discourse, on December 30, 2013, *New York Times* writer Douglas Quenqua reported, "Researchers have identified gene mutations that may explain why Latinos are almost twice as likely to develop Type 2 diabetes as Caucasians and African-Americans. And in a twist, the quirk can be traced to Neanderthals." Then, in her bluntly titled blog post "*The New York Times* and NPR Are Still Clueless about Latinos," Latina novelist Alisa Valdes (2014) responded that although Quenqua's report uses the term "Latino" to refer to a racial category, "There is no single 'type' or 'race' of human being in Latin America, and as a result Latinos are 'racially'/physically as diverse as the United States population as a whole—or as the entirety of humanity." The *Times* report opposes Latinos to Caucasians and Africans, but innumerable Caucasians and Africans are Latinos. As Valdes explains, the report reflects the high Type 2 diabetes rate among indigenous Mexicans; "Latino," though, should not be reductively confused with "Native American." The study's authors themselves do not commit the terminological confusion exhibited in the *Times*, which suggests that whereas experts understand such distinctions, the *Times* and the general public to which it caters perceive little difference among Hispanophone peoples. For Valdes, the report exemplifies pervasive US misunderstanding of the racial status of Latinos/as.

Although this *Times* report is not a celebration of imperialism or xenophobic immigration anxiety, Valdes's concern is well placed. Are not those who see Latino immigrants through reductive racial lenses less likely to recognize that each immigrant is a unique individual who has made challenging choices to get to where s/he is today? Are not individuals who view Latinos through such lenses also unlikely to recognize that systemic global economic trends drive immigration, in failing to do so directing their resentment of the perceived economic and social ills of immigration toward unfairly demonized immigrants rather than the corporate and political powers that engineer an inequitable global economy? This tendency to blame the immigrant rather than the system has made it possible for anti-immigrant rhetoric to attain great currency. Texas lieutenant governor Dan Patrick stoked Anglocentric racial fears by describing undocumented immigration as an "illegal invasion" while campaigning (Ura and Smith 2014). President-elect Donald Trump made Hispanophobic rhetoric a key element in his campaign announcement, stating that "when Mexico sends its people, they're not sending their best. They're not sending you. They're not sending you. [*sic*] They're sending people that have lots of problems, and they're bringing those problems with us. They're bringing drugs. They're bringing crime. They're rapists. And some, I assume, are good people" (Lee 2015). Trump continued to rely upon such language during his improbable run toward election, which illustrates the rhetoric's popularity among his Anglo-American coalition.

As suggested by the fact that Trump is mistaken that immigrants are any more likely to commit crimes than US citizens (Lee 2015), the assumption that Latinos pose an ominous racial threat is misleading. A recent study suggests that US Americans may be more likely to support intrusive immigration inspection against documented immigrants or US citizens perceived to be of Latino "racial" origin (for instance, via Spanish names) than undocumented immigrants of perceived Canadian origin (Mukherjee, Molina, and Adams 2013). Supporters of harsh immigration policy claim an unbiased desire to uphold the law, but "that support for tough policy varie[s] with detainee identity suggests that it instead reflects concern for ethnocentric exclusion" (327). Despite the confusion inherent in Anglo-American racial views toward Latinos, Anglocentric US Americans confidently believe that the racial threat perceived simply in the Spanish language is sufficient to deny rights to Latinos. The enforcement patterns enabled by their views lead to two undesirable outcomes, the unwarranted detention of US citizens and legal immigrants of Latino origin and undeserved privilege experienced by law-breaking immigrants of Anglo or European origin who escape questioning and punishment (321).

The persistence of Hispanicism reflects and feeds how international relations between the United States and Spanish America remain strained. Such tensions are evident as US Americans anxiously debate immigration policies while supporting expansion into Spanish America. In recent years, expansion has taken the paternalistic, neo-imperial form of "freetrade" agreements such as NAFTA and the lending policies of the International Monetary Fund, the effects of which have spurred the very migration xenophobes fear. Ignorance regarding these policies' impact and the self-congratulatory rhetoric used to defend them powerfully illustrates Hispanicism's delusive effects. For instance, Fox News personality Bill O'Reilly stated in response to anti-US sentiment in Mexico that "for what we've done for this country, it makes me fairly angry." In Spanish America resentment toward such policies manifests itself in revolutionary demonstrations such as the Chiapas Zapatista movement. It moreover is apparent in the recent "pink tide" of support for anti-US, socialist politicians such as the former president of Venezuela Hugo Chávez.

As a literary critic, I do not offer policy answers for the complex contemporary issues of immigration and international relations with Spanish America. My study reveals the delusive and violent historical effects of the rhetoric that is reemerging today. This history reveals to us that the language of Hispanicism is not a productive way to talk about the challenges we face. Said concluded his introduction to *Orientalism* stating that what he wanted "to have contributed here is a better understanding of the way cultural domination has operated. If this stimulates a new kind of dealing with the Orient, indeed if it eliminates the 'Orient' and the 'Occident' altogether, then we shall have advanced a little in the process of what Raymond Williams has called the 'unlearning' of 'the inherent dominative mode'" (Said 1979, 28). My study contributes to unlearning the discursive modes of Hispanicism. These modes make it difficult for US Americans to see the Hispanophone world in an undistorted manner and enable xenophobes and imperialists to defend destructive actions on false premises.

Attending to moments of uncertainty and agency is here key. Scholarship regarding racialism and imperialism is generally driven by progressive sentiments, but the argument that these discourses overdetermine US literature undermines such goals. If these discourses inevitably co-opt an author of Melville's acuity, how are we to escape a similar fate? Some critics making such Foucauldian arguments claim a place outside these totalizing logics, but their theoretical and methodological presuppositions render this claim problematic. As Levine complains, "Does the simple act of claiming to 'see' or locate a historical trajectory through a retrospective imposition of a fixed narrative history somehow free us to create better futures? Or might such a vision of writers locked into their respective historical moments simply confess to our own profound sense of futility and entrapment, a conviction that our own histories are in various ways overdetermined and that hopes for change at the current moment are grim?" (Levine 2008, 22). Levine's insight that imposing fixed narratives on the past enforces a sense that we are also controlled by overdetermining discourses says much about the critic's loss of a sense of significance as someone with something consequential to say about the politics of culture.

By recognizing that at its best literature exemplifies ways of examining and contesting destructive discourses, we can restore a sense of possibility not only to the periods and texts we study but also to our present circumstances (Levine 2008, 22).[12] Possibility's presence in the past suggests that history could have turned out differently than it did and thus that we ourselves have multiple potential futures. Considering the study of literature or history as a way to fashion a better future may seem naive. Given the stakes of our current moment, we must find a more impactful way of doing our work. The study of literature reveals that we are not trapped, and we need to remember that today.

PART I

The Black Legend, Hispanicism, and the Emergence of National Identity in the Early United States

1

Joel Barlow's *The Vision of Columbus* and *The Columbiad*

US National Identity and Spain

Joel Barlow's long Columbian poems *The Vision of Columbus* and the later, more doctrinaire revision *The Columbiad* are among the first examples of US literary nationalism. His work's foundational role suggests meaningful questions despite the poetry's derivative, tedious neoclassicism. At this early moment, how would Barlow conceive US nationality? What stories would he tell, and what forms would those stories take? How does his work relate to later literary nationalisms?

William C. Dowling provides a useful paradigm for understanding the political and philosophical dimensions of Barlow's poetry. Dowling argues that what most marks Barlow's work is its insistent faith in history's progress toward a secular millennium defined by universal liberty. Dowling, moreover, emphasizes Barlow's relentless, merciless demystification of all religious and philosophical systems that impede this millennium. Dowling explains that Barlow took aim at Christian, classically republican conceptions of cyclical history as impediments to progress (Dowling 1990, 100). Although Barlow was writing during the age of republicanism, he can be viewed as a liberal, a term more frequently applied to later thinking. Many of his contemporaries, such as his fellow Connecticut Wits, exhibited the tradition-focused, inward-looking tendencies characteristic of republicanism. The anticonventionalist Barlow, though, looked outward. His work may have been aesthetically conservative, but it was politically radical (Sutton 1980, 75).

The liberal, secular millennium that Barlow saw as history's ultimate outcome was a cosmopolitan moment. It would, upon its achievement, bring humankind together under terms of brotherhood and equal opportunity. Barlow believed that the expansion of commercial enterprise was slowly bringing the peoples of the world into contact with one another, and he thought such interaction would bring about cosmopolitan utopia (Bloch

1985, 97). Difference would break down as part of a march toward the human perfection that is achieved when liberty becomes ascendant.

Existing along with this cosmopolitanism, however, is Barlow's nationalism. These poems are works of literary flag-waving, written to formulate US identity and to give that identity neoclassical cachet. They highlight the United States' role in Barlow's world-historical narrative; Barlow figures the American Revolution as this story's central moment. This dual commitment to nationalism and cosmopolitanism, particularism and universalism, may seem paradoxical. US identity, for Barlow, is an identity of nonidentity. To Barlow, though, this conception was natural. In Barlow's narrative, the American Revolution marks the peak of liberal progress, a moment pointing toward the day when men realize that they are all truly created equal and are entitled to life, liberty, and the pursuit of happiness—a future in which men have even adopted the same "manners, feelings, and languages" (Barlow 1970b, 343). Thus, Barlow tethers nationalism to cosmopolitanism. This is an Enlightenment as opposed to a romantic view of the nation, one focused on ideas rather than blood and soil.

Yet the extent to which Barlow's understanding of nation relies on difference attests to how it is not a purely Enlightenment conception of a cosmopolitan nation and rather resembles the expansionist nation. To understand Barlow's cosmopolitan nationalism, we must attend to how his poems represent Spain and Spanish-ness. Barlow, drawing from the Anglophone Black Legend tradition, represents Spain as a depraved, backward nation. By doing so, he holds up the virtues of the cosmopolitan identity epitomized in the American Revolution's triumph for liberty. Barlow defines Spanish-US difference by the oppositions particular/universal, monarchical/republican, autarkical/liberal, and reactionary/progressive. This last coupling deserves particular notice. Barlow's understanding of the achievements of the Revolution as the peak of a secular-millennial world-historical narrative relies on figuring Spain as a recalcitrant impediment to that narrative's realization. Spain is an antagonist that the United States must transcend to fulfill its destiny. Spain's defeat leaves it on the wrong side of history. Barlow's construction of US identity provided the basis for a narrative by which his nation could understand itself, in that sense answering his literary-nationalist motives.

This understanding of difference would also provide the material by which he could construct a viable imperial identity. Over the course of the final years of the eighteenth century, Barlow became interested in imperial enterprises in Spanish territories. However, his commitment to both liberalism and imperialism posed a dilemma: How could he both respect Spanish state sovereignty and national self-determination and, at the same time, promote US appropriation of Spanish territory? The conception of national identity as cosmopolitan and liberal that Barlow constructed vis-à-vis figures of Spain provided the solution. By representing Spain as the antithesis of the values he sought to promote, Barlow constructed a discourse by which he could make acceptable the imperialist dispossession of Spanish lands.

Barlow's revisions to *The Vision of Columbus* in *The Columbiad* indicate a shift to a more nationalistic perspective. This shift reflects a general tendency in the period's culture and foreshadows the exceptionalism that would characterize antebellum discourse. Whereas republicans skeptically questioned the triumphalism of exceptionalist claims and Enlightenment cosmopolitanism stressed commonality over differences, the exceptionalist cosmopolitanism that Barlow most forcefully articulates in *The Columbiad* holds that the United States is different in its commitment to cosmopolitanism. Addressing this matter, Eric Wertheimer (1999) may in a sense be correct that Barlow's revisions indicate his growing uncertainty about cosmopolitan nationalism, an uncertainty that reflects the United States' shift from dealing with the necessities of postcolonial national consolidation to its growing status as an imperial power. This argument usefully helps us to understand the stakes involved in the early national transition between an unbound, cosmopolitan sense of national identity to the more bound, discrete understanding that would mark the antebellum period. However, two points must be noted. First of all, whereas for Wertheimer the principal difference between *The Vision of Columbus* and *The Columbiad* resides in how they tell the story of the Inca Manco Capac, I locate that difference in their understandings of Spain and their relationships to the epic tradition. Moreover, whereas Wertheimer sees a shift from cosmopolitanism to nationalism in these revisions, I instead suggest that they do not exactly exhibit a shift from one to the other but, instead, a more forceful evocation on Barlow's part of how these concepts can be realized in an interrelated manner in the practices of an exceptional nation.

Columbus, Spain, and US Identity

Despite their differences, the two poems feature the same plot. Both open with a prose introduction that describes Columbus suffering the indignity of being imprisoned by Spanish authorities in a Valladolid dungeon. This treatment follows many other conflicts with Spain. After discovering the New World, Columbus finds his plans to establish a beneficent, productive colonial regime frustrated by retrograde Spanish adversaries. First, self-interested discontents treat him treacherously at Ferdinand and Isabella's court, prompting Ferdinand to strip Columbus of authority. Then, the men

Ferdinand puts in Columbus's place wreak havoc upon Columbus's work in the West Indies by stifling commerce and butchering Native Americans. The devastation mortifies the discoverer. This dissension is groundwork for the poems proper, in which an angel provides the explorer with a consolatory vision of how "that change in the political face of Europe, that liberality of sentiment, that enlargement of commercial, military and philosophical knowledge, which contrast the present with the fifteenth century, are but so many consequences of" his voyages (Barlow 1970b, 103). The vision culminates in the American Revolution, which heralds the prospect of a secular millennium; this turn of events, the angel tells Columbus, is the ultimate benefit of his toil. The thought is Columbus's solace for ills that regrettably cannot be remedied in his lifetime. Spaniards continue to serve as antagonists in the vision. Barlow differentiates US national identity as liberal and cosmopolitan by contrast to Spanish antiliberalism and tribalism.

Understanding how identity works in these poems requires examining how Barlow characterizes their major players, as identity takes shape here by way of a web of relationships between Columbus, the United States, and Spain. Columbus is seen most prominently in the poems' introductions. Despite being the ostensible protagonist, he plays only a small role in the visionary narrative proper. That narrative presents New World progress, culminating in the US Revolution, as Columbus's legacy. Barlow sets up this relationship by using the introductions to depict Columbus as being ahead of the curve. The admiral sees things others do not, and he is willing to go to great lengths to act on his intuitions: "Columbus, by an uncommon exertion of genius, formed a design no less astonishing to the age in which he lived, than beneficial to posterity" (Barlow 1970b, 108). Columbus undertakes his actions for the greater good. He is often challenged, though, precisely because he is so ahead of his time. His collaborators fail to understand the gravity of his project, and "the preparations . . . were by no means adequate to the importance of the expedition" (112). On the voyage itself, he must deal with the constant prospect of mutiny, as his sailors lack the courage that Columbus's vision, ambition, and desire give him. That courage is needed to brace them for the challenge. As Barlow writes, "from the nature of the undertaking, every man had leisure to feed his imagination with all the gloominess and uncertainty of the prospect. They found, every day, that the same steady gales carried them with great rapidity from their native country, and indeed from all countries of which they had any knowledge" (114). These sailors fear the uncertainty that Columbus is so at home with. Such fears threaten to terminate Columbus's voyage before it succeeds, but Columbus's leadership enables him to assuage the sailors' concerns.

The story of Columbus enacts in miniature what Barlow viewed as his poetry's overall aim, that of displaying the benefits of a progressive unmasking of conventions that constrain the march toward the secular millennium. The pernicious role of tradition was for Barlow the most significant lesson history teaches. Columbus's efforts pointed up a productive tension between convention and progress, as his successful struggle against custom enabled him to make the discovery that was the most important step toward human perfection. Columbus's story is not the only such historical flashpoint, however; Barlow frequently highlights tradition's opposition to progress when discussing other Renaissance and Enlightenment stories of success against the odds, such as those of scientific thinkers such as Galileo and Copernicus. Barlow believed that convention would necessarily fail against the coming millennium (Barlow 1970b, 107).

Columbus's troubles with the sailors exemplify what Barlow took to be a crucial broader conflict between innovation and custom. In the extended footnote in Book IX of *The Vision of Columbus*, Barlow elaborates the idea when he propounds a progressive view of history. First of all, he discusses his secular millennialism, claiming, "It has long been the opinion of the Author, that such a state of peace and happiness as is foretold in scripture and commonly called the millennial period, may be rationally expected to be introduced without a miracle" (Barlow 1970b, 342). Barlow, in other words, believed in the Judeo-Christian commonplace of prospective perfection on earth. As a religious skeptic, he thought it would come about not through divine intervention but through human agency—specifically, commerce. As Barlow rapturously explains, "The spirit of commerce is happily calculated by the Author of wisdom to open an amicable intercourse between all countries, to soften the horrors of war, to enlarge the field of science and speculation, and to assimilate the manners, feelings, and languages of all nations" (343). Barlow's millennium is a world in which all men and women are united in a quest for material happiness, one in which all restraints against unity and collaboration are antiquated. This shared desire would produce the apex in human happiness.

Barlow's millennium is deeply cosmopolitan. Also in the Book IX footnote, Barlow writes, "It seems necessary, that the arrangements of events in civilizing the world should be in the following order. *First*, all parts of it must be considerably peopled; *secondly*, the different nations must be known to each other; and *thirdly*, their imaginary wants must be increased, in order to inspire a passion for commerce" (Barlow 1970b, 343). Barlow, here, contends that the fruition of his secular millennium required increasing interaction between the globe's peoples. This circulation would inspire shared desires that commerce could satisfy. Cosmopolitan commerce brings the desires of the formerly disparate masses together at the moment of millennium.

This march toward millennium requires the effacement of particular identities. Barlow understands identity and global commerce in inverse relation. Identity forces humanity apart, separating it into discrete, mutually exclusive parcels that oppose those who do not share their own identity. This division forces people to act against the interests they mutually share with members of communities other than their own, interests they could better fulfill by working together. When they participate in global commerce, though, they find that what each community shares with other communities is in fact more fundamental to their individual prosperity and happiness than the superficial differences that divide them. This realization spurs them to work together for their mutual benefit. Identity recalcitrantly hinders progress, whereas global commerce—facilitated by liberalized trade policies—enables it. (By contrast, as we will see in chapter 5, José Antonio Saco argues that although political and economic liberalization and commerce are desirable, true liberty can only be achieved via the zealous maintenance of boundaries between identities. To whatever extent liberalization entails the loss of such identities, it must be opposed.) This context sheds light on Barlow's diatribes against convention, which he often explicitly ties to attacks on identity. Barlow's thought, in this regard, reflects a common Enlightenment opposition between reason and superstition in which religions, customs, and folkways blind people to their true needs. For example, such narratives regarding Galileo construe religion as being opposed to science, which offers truly meaningful benefits. This paradigm holds true in Barlow's understanding of Columbus's first voyage. Barlow emphasizes that superstitious ignorance about the seas almost leads Columbus's sailors to prevent the discovery of the New World, which for Barlow is the event most important in the spread of progress-initiating global commerce. Happily, for Barlow, the march of progress will always eventually triumph over these stumbling blocks; cosmopolitanism will always supplant identity.

Considering Barlow in light of Paul Gilroy's work on identity is revealing. Barlow is a forerunner of Gilroy and others who have sought to revive the cosmopolitan spirit. In *Against Race* (2000), which represents a revival of Enlightenment universalism, Gilroy critiques what he perceives as a growing market in essentialized black identity. Gilroy sees the identity politics buttressing this market as similar to racial essentialism in that it divides humanity's commonality. He damns this manner of thinking as counterproductive by likening it to fascist fetishes for identity. Such identity politics do not empower the subaltern. At best, it comprises an impoverished critique of modernity's terrors. Not only does identity politics offer "only the shallowest comfort and short-term distraction," it in fact reproduces "the same repertory of power that produced [the subaltern's] sufferings in the first place" (Gilroy 2000, 6). Gilroy instead advocates cosmopolitan "planetary humanism." He argues that even if historical actors making appeals to abstract equality and human commonality come up short of our standards in various ways, such appeals remain the best ways to conceptualize social justice. Dividing the world according to identity "destroy[s] any possibility of human mutability and cosmopolitan democracy" (7).[1]

Gilroy's work hearkens to that of Thomas Paine (*Common Sense* and *Rights of Man*), C. F. Volney (*The Ruins*), and, indeed, Joel Barlow, who was, along with Thomas Jefferson, one of the exemplars of such thinking in the early national United States. Barlow's cosmopolitanism, surprisingly, provides the context for his nationalism. Because of fascism, we conventionally think of nationalism as being premised on essential difference and chauvinistic antagonisms. For instance, exceptionalism is considered a crucial component of nationalist conceptions of US identity; according to this idea, the United States is different and better than other nations. Although there are elements of this kind of thinking in his work, it would be a mistake to oversimplify Barlow's nationalism in these terms. Rather, "Barlow's dream of America [was that it was] ushering in a great millennial morn . . . a 'commonwealth of man' in which all distinctions of nation and class will dissolve and universal brotherhood will emerge on earth" (Dowling 1990, 10). Barlow did see the United States as different from and better than other nations. For Barlow, though, this difference resided in how the nation was at the vanguard of a progressive narrative that would culminate in the obliteration of difference once abstract equality was established. Barlow saw the United States as serving as a city on a hill, but he did not see it as different in the sense that the term "difference" signifies in romantic and fascistic discourses. For Barlow, such notions hinder progress by blinding people to shared interests.

Columbus's exploits provided a useful genealogy for Barlow's nationalism. Columbus's discovery of the New World, first of all, facilitates the colonial project that results in the American Revolution. The poems figure Columbus as the Revolution's progenitor, constructing a historical narrative that draws a direct line between his exploits and the actions of Barlow's present. This present is Columbus's consolation; as Barlow writes a conversation between the angel and Columbus in Book I of *The Vision of Columbus*, "Though still to virtuous deeds thy mind aspires, / And heavenly visions kindle new desires; / Yet hear with reverence what attends thy state, / Nor pass the confines of eternal fate. / Led by this sacred light thy soul shall see, / That half mankind shall owe their bliss to thee, / And joyous empires claim their future birth, / In these fair bounds of sea-encircled earth" (Barlow 1970b, 138). Forecasting the poems' eventual focus on North America, these lines illustrate that eighteenth-century progress is the prime solace with which the angel demonstrates to a despondent Columbus that his actions have not been in vain. Throughout the books that focus on the events that occur in the North American colonies, Columbus views the colonists as his endowment to history. He "hail'd them with a father's smile, / Fruits of his cares and children of his toil" (251). This relationship is particularly emphasized in the sections pertaining to the Revolution, which provokes Columbus's concern for his heirs. For instance, Barlow writes, "The great Columbus, with an anxious sigh, / Saw British ensigns reaching round the sky" (287). Columbus earnestly desires his work's fruition in the revolution's success.

Barlow further points up the filial tie between Columbus and the United States by establishing a conceptual linkage between them. Both share progressive desires and the ability to transcend the pressure that convention and identity impose upon progress. Just as Columbus must struggle against the religious and epistemological conventions of his early modern historical moment, so must the United States against that of its late eighteenth-century one, particularly those of a corrupt British political system. Similarly, as Columbus's discovery opens the possibility of commercial circulation between peoples of diverse identities, so does the Revolution provide the political grounds that are most conducive to realizing those possibilities by facilitating the establishment of liberal democracy and, thus, a society based on the mutuality of human needs and desires. The very fact that Barlow chose a Genoese as the nation's father figure says much about his understanding of Columbus's and the United States' relationship to cosmopolitanism. Columbus's nationality is of little import to Barlow. What matters is what Columbus and the United States share. These common goals explain Columbus's affection for his North American progeny.

In his sense of history as inexorably progressing toward a secular-millennialist, cosmopolitan utopia, Barlow was a radical in his time; differing much from his republican contemporaries, he was alternately ridiculed and feared. The way his work anticipates that of Gilroy and other anti-identity intellectuals illustrates his radicalism. Gilroy hints toward a difference between the two when he distinguishes himself from his Enlightenment forebears: "While I value [the Enlightenment's] political pedigree, I want to try to be clear about exactly where [my] line of thought departs from its noble precursors in those traditions that have contributed so extensively to the ideas and the practice of antiracism. All the earlier arguments conform to the same basic architecture. They posit the particular, singular, and specific against the general, universal, and transcendent that they value more highly. In contrast, the approach I favor attempts to break up these unhappy couples" (Gilroy 2000, 29). Regardless of whether Gilroy has read him, this criticism unquestionably applies to Barlow. Barlow's cosmopolitanism relies heavily on figuring Spain as the inferior second term that differentially illustrates the virtues of the cosmopolitan United States. Barlow devotes much of his poems to the Spanish, whom he vilifies as the enemies of Columbus, the United States, and other proponents of progress. Attending closely to this representational strategy is crucial to understanding Barlow's nationalism. The strategy suggests how that nationalism, although relying on Enlightenment conceptions, still forefronts difference.

Barlow's understanding of the Spanish proceeds from his reading in New World history. Earl E. Fitz has described Barlow as "one of the earliest scholars of Inter-American literature" (Fitz 1991, 53), as from his days at Yale College, Barlow avidly consumed writing about the Americas. These readings encompassed not only well-known histories such as Bartolomé de las Casas's *Brevísima relación de la destrucción de las Indias* (1552) (Barlow read Spanish works in translation) and William Robertson's Buffonian *History of the Discovery and Settlement of America* (1777), the latter of which appeared in five US editions by 1788 and thirteen by 1817 (Bauer 1995, 205, 223–24n9; Bernstein 1985, 215), but also other significant, lesser-known works. These include the Inca Garcilaso de la Vega's *Comentarios reales de los incas* (1688), which Barlow had access to via a rare North American copy housed at Yale (Bauer 1995, 205).[2]

Barlow's reading informed his poetry's historical vision. These texts share, along with other key points of reference such as Girolamo Benzoni's *La historia del mondo nuovo* (1565), a formative role in shaping the themes, modes of characterization, and rhetorical motifs of the Black Legend. Charles Gibson identifies seven manners through which the Black Legend represents Spain. These include figuring the Spanish as decadent, authoritarian, politically corrupt, religiously bigoted, indolent, cruel to Amerindians during their colonial conquest, and persistent in that cruelty after conquest (Gibson 1971, 21–27). Barlow's poems follow all of these patterns, most prominently the last two. Barlow is thus consistent with the discourse at large. Although the idea of unique Spanish depravity was later applied to other contexts, it found its origins in Las Casas's denunciations of the Spanish treatment of Native Americans. Barlow follows this tendency by devoting space in Books II–IV in both poems to representing Spanish atrocities committed against the Incas and Aztecs. Book II opens with the angel showing Columbus the indigenous peoples of the Americas, which prompts a conversation about human difference after Columbus finds himself surprised by the customs of the more "primitive" natives. Columbus, though, is quite pleased by the Aztecs. He expresses hope to the angel that their worthy civilization will not suffer the fate of the natives who were butchered after treacherous Spaniards divested him of his West Indian leadership, saying "May no gold-thirsty race thy temples tread, / Nor sustain thy streams nor heap thy plains with dead; / No Bovadilla seize the tempting spoil, / Ovando dark, or sacrilegious Boyle" (Barlow 1970b, 160–61). His wish is upset, however; the seraph must reveal to him the Aztecs' fate, saying,

So the dire hosts, that trace thy daring way,
By gold allured to sail the unfathom'd sea,
Power all their aim and avarice all their joy,
Seize brightest realms and happiest tribes destroy.
Thine the dread task, O Cortez, here to show
What unknown crimes can heighten human woe,
On these fair fields the blood of realms to pour,
Tread scepters down, and print thy steps and gore,
With gold and carnage swell thy sateless mind,
And live and die the blackest of mankind. (Barlow 1970b, 162–63)

This passage is rich in Black Legend tropes. Cortez and his band are motivated by greed for power and gold. The crimes they perpetrate rewrite the book of evil. Barlow describes Cortez with bombastic hyperbole. In all manners of iniquity, these men supersede all precedent. Columbus, understandably, sheds tears at this scene (163).

The vision then moves to Peru and the Incan civilization, which is even more fascinating and admirable to Columbus than that of the Aztecs. The poems' praise of Incan virtues occurs both in the poetic vision proper and in a "Dissertation on the Genius and Institutions of Manco Capac," in which Barlow provides an extended prose celebration of the Incan Empire's founder. The "Dissertation" comes between Books II and III in *The Vision of Columbus* and as a footnote to Book II in *The Columbiad.* (I will later return to this shift, which is significant.) As with the Aztecs, Spanish terror under Pizarro upsets Columbus's pleasure at viewing this civilization, as the angel must sadly report that "another Cortez shall the treasures view, / The rage rekindle and the guilt renew— / His treason, fraud, and every dire decree, / O curst Pizarro, shall revive in thee" (Barlow 1970b, 165). Pizarro's crimes against the Incas repeat those of Cortez against the Aztecs.

By repeating these representations, Barlow fixes a transhistorical Spanish identity. He thus keeps step with general tendencies within Black Legend discourse. As Gibson describes these tendencies, "When Las Casas' *Brevísima relación* was republished by Spain's enemies in the sixteenth century, during the Thirty Years' War, in 1898, and at other times, the implication—indeed at times the explicit statement—was that Spanish brutality had remained unchanged from the time of the American conquests" (Gibson 1971, 14). Barlow's point, here, coheres with identity discourses generally. Recalling Homi Bhabha's argument that the repetition of shared narratives supplements the instability of national identities, and Dana D. Nelson's claim that racializing identity relies on obscuring the variability of the histories experienced by the identity in question, reductiveness is fundamental to identity discourses (Bhabha 2004; Nelson 1993, esp. xii). To this end, Barlow's poems take a set of hyperbolically presented incidents in Spanish history—in addition to what I have mentioned, he also notes the Inquisition (e.g., Barlow 1970a, 536)—and present them as expressions of the Spanish type. Barlow thus figures the Spanish as timelessly inimical to the progressive history he constructs.

This conflict spurs the poems' broader trajectory. Opposition between Spanish antagonist and progressive protagonists plays out, in the first instance, as Spanish political corruption thwarts Columbus's benevolent rule in the West Indies. In the poems' introductions, Barlow describes how Columbus's self-reliance results in the opening of the New World for the exploration and global commerce that will usher in modernity and the secular millennium, but the Spanish frustrate Columbus. Here, political corruption, one of Gibson's elements of Black Legend discourse, rears its ugly head. Although Columbus works for progress in the West Indies, "some discontented persons, who had returned from the colony to Spain, together with his former enemies in that Kingdom, conspired to accomplish his ruin" (Barlow 1970b, 117). These men deal treacherously with Columbus, relating "his conduct in such a light at court, as to create uneasiness and distrust in the jealous mind of Ferdinand, and made it necessary for Columbus again to return to Spain, to counteract their machinations, and to obtain such farther supplies as were necessary to his great political and benevolent purposes" (117). More such problems follow, finally resulting in Columbus's deportation to Spain and subsequent penury. Crucially, Spanish corruption is the immediate antagonist of not just Columbus himself but the progressive nature of Columbus's exploratory and commercial projects, a nature that forms the foundation of the poems' message. Whereas Columbus moves history forward, "form[ing] and thoroughly digest[ing] a plan, which, in its operation and consequences, unfolded to the view of mankind one half of the globe, diffused wealth and dignity over the other, and extended commerce and civilization through the whole" (109), the Spanish seek to hold him in check. The narrative's very inception is in Spanish-progressive conflict—Spanish treachery necessitates the consolation that the angel provides Columbus.

In detailing Columbus's travails with Spain, Barlow fixates on Spain's opposition to a cosmopolitan politics. For instance, he emphasizes that Spanish policy with the Incas entails clashing with a cosmopolitan, politically progressive people. In the "Dissertation on the Genius and Institutions of Manco Capac," Barlow asserts that readers should admire Capac because he successfully erected a political edifice that organized what had once been an unruly people. His success exemplifies progressive thinking, as, due to his unpropitious situation in "savage" Native America, his effort is "the most surprising exertion of human genius to be found in the history of mankind" (Barlow 1970b, 191). His reforms facilitate the agriculture and commerce so important to Barlow's understanding of a society most attuned to mankind's shared interests; he successfully brings together diverse peoples, establishing the cosmopolitan circulation characteristic of such a society (181). Barlow's view of the Incan empire as cosmopolitan is also evident in the historical genealogies he constructs for Capac. Barlow contrasts Capac's exploits favorably with Western history, writing that "we find the political system of Capac at least equal to those of the most celebrated ancient or modern lawgivers" (187). Barlow proceeds to evaluate Capac against several Western thinkers and leaders to Capac's advantage. These genealogies place Capac in a cosmopolitan history of reform. They also, considering Spain's brutality in colonial Peru, place Spain at odds with that history. Spain again acts the role of timeless villain in an epic of historical progress.

Many of the Black Legend's charges are valid. Spaniards committed atrocities in the New World. The colonial iniquity Barlow attributes to Spain, though, was universal to the colonial enterprise. As Roberto Fernández Retamar puts it, the Spanish conquest is no different than "the depredations of Holland, France, England, Germany, Belgium, and the United States." In "the magnitude of the crimes," these nations "are all worthy rivals" (Fernández Retamar 1989, 58). The Black Legend was ideological. From its inception, it provided non-Hispanic colonizers with the means to contest the moral legitimacy of Spanish colonial hegemony, a particularly urgent desire in an Anglophone world eager to assert its own claims to colonial power. Even as Spanish colonial influence waned during the eighteenth century, the Black Legend continued to find a ready audience among those who desired either to appropriate Spanish territories and/or to repress their own complicity in the horrors of colonialism (Shields 1990, esp. 175–94).

The Black Legend's cultural work was to produce identity, to split the essential commonality of the European colonial experience into fictive hierarchies of virtue and iniquity. Barlow's deployment of the Black Legend must be read in this context. Appropriately here, Nelson writes of the "'violence of representation' that occurs in texts about race, the oppressive reduction of the apparently infinite diversities among humans to an oppositional binary, always hierarchically figured. My most basic point is that while the *word* is black and white, people most certainly are not" (Nelson 1993, xii). Although Nelson's work is specifically about race and Barlow's representation of the Spanish is protoracialist, her claim is relevant to identity discourses generally, including the discourse we find in Barlow. By denigrating Spain, Barlow dichotomizes US and Spanish identity. The United States is progressive; Spain is historically recalcitrant. The United States is protean and cosmopolitan; Spain has a fixed identity. The United States favors a classically liberal open market; Spain is autarkical. Barlow's construction of US identity—the explicit aim of his nationalist poetry—rests on these tensions. Through them, Barlow represses colonial Anglo-America's own investment in violence, thus conceiving an ideal New World identity for the United States.

Anne Norton's concept of liminality is useful for understanding Barlow's conception of US identity. As Norton writes, "political identity is shown to emerge with the greatest clarity when the polity confronts individuals whose inclusion in the polity is ambiguous. . . . The people on the boundaries—territorial, cultural, ideological—thus serve to mark the boundaries they prompt the polity to draw" (Norton 1988, 4). Elaborating on this idea, Norton writes, "At once other and like, they [liminars] provide the occasion for the nation to constitute itself in reflection upon its identity. Their likeness permits contemplation and recognition, their difference the abstraction of those ideal traits that will henceforth define the nation" (54). For Barlow, Spain, the Hispanophone Americas, and Spanish-ness are not only debased but also liminal. Both European and not European, Western and non-Western, American and not American, modern and not modern, Spain serves a paradigmatically ambivalent role both in Anglophone discourse in general and in Barlow's US twist on the Black Legend. Spain and its New World empire were on the borders of Europe and the revolutionary United States, and Spanish-ness plays a similarly limiting role in terms of identity. Spain provides the mirror through which Barlow both abstracts an idealized conception of US identity through recognition of the United States' reflection of Spain's attractive aspects—Spain is an example of an empire—and rejects the Spanish traits with which he wishes to disidentify.

Barlow, with characteristic proclivity for adding historical depth to his identity narratives, emphasizes this opposition not only by dichotomizing US and Spanish identity but also by positing an antagonistic relationship between Spain and the United States' hemispheric forebears, Columbus and the Incas.[3] Like Columbus, the Incan civilization prefigures the United States in its progressivism and cosmopolitanism, which the United States takes up in its successful Revolution. In his celebrations of the Aztecs and particularly the Incas, Barlow provides an early example of the inter-American tradition of looking to Native America for a usable past with which to conceive nationality. Not only, though, do the States take up the ideals propounded by the Incas; they also take up their resistance to Spain, not in direct combat but rather by a contrast in historical mission and identity. Through this focus on the Incas, furthermore, Barlow displaces onto Spain the United States' own questionable interactions with Native America, thus abstracting an ideal US identity.

Identity and nationalism offered order in an unstable early national United States. In the chaotic post-Revolutionary years, US Americans sought a paradigm that could guide virtuous lives and provide the cultural authority that could ennoble the nation vis-à-vis Old World powers. They desired cultural consolidation, a unifying core in national identity.[4] Barlow was one voice among this tumult. Although Van Wyck Brooks's usable past concept (Brooks 1918) is dated, it remains suggestive. Early US writers often not only celebrated the United States' newness and potential but were also painfully aware of how that very newness left the nation without a defining history. This awareness prompted them to search for a usable national past that could provide such a historical foundation. This bedrock came in many forms, such as Puritan history and the noble savage trope. As we can see by his deep interest in imagining historical narrative, Barlow clearly desired to develop a usable past. With his concern for progress, his historical narrative highlights his sense of the United States' position at history's vanguard. In this narrative, he differentially emplots the United States, Columbus, Spain, and the Incas. These identities, mediated to Barlow through the Black Legend, provided the requisite usable past.

Joel Barlow's Black Legend: Poetry, Nation, Conspiracy, and Empire

Although the need to solidify national identity in the post-Revolutionary period provides a crucial context for understanding Barlow's representation of Spain, he also exploited the Black Legend in service of his imperial activities; his investment in constructing US identity through nationalist poetry was no merely benign patriotism. In attempting to construct a progressive cosmopolitan identity for the young nation, one by which he could promote the extension of liberal political and economic rights to a humanity whose local traditions, he believed, should be leveled, Barlow was also formulating an imperial identity. He sought to negotiate the vexing issue of denying territorial sovereignty to Spain while promoting liberal values that might seem at odds with expansion.

We typically think of the United States' major territorial concerns in this period in terms of the nation's fight to maintain its recently won sovereignty over the lands comprising the thirteen states. Conversely, we tend to view US imperialism as an antebellum and, even more so, late nineteenth-century phenomenon. However, no sooner than they had put the finishing touches on their Revolution against Great Britain, US Americans quickly turned their eyes to the south and west and began thinking about expanding across the continent. These territories included what was then Spanish Louisiana, which Spain had acquired during the aftermath of the Seven Years' War. This area, with its natural resources and access to the Mississippi River and Gulf of Mexico, was very desirable. Just as the colonial-era British used the Black Legend to contest Spanish hegemony in Europe and the New World, Barlow put the Legend to imperial purposes by employing it to question Spain's control of Louisiana.

Barlow's involvement in Louisiana was preceded by other territorial ventures, such as his well-documented involvement in the Scioto Company debacle. While abroad in France in the late 1780s and early 1790s, Barlow served as publicist and broker for William Duer's ill-fated Scioto Company, which sought to sell land in the Ohio Country to French colonists. Duer attempted to purchase a 4,000,000-acre tract for French settlement from the Ohio Company, but the deal and the Scioto Company itself collapsed in early 1790 due to the Scioto Company's failure to make payments according to its contract. Barlow, though, knowingly sold worthless deeds to French emigrants, who discovered the situation upon arrival in the Ohio Country in 1792. The settlers eventually negotiated deeds with the Ohio Company and the US government (Jones 1992, 141–206; Sioli 2003, 552–53). Barlow's involvement in this infamous episode of early national land speculation puts a suspicious dye on his professed faith in global commerce's potential to better society. That apparent conviction may have masked Barlow's self-interest.

Barlow's activities in Louisiana were also illicit. As David S. Shields (2006) suggests in a brief history of the print culture of early national filibusterism, Barlow may have engaged in secretive negotiations with French agents to foster filibustering activity in Louisiana. Barlow probably authored a "Plan proposé pour faire une revolution dans la Louisiane" / "Proposal to Incite a Revolution in Louisiana" (1792), which details the plan's aims and methods. The document proposes to transfer control of Louisiana from the Spanish back to the French by inciting a rebellion against Spanish dominion among the region's English and French population. The document recommends that Citizen Genêt provoke the insurrection; that Cumberland, Marietta, and Scioto serve as recruitment centers; that General James Wilkenson serve as chief of the operation; and that H. H. Brackenridge possibly help as well (Shields 2006, 251). Barlow's authorship is not 100 percent certain, but Shields convincingly argues that "Barlow's deep involvement with the ill-fated Scioto land company, his advocacy in other places of a revolutionized hemisphere . . . [and] his connection with Brackenridge strongly argue authorship" (251n44).

Attending to Barlow's involvement in this little-known conspiracy in early national history sheds light on the imperial resonances of his understanding of identity. Like the Scioto incident, the plot says much about Barlow's commitment to these kinds of projects, as it presented significant legal barriers. Two years after Barlow composed the document, Washington would sign the United States Neutrality Act into law. The legislation was specifically provoked by further, more public filibustering attempts by Genêt to reestablish French control of Louisiana. However, the act more generally responded to the myriad such activities that were taking place in the western territories, activities of which Barlow's plot is one example. The act criminalized "the organization of a military expedition by a person within the United States territory aimed at a foreign dominion with which the United States was at peace" (Act of June 5, 1794, Cha. 50, section 5, 1. Stat. 381 384). The act had not yet gone into effect when Barlow planned the plot, but he tested risky waters by violating the United States' aloof position in the Spanish-French conflict. He was aware of these risks, asking in the document, "Pouvons nous agir sur l'ohio sans compromettre la neutralité des Etas unis?" / "Can we take action around the Ohio without compromising the United States's neutrality?" (Barlow 1896, 950).[5] Barlow recognized legitimate diplomatic methods of achieving his aims (946) but was willing to adopt more drastic methods instead of relying on conventional ones.

These plots are the material context that spurred Barlow's conception of identity in his poetry. A clear parallel presents itself between how Barlow elaborates US identity in the poems and the contrast he draws between cosmopolitan revolutionism and Spanish monarchical autarky in the plot document. Barlow, first of all, presents the plot as a necessity because the Spanish misuse their sovereignty over Louisiana. Discussing the enterprise's grounds, Barlow identifies a tactical advantage in "la disposition des habitans, presque tous François ou Anglo-Americains, ennemis jurés d'une poignée d'Espagnols qui à la verité ne les oppriment pas, mais genent leur industrie et leur commerce" / "the disposition of the inhabitants, almost all French or Anglo-Americans, sworn enemies of the grip of Spaniards who, granted, do not violently oppress them, but do restrict their industry and commerce" (Barlow 1896, 946). Spain shows its iniquity, if not through the barbarous tortures of the Conquest and Inquisition, through autarkical overreach over the region's inhabitants. Spain is, as in the poetry, defined by its commitment to identity. That commitment is apparent in a mercantile economy that subjugates all production and trade to the goal of enlarging the crown's coffers, as opposed to a liberal open market whose participants are freer to act on their individual interests. Rhapsodizing over the immense resources available in Louisiana (950), Barlow presents Spain as unfit to exercise sovereignty in the region. Indeed, he writes of all of the Hispanophone Americas, "Sans doute ces immenses possessions ne resterout pas toujours sous le joug Espagnol," but finally concludes, "Mais il ne depend pas de nous de les delivrer aujourd'hui" / "Without a doubt these immense possessions should not always remain under the Spanish yoke. But it is not our job to deliver them at this time" (946), leaving redemption for a later day.

Barlow's discussion of the non-Spanish inhabitants of Louisiana follows the pattern of progressive, cosmopolitan US identity construction the poems establish. Barlow writes of these inhabitants, "Le caractere des habitans qui resemble beaucoup à celui des Anglo Americains, ils sont robustes, entreprenans, bons chasseurs et amis de la liberté, d'ailleurs tous armés" / "The character of the inhabitants very much resembles that of the Anglo-Americans: They are robust, enterprising, good fighters and lovers of liberty, and all armed" (Barlow 1896, 947). From a logistical standpoint, Barlow emphasizes the ability of these inhabitants to take part in a successful revolution against Spanish rule. This belief, reiterated multiple times, was not mistaken, as the region was indeed largely populated by communities of Franco- and Anglo-Americans who outnumbered and had little love for Spain. Furthermore, the cultural identities of these peoples cohere with Barlow's logistical scheme. The vocabulary Barlow uses in this excerpt suggests, first of all, that he believed that the English and French in the region, unlike the Spaniards, exemplify dedication to natural rights, as they are "lovers of liberty." The repetitive use throughout the document of the terms "libre" and "joug" to describe, respectively, the non-Spaniards and Spaniards further points up this opposition. The non-Spaniards' freedom-loving identity shows that, for Barlow, they should resist Spanish restrictions upon their commerce. Barlow also emphasizes their "robust, enterprising" character, figuring them as the ideal participants in the open market that Barlow believed his revolution would produce. These peoples would transcend Spanish limitations and thus deserved power that would be granted by French sovereignty.

The convergence between how the poetry and the filibustering document construe identity suggests that Barlow was invested in an understanding of US identity as not only liberal but also imperial. He deployed this concept of identity in the service of a revolutionary territorial politics through which the United States could challenge Spain's sovereignty in Louisiana. Disputing Spanish sovereignty was a vexing imperative, as the promotion of self-determination and freedom from domination central to US republicanism and liberalism rendered imperialism like Barlow's problematic. Although purportedly aimed at expanding liberty into strongholds of despotism, these ventures also denied self-determination to sovereign nations. This denial was at odds with both liberal and republican values. Thus, despite his belief that filibustering means expanding liberty, Barlow at times registers uncertainty over the implications of his methods. He resolves this tension through a logic of US-Spanish identity that figures the United States and France as dedicated to cosmopolitan liberalism and Spain to autarkical devotion to identity. The plot document thus inverts imperial roles, obfuscating US aggression and Spanish subjugation and emphasizing US-French victimization and Spanish domination. The convergence seen here between poetry and plot suggests that the poetry provides not merely the means for national consolidation but also the cultural basis for a vision of US empire in the Hispanophone Americas.

This connection between poetry and US empire may seem surprising given that the plot was designed to transfer control of Louisiana to France rather than to the United States. How can a plot with such aims attest to the imperial politics of US identity formation? First of all, although his goal was to reestablish French sovereignty in the region, Barlow viewed the filibustering project as one that could serve US aims. After asking "quelle doit *être* notre conduit a l'egard des Etats Unis?" / "what should our conduct be in regards to the United States?" (Barlow 1896, 950) and ruminating upon the risks of violating neutrality, Barlow represents the benefits the United States would enjoy from a transfer of sovereignty. He implies that in the event of diplomatic and legal emergency, such benefits would absolve the perpetrators. Barlow enumerates a series of such benefits, emphasizing particularly that France would provide open shipping on the Mississippi waterways and thus access to numerous resources and markets (950–51). Clearly, this is a plot invested as much in US as French interests, one not to be easily dissociated from the nationalism of Barlow's other writings. Second of all, and more fundamentally, regardless of the plot's particular aims, the confluence of the understandings of identity between the poetry and the plot suggests that Barlow's aesthetic work was invested in formulating a view of identity that could be deployed for imperial aims.

A Poetry of Identity: Barlow's Turn to Epic and Particularist Cosmopolitan Liberalism

Thus far I have largely considered Barlow's *The Vision of Columbus* and *The Columbiad* as one. Although the works are generally similar, there are significant differences to account for. Given that Barlow undertook the revision in the wake of the Constitutional Debates and during a period of intense conflict and consolidation as the nation attempted to gain its moorings, what can historicist analysis of these revisions tell us about this crucial period in the nation's formation? How did Barlow's literary choices represent concrete engagements with broader cultural forces? I have shown that the notion of identity that Barlow constructed in the poems relied on concepts such as cosmopolitanism, nationalism, liberalism, and imperialism. Although significantly articulated in various ways, these conceptual schemes could be said to be mutually exclusive. Would this version of identity hold up under the pressures of the Crisis Period, and, if so, how would Barlow address its inherent tensions?

Eric Wertheimer argues that Barlow's revisions indicate an increased sense of particularist, exceptionalist nationalism and a consequently decreased cosmopolitanism. Wertheimer ascribes this shift to the increased pressures to expand westward in the post–Louisiana Purchase years during which Barlow published *The Columbiad.* Wertheimer's reading hinges on a conspicuous revision: Barlow's choice to move the "Dissertation on the Institutions and Genius of Manco Capac" from between the second and third books in *The Vision of Columbus*—a placement that for Wertheimer highlights the "Dissertation"—to a footnote in *The Columbiad.* Wertheimer argues that this revision deemphasizes Barlow's earlier nationalist identification between the United States and Native America, as that identification had become ideologically inexpedient as US expansionists began strongly to desire Indian lands (Wertheimer 1999, 53–54). In thus minimizing the cosmopolitanism exhibited in *The Vision of Columbus, The Columbiad* exhibits a shift from an Enlightenment nationalism to a more particularist one that would characterize US nationalism as the nineteenth century pressed on (53, 76).

Although Wertheimer makes a compelling argument, his choice to focus on the poems' representation of the Incan Empire obscures the centrality of Spain as the poems' primary national Other and imperial antagonist. Wertheimer does acknowledge the poems' engagement with the Black Legend and issues of Hispanophone and Anglophone intercolonial politics. However, he views these issues principally as they inflect the United States' engagement with Native America and emergent Indian Removal politics, that is, with how the Black Legend enables identification with a noble Incan usable past that became impolitic in the face of increased western expansionism (Wertheimer 1999, 87–89). (I note that, whatever the virtues of Wertheimer's reading, his argument seems to neglect acknowledging the extent to which the noble savage trope remained popular even during the most brutal moments of westward expansion and expropriation, in that it suggests that Barlow's disaffection for the trope reflects a more general trend that was spurred by expansionism.) This approach reflects the idea that we should view US identity and territorial politics according to a red-white binary. The poems' principal national Other, though, is not Native America but Spain.

Consistent with this misdiagnosis, Wertheimer's claim that Barlow's 1807 revision bears witness to increased territorial agendas implies that the 1787 version did not evince such ambitions. As we have seen via its relationship to the plot document, *The Vision of Columbus* does exhibit an emergent imperialism. To acknowledge this, we must look not just to the frontier of Native America but also to that of Spanish Louisiana. What is more, Wertheimer's suggestion that we view the revisions Barlow undertook as exhibiting a shift from cosmopolitanism to imperialism would seem to suggest that the two concepts are mutually exclusive. Again, as the foregoing indicates, this is not true. Imperialism, for Barlow, is articulated to liberal cosmopolitanism, as the imperial elimination of identity-fixated Spanish sovereignty paves the way for the spread of cosmopolitan values, values that include a liberal commitment to opening markets.

This is not to say that the latter poem does not exhibit increased particularism. We should, though, reconsider where that intensified nationalism is located. It is worth remembering that, as almost anyone who reads the two poems notes, there is something undeniably more doctrinaire about *The Columbiad*. As Wertheimer felicitously puts it, "there is a new confidence to *The Columbiad*, a mature arrogance of nationalized civilization that before seemed elusive or ideologically distasteful" (Wertheimer 1999, 83). Any analysis of national identity in these poems must contend with this fact. I argue that the most meaningful shift between the two poems is Barlow's turn to epic in the later version. This shift has been remarked, including by Wertheimer (62), but its import remains underemphasized.

Which revisions constitute this shift? Barlow was ambivalent about embracing epic in *The Vision of Columbus*. As he writes in its introduction, "The author, at first, formed an idea of attempting a regular Epic Poem, on the discovery of America. But on examining the nature of that event, he found that the most brilliant subjects incident to such a plan would arise from the consequences of the discovery, and must be represented in vision" (Barlow 1970b, 121). Barlow recognizes a generic conundrum. Although he projects to write a long narrative poem with a lofty tone, the subject on which he wishes to focus—a sweeping historical narrative featuring the growth of global commerce and the consequent progress toward the secular millennium—does not conform to the typical material of epic. As conceived by the Homeric, Virgilian, and Miltonic traditions that were Barlow's reference points, the epic assumes a more limited historical scope and a focus on the heroic action of the quest for glory and honor via martial valor (Bowra

1952, esp. 1, 4, 53, 97). Episodes in the discovery of the Americas such as the conquest of the Aztecs might conform to this tradition, but Barlow did not wish to focus on those events. His antimilitarism mitigated against typical epic subject matter. Indeed, he saw traditional epic as setting a pernicious example by glorifying the bloody pursuit of honor and dominance (Sutton 1980, 76; Wertheimer 1999, 62), in this sense reflecting a tendency among democracy-inclined US writers of epic (Pearce 1959, 362–63). This view led to ambivalence about the books in his poems representing the Revolution, the most traditionally epic portions of the work. Celebrating such action did not accord with Barlow's moral views.

By the time Barlow took up revising *The Vision of Columbus* as *The Columbiad*, however, his position had changed. In the latter poem's preface, Barlow is less hesitant to call his poem an epic. Here, although he dissembles that "I shall enter into no discussion on the nature of the epopea, nor attempt to prove by any latitude of reasoning that I have written an Epic Poem," he proceeds to imply that he has indeed done so, writing, "The subject indeed is vast; far superior to any of those on which the celebrated poems of this description have been constructed; and I have no doubt but the form I have given to the work is the best that the subject would admit" (Barlow 1970a, 376). Although he recognizes that his subject matter is not that of conventional epic, he suggests that the grandeur of his subject makes it more appropriate for the lofty tone and aims of epic than the form's conventional material. He goes on to assert that he has followed the unities of time and space. Although Columbus's vision spans New World history since European discovery, the actual time and space of the poem are, according to Barlow, confined to Columbus's interactions with the angel who gives him his vision and the location in which these conversations occur (Barlow 1970a, 376; Sutton 1980, 77). Barlow proceeds to describe the poem's content and aims in manners consonant with those of the earlier poem: "its aim is to inculcate the love of rational liberty, and to discountenance the deleterious passion for violence and war; to show that on the basis of the republican principle all good morals, as well as good government and hopes of permanent peace, must be founded; and to convince the student in political science that the theoretical question of the future advancement of human society, till states as well as individuals arrive at universal civilization, is held in dispute and still unsettled only because we have had too little experience of organised liberty in the government of nations to have well considered its effects" (Barlow 1970a, 382–83). The general purport of the preface is that such themes are appropriate for epic; although Barlow still evinces distaste for traditional epic subjects, his desire to embrace the form's lofty tone as the proper mode of singing his subject's glories supersedes those worries.[6]

The Columbiad proper adheres to the tenor established by its preface, generally following *The Vision of Columbus* in terms of content and thematics but more forcefully embracing an epic tone. This shift is evident in the work's new title, which signals Barlow's move from his earlier understanding of the poem as a "vision" to his understanding of the later version as the modern iteration of the classical epic tradition. Barlow adopts a number of other classicisms. Most obviously, he selects a new title that resonates with classic epics such as *The Iliad* and *The Aeneid.* Moreover, he opens with an invocation to the Muses. Then, instead of referring to the vision-revealing angel as "the seraph" as he did in *The Vision of Columbus*, he renames the angel Hesper. The name is rooted in ancient Greek and Latin terms meaning "western," and Barlow uses the classical name to signal that the tale is an epic of the Western world. He also more frequently adopts epic rhetorical conventions, as when he apostrophizes a deified Freedom: "Sun of the moral world! Effulgent source / Of man's best wisdom and his steadiest force, / Soul-searching Freedom! here assume thy stand / And radiate hence to every distant land" (Barlow 1970a, 549). Similarly, epic simile and epithet become more common, with one simile, telling in its classical reference point, comparing the convening of the Continental Congress to Caesar crossing the Rubicon (579). Finally, if there is a significant shift in content focus, it is undoubtedly the move to discuss the martial exploits of the French and Indian War and the Revolution at greater length. Although Barlow remains committed to antimilitarism, he at the same time is more inclined to celebrate the United States' founding military moments as aspects of the world-historical narrative he develops. The books taking the Revolution as their focus, not coincidentally, are the most heavily classicized, signaling Barlow's choice more openly to embrace the Revolution's heroic aspects.

This last revision indeed signals a thematic shift toward what we might now recognize as a more trenchant nationalism, but it remains true that the poem is ambivalent about the Revolution and chauvinism. Its nationalism is still rooted in the progressive cosmopolitanism that had characterized *The Vision of Columbus.* Barlow does not deemphasize this aspect of the first poem in its revision. Even the repositioning of the "Dissertation on the Institutions and Genius of Manco Capac" in the footnotes, which Wertheimer takes to signify a move away from cosmopolitanism, could signal a strengthened cosmopolitanism. Barlow's inclusion of notes in *The Columbiad* attests to his desire, as a didactic poet, to establish a scholarly pedigree; in moving the "Dissertation" to the footnotes, Barlow reaffirms his commitment to cosmopolitan Native American nationalism, as he intended for readers to attend to the information presented in the notes and to take what they found there seriously.

Even though *The Columbiad* thus largely retains the earlier poem's thematic and philosophic commitments, the shift to a more epic register still warrants remark. What should we make of this shift? Post-oral literary epics seek to convey general truth and a sense of objective facticity about the values their narratives promote (Bowra 1948, 19), and Barlow's move to embrace the epic form signals his greater commitment to the cosmopolitan nationalism of *The Vision of Columbus*. The content of the United States remains the same in *The Columbiad*, particularly the nation's commitment to liberal cosmopolitanism. Barlow, though, plots that content in a more defined epic register, which indicates his strengthened commitment to celebrating those values as the significance of a story of the Western Hemisphere that ends in the American Revolution. The revisions, in other words, do not exactly evince a shift from cosmopolitanism to particularism. These two concepts are mutually dependent for Barlow. The poems, rather, express nationalist sentiments with different tones.

To say that Barlow sees cosmopolitanism and particularism as mutually dependent, however, is not to say that he never perceived contradictions in his position. This US son of the philosophes was not thus obtuse. Barlow's qualms that the epic is not the form proper for his story and is, in fact, distasteful in *The Vision of Columbus*'s preface register a more fundamental concern that particularist nationalism is at odds with cosmopolitan liberalism. Although the manner in which I have arrived at the conclusion that the proper terms for discussing the difference between the two poems resides in the tension between nation and cosmopolis is different from that of Wertheimer, he remains correct that these are the appropriate terms. Barlow's reservations in *The Vision*'s preface demonstrate that he viewed the epic as the genre of national particularity, and Barlow's move to epic suggests that he had put aside his earlier anxieties. The move proves useful to Barlow in that it enables him to see nationalism and cosmopolitan liberalism not as at odds but, rather, as articulated in the manner that his poetry had already begun to indicate. The more stringent literary nationalism of the later epic version more openly particularizes cosmopolitan liberalism as the United States' exceptional provenance.[7]

The Columbiad melds this new form and tone with the discourse regarding Spain and the United States already being constructed in *The Vision of Columbus*. Along with capitulations to epic form and increased focus on Revolutionary military exploits, *The Columbiad* also features greater reliance on the Black Legend than does its predecessor. The later poem contains a number of passages representing Spanish iniquity to which Barlow adds poetic flair by revising more inconspicuous sections from the first poem according to his newfound acceptance of the classical and epic traditions. For example, in Book Four, Barlow decries the horrors of Peru and the Inquisition as follows: "Led by the Dark Dominicans of Spain, / A newborn Fury walks the wide domain, / Gaunt Inquisition; mark her giant stride, / Her blood-nursed vulture screaming at her side" (Barlow 1970a, 536). Here, no longer satisfied simply to deplore Spain through graphic, vivid catalogues of her sins against humanity, Barlow draws from classical mythology and figures the Inquisition as a modern-day Fury. He then extends the conceit over the course of the following lines, melding classical resonances with vivid, gothic depictions of painful tortures: "Lasht on the pile their writhing bodies turn / And veil'd in doubling smoke begin to burn. / Where the flames open, lo their limbs in vain / Reach out for help, distorted by the pain" (537). This example is only one of many such revisions in *The Columbiad* in which Barlow either expands his representation of Spanish depravity or vivifies it through the use of figurative language. It is no mistake that Barlow combines this increased focus on Spain with added epic resonances. The moves work together to particularize a supposedly universal cosmopolitanism as the United States' special provenance.[8]

Both moves can also be seen in terms of the poems' relationship to Barlow's imperial politics. The increased certainty about nationalism that Barlow's revisions indicate adheres with a post–Louisiana Purchase moment in which, as Wertheimer illustrates, US Americans looked westward with increasing certainty regarding their ability and right to dispossess the national Others living to the west of the original states. The differential understanding that Barlow most forcefully expressed in *The Columbiad* is an early iteration of a model that others would deploy to argue the inability to exercise the duties of sovereignty of not only Hispanophone peoples but also of others of supposedly limited capacity for liberal democracy.

Conclusion

I have argued that Joel Barlow types Spain as being opposed to progress and devoted to identity, in doing so holding up the United States as being committed to cosmopolitan liberalism. Barlow deployed this discourse to rationalize his imperial agenda. What is more, his later poetry evidences more certainty about the discourse's validity. In terms of the literary history I am constructing in this study, Barlow's work, first of all, is an important early example of a tradition that developed in the early national period of thinking about US identity vis-à-vis that of Spain. This tradition has persisted in US literature and culture. Scholars have tended to think about questions of race and nation in the United States in terms of black-white and red-white dyads, but Barlow's legacy suggests that we should not let the significance of those oppositions cause us to ignore a significant Spanish-US pairing. Considering this tradition in the manner in which I have read Barlow, second of all, illustrates how US identity has been particularized according to the universals of liberalism such as progressivism, cosmopolitanism, and the open market. The representation of Spain as dedicated to these concepts' inverse was particularly invested in constructing US identity along these liberal lines. Barlow's work can be understood in terms of a shift from the republican conceptions of national identity prominent in the revolutionary period to the blend of Enlightenment cosmopolitanism and liberal exceptionalism that would become more prominent in the nineteenth century.

Thirdly, the relationship seen between Barlow's discourse on national identity and his territorial politics is another that would become a larger part of US literature and culture throughout the nineteenth century. Whereas we tend to think of these phenomena as pertaining to later periods in US history, they have in fact been central to US literary history since the beginning. The nineteenth century would see the United States turn imperial eyes toward many Spanish and Spanish American dominions, and those desires would always run up against its liberal self-understanding and concomitant respect for territorial sovereignty. Barlow's answer to this double-bind—this dual commitment to liberalism and imperial expansion—was to represent the Spanish as incapable of a territorial sovereignty in Louisiana that was in his view properly the domain of France and the United States. Barlow's formulation represents an early national template for how nineteenth-century writers would work through this issue. His thought would feature the Enlightenment, Jeffersonian concept of the empire for liberty—Barlow's dream is a cosmopolitan utopia of shared desires. Yet the logics of difference and consequent denial of self-determination to Spaniards suggest that this empire for liberty was, simply, an empire. This tension between universal liberty and expansion would persist in US imperialism.

In closing, I consider one final moment in Barlow's career. In 1811 Barlow served as US minister plenipotentiary to France, charged with negotiating a commercial treaty. During Napoleon's fatal eastern campaign, Barlow was summoned to see the emperor at Vilnius. However, he became involved in the French army's disastrous retreat and died of exposure in Poland. Barlow left behind a striking poem recording his impressions of the carnage Napoleon's campaign produced. The poem's title is "Advice to a Raven in Russia, December 1812." Barlow apostrophizes a raven he comes across in the snowy tundra, suggesting that the bird has followed him to Russia because Napoleon will fight his last war there and thus will leave behind no more carrion in western Europe: "You fear perhaps your food will fail you there, / Your human carnage, that delicious fare / That lured you hither, following still your friend / The great Napoleon to the world's bleak end. . . . You fear he left behind no wars, to feed / His feather'd cannibals and nurse the breed" (Barlow 1995, 68). Barlow consoles the bird that it need not go to the ends of the earth to find food: "Fear not, my screamer, call your greedy train, / Sweep over Europe, hurry back to Spain, / You'll find his legions there; the valiant crew / Please best their master when they toil for you" (68). The poet then informs the raven that with knowledge of mankind's history, the raven need not fear the end of war: "How could you fear a dearth? Have not mankind, / Tho slain by millions, millions left behind?" (69). The poem ends in hopes that one day man will stop the war-hungry emperor.

This is, clearly, not the usual Barlow. The optimism that pervades his work is entirely inverted in "Advice to a Raven in Russia," which is instead deeply cynical regarding human coexistence. Moreover, whereas Barlow's understanding of history in the earlier poems had been profoundly progressive, here it becomes strikingly cyclical. This is apparent when Barlow describes how the raven need not fear that a world without human remains to feed upon is coming because there are still plenty of people left behind to cause further destruction; as Barlow strikingly writes of humanity, "Tho slain by millions, millions left behind." The chiasmic structure of the line syntactically emphasizes cyclicality. Here, Barlow's millennialism becomes apocalyptic mania as he regards the prospect of perpetual carnage.

Given its strong contrast with the perspective Barlow presents in his earlier work and its biographical-historical context in Napoleon's imperial enterprise, it is difficult not to read this poem as a commentary on the failures of the Enlightenment and the late eighteenth-century revolutionary moment. One senses Barlow's deep disillusionment with modernity's promise of progress. He seems to imply that Enlightenment-promoting France has become what it set out to supplant, with Spain now a victim of French depredation rather than the imperial villain it had formerly been for Barlow. In this regard, the poem has something to tell us about US national identity as Barlow and others after him would conceive it. Although it might seem that a poem about Napoleon's Russian disaster is unrelated to questions of US nationality, this is not true. The Enlightenment perspectives and values that Barlow found insufficient to stay Napoleon's hand in Russia were the same by which he would construct US identity, which he viewed as exceptional in its dedication to those values. Reading this poem, one can only wonder what Barlow would have thought of the tragedies of the nineteenth-century United States, many of which were performed in the name of the liberal national identity that from our perspective they compromised. These tragedies may have provoked uncertainty in or rebukes from Barlow regarding whether his nation failed to live up to the standard that he differentially constructed vis-à-vis Spain. I will take up such concerns, which would become a common theme in Hispanicist representations, in greater depth in the forthcoming chapters.

2

James Fenimore Cooper's *Mercedes of Castile* and *Jack Tier*

Realism and Hispanicism

Scholars are generally familiar with James Fenimore Cooper's 1840 *Mercedes of Castile; or, the Voyage to Cathay*, a historical novel concerning Columbus's first voyage to the New World, via Edgar Allan Poe's 1841 *Graham's Magazine* review. In this merciless critique, Poe writes, "As a history, this work is invaluable; as a novel, it is well nigh worthless. The author deserves credit for presenting to the public, in a readable form, so much historical information, with which, otherwise, the great mass of the community would have never become acquainted; and he ought, also, to receive proper condemnation for having woven that information in any way whatever, into the narrative of a novel. . . . It is, if possible, the worst *novel* ever penned by Mr. Cooper" (Poe 1841, 47). Poe's criticism has been decisive. *Mercedes* is one of the most infrequently discussed of Cooper's works, with the few responses it has provoked echoing Poe by referring to *Mercedes* to illustrate Cooper's nadir (Anonymous 1840, 1005; Anonymous 1841, 137; Goodfellow 1940, 319; Harthorn 2004, 5, 7; Lounsbury 1882, 242; Madison 1985; Philbrick 1961, 125–26; Ringe 1962, 80; Schultz 1991, 33, 40).

Yet Poe's bluster obscures an important insight. In his estimation, *Mercedes of Castile* is not a terrible *book*; it is a terrible *novel*. Poe praises the work as a history, noting its utility in exposing a wide range of readers to foundational events in the history of New World exploration. "To describe this voyage," Poe observes, "was manifestly the sole object of the author in writing this work. Availing himself of the journal of the admiral, and mingling just enough of fiction with the incidents recorded there, to make it generally readable, Mr. Cooper has succeeded in producing the most popular, detailed, readable history of that voyage which has yet seen the light" (Poe 1841, 47). Poe's problem is that the work is not principally a history. It is a novel, and as such, it has many flaws. In particular, to create a historical romance out of the Columbus story, Cooper grafts the fictional love story of Luis de Bobadilla and Mercedes onto the story of the admiral's exploits, with the ne'er-do-well Luis joining Columbus's expedition to win the approbation of his mistress's guardians by doing great deeds in service of cross and crown. This is not a compelling plot line, Poe writes, because as a protagonist Luis pales in comparison to the admiral (47). Moreover, the narrative suspense Luis's seemingly doubtful attempt to impress his mistress's guardians should create is lost because the reader knows Columbus will succeed (48). Poe concedes Cooper's inventiveness in including Luis's dalliance with the Indian princess Ozema as a way to manufacture suspense. Yet Poe finds that this element of the story, too, fails because Cooper does not introduce it until the novel's end, the work's preponderance being devoted to minute examinations of the intellectual and political debates regarding Columbus's theories. "The interest of a novel should continue . . . throughout the whole story," but, Poe writes, "in *Mercedes of Castile* it does not begin until we are about to close the book" (48). In short, Cooper fails to navigate intrinsic challenges to achieving historical fidelity within the novel form.

Poe's analysis of *Mercedes of Castile* as a failed work of historical realism calls attention to Cooper's 1840s turn to realism. The novel, in this respect, can be read alongside another of Cooper's late nautical works, *Jack Tier; or, the Florida Reef* (1848). Concerning treasonous trade off the Florida Keys during the US-Mexican War, *Jack Tier* was the only novel Cooper released serially, which he did during the war years before publishing the work in book form at the conflict's close. Although both books include many sensational, even ludicrous aspects at odds with realism, and neither reaches a high-realist standard of psychological complexity, they also varyingly exhibit some of the major elements of the realist tradition such as unidealized, oftentimes middle- and lower-class characters (this is less true of *Mercedes* than *Jack Tier*); plots that treat the everyday and mundane rather than the transcendent (again less true of *Mercedes*); and a focus on reality as apprehended by the rational, observant mind (true of both), making them among the more realist works in Cooper's oeuvre and thus characteristic of his later tendencies. With its decidedly unromantic characters (even *Jack Tier*'s hero and heroine, Harry and Rose, are middling by contrast to other such lovers in Cooper's oeuvre), attention to maritime war strategy, and descriptions of nautical terminology and the art of sailing, *Jack Tier*'s realism was noted in its time. During the 1852 memorial to Cooper at the Metropolitan Hall in New York City, William Cullen Bryant (who summarily dismissed *Mercedes* as "possessing none of the stronger characteristics of Cooper's genius" [Bryant 1852, 64]) praised *Jack Tier* as being "as full of spirit, energy, invention, life-like presentation of objects and events, 'The vision and faculty divine,' as anything he had written" (65). Bryant clearly appreciated the novel's verisimilar qualities. Yet he devotes much less time to this novel than to others, particularly Cooper's famous frontier romances, which suggests lack of enthusiasm. Moreover, although held in higher critical esteem by contemporaries than *Mercedes*, *Jack Tier*'s mundane characters failed to excite the public, resulting in commercial failure despite the novel's timely subject matter (Johannsen 1985, 203; Oberholzter 1906, 273). The book has retained this reputation; like *Mercedes*, it is one of few Cooper novels not yet republished in the SUNY series of critical editions. Scholars have rarely had as much as Bryant to say about it and even more rarely have had as much praise for it. Its detail-oriented nature is considered taxing, much less preferable than Cooper's romances (Philbrick 1961, 318n2; Walker 2010, 12).

Whereas these works' realism can be considered a defect not only because it does not exhibit Cooper's talents for romance but also because the works' predictable characters fail to measure up to high realism's standard of psychological complexity, I contend that this realism appears more meaningful when read against the 1840s intensification of US imperial ambitions. Cooper is often considered a key literary commentator on westward expansion, but *Mercedes of Castile* and *Jack Tier* demonstrate his interest in southern expansion. During this period, US imperialists turned their attention not only to the Native American lands of the western territories but also to the Spanish- and Mexican-controlled Caribbean and the Southwest. These desires exploded in the Texas Revolution and the eventual US-Mexican War, after which the United States took control of large portions of Mexico's northern frontier. *Mercedes* and *Jack Tier* comment on the period's imperial discourse.

One notable aspect of this discourse was its mythology of US national greatness and imperial rights. Such fantasies are exemplified in the writings of John L. O'Sullivan, who founded the expansionist *Democratic Review* and coined the term "Manifest Destiny." O'Sullivan did not use that term itself until "Annexation" (1845), a polemic against Whig cautions against the US annexation of Texas. However, the underlying concept originated in "The Great Nation of Futurity" (O'Sullivan 1839). Published shortly before *Mercedes*, this essay opens with the claim that "we have, in reality, but little connection with the past history of [powerful European nations and empires], and still less with all antiquity, its glories, or its crimes. On the contrary, our national birth was the beginning of a new history, the formation and progress of an untried political system, which separates us from the past and connects us with the future only; and so far as regards the entire development of the natural rights of man, in moral, political, and national life, we may confidently assume that our country is destined to be *the great nation* of futurity" (O'Sullivan 1839, 426). For O'Sullivan, the United States represents a break with history, a new sort of nation premised on commerce, self-determination, and free civic institutions. The nation is positioned to evade Old World failings, such as monarchy, militarism, and the degradation of the producing and commercial classes. "America is destined for better deeds," O'Sullivan writes, continuing, "It is our unparalleled glory that we have no reminiscences of battle fields, but in defence of humanity, of the oppressed of all nations, of the rights of conscience, the rights of personal enfranchisement. Our annals describe no scenes of horrid carnage, where men were led on by hundreds of thousands to slay one another, dupes and victims to emperors, kings, nobles, demons in the human form called heroes" (427). Given its profound innocence, O'Sullivan claims the future for the nation: "The expansive future is our arena, and for our history. We are entering on its untrodden space, with the truths of God in our minds, beneficent objects in our hearts, and with a clear conscience unsullied by the past. We are the nation of human progress, and who will, what can, set limits to our onward march?" (427). As these passages suggest, evidence-based argument is not O'Sullivan's chief mode. His descriptions of US character and prospects are composed of such hyperbolic abstractions of "human progress" and "futurity" as to permit nothing but faith as a basis.

"Annexation" (1845) and, later, "The War" (1847) apply these notions to US imperial interests in the Southwest. Unlike more aggressive expansionists, O'Sullivan was not a warmonger and generally insisted that Manifest Destiny should be carried out peacefully. During this time of armed conflict with Mexico, he found a silver lining in the intoxicating prospect of a speedy extension of US territory. Illustrating these views is "The War," an argument for a speedy resolution to the US-Mexican War, such a resolution being necessary in part, to O'Sullivan, to avoid sullying national character by participating in a prolonged war. According to this essay, annexation of Mexican territories will provide a safety-valve opportunity for hardy, pioneering eastern settlers whose outlets for agrarian self-determination are limited at home due to urban overpopulation and industrialization (O'Sullivan 1847, 99–100). These settlers, O'Sullivan writes, will introduce possessive individualism, industry, and commerce to the region and thus make better use of local resources than Mexicans (101), who thus have less right to the land. In fact, in a characteristic mood of Manifest Destiny, O'Sullivan writes that Mexicans are not only incapable of properly turning the land to issue, they are also doomed to extinction. Anglo-American settlers from the East will not tolerate "political union with the degraded Mexican-Spanish." Instead, Mexicans must "amalgamate and be lost in the superior vigor of the Anglo-Saxon race or they must utterly perish. They may postpone the hour for a time, but it will come, when their nationality shall cease. It is observable that, while the Anglo-Saxon has overrun the northern section, and purged it of a vigorous race of Indians, the Spaniards have failed to make any considerable progress at the south. . . . The proud, rapacious, and idle Spaniards have but poorly fulfilled their mission. They have neither civilized nor christianized the people, nor reclaimed the country, in the possession of which they have been undisturbed for centuries. The descent of the northern race . . . threaten[s] speedily to change this state of things" (O'Sullivan 1847, 100). Figuring imperial expansion into the Southwest in terms of the two races' providential fate, O'Sullivan again expresses his ideas not through logical argumentation but rather through myth. His unequivocal certainty reflects this fact.

These arguments display a trenchant Hispanicism. For O'Sullivan, US Americans and Hispanophone peoples are irremediably opposed. One is committed to free institutions and the vigorous, rational development of agriculture and industry, the other enslaved to aristocracy and economic inefficiency. Mexico thus serves as a proving ground for the national greatness O'Sullivan touts; there, the United States can demonstrate the validity of its national model over that of its Hispanic neighbor, thus illustrating that the United States is the "great nation of futurity." This idea was not original—we saw it in Joel Barlow. However, O'Sullivan voiced a newly vigorous, racialized sense of nationality that emerged in the antebellum period. He figures Spanish and Mexican difference in essential, racial terms. In "The War" the term "race" is used several times to describe national identities and prospects: "The Mexican race now sees, in the fate of the aborigines to the north, their own inevitable destiny" (O'Sullivan 1847, 100); "the superior vigor of the Anglo-Saxon race" (100); "the Spanish race, to maintain their slothful possession of the country they hold, have, in the madness of their pride, attacked the colossal power that is about to overwhelm them" (100). This language connotes that difference is rooted in blood. Such notions were new to the nineteenth century. Barlow may display a stringent belief in difference between national types and a pride in special US accomplishments, but his work does not prominently display the language of blood and race. O'Sullivan's claims, by contrast, reflect the growing acceptance of polygeneticist racial science. Such ideas enable O'Sullivan to view US national greatness and prospects with confidence, as national differences are now innate and essential. This assumption prompts O'Sullivan to explain every US victory, every Mexican weakness as a product of racial-national characteristics intrinsic to the Anglo-American and Hispanic types. Self-assured in such notions, O'Sullivan's Hispanicist arguments display a newly brash certitude that forecasts 1898's aggressive Hispanicist imperialism.

Racialism and nationalism were at the heart of the antebellum Anglo-American worldview, and it was uncommon for this era's US Americans to view the world outside this frame. However, multiple, oftentimes complexly related positions were available within this broader discursive terrain. Many generally nationalist writers took O'Sullivan's views to task; one was Cooper. Cooper's late realist turn coincided with a shift from literary nationalism to an interest in using literature as a vehicle for political and social critique (Railton 1978, 178), and in *Mercedes* and *Jack Tier*, Cooper uses the complex mode of interrogating reality offered by realism as he conceived it not only to anxiously acknowledge but also to angrily challenge O'Sullivan's Hispanicist oversimplifications.

It would be a mistake to overstate the differences between Cooper and O'Sullivan. Cooper supported the Democratic Party, and, albeit with reservations, he also favored expansion and the US-Mexican War. Somewhat akin to O'Sullivan, Cooper viewed US expansion as a matter of necessity; just as the nation had supplanted the Native Americans of the eastern United States, a process Cooper comments upon at length in the Leatherstocking Tales and other works, so would it inevitably make its growing influence felt to the south. Although he may not have presented them in as vitriolic a manner as some of his contemporaries (Mann 2007, esp. 155; Wallace 1995, 193), Cooper's racial views, like O'Sullivan's, reflected the antebellum popularity growth of racial science (Person 2007, 17; Tawil 2006, 69–91 and 129–51). Descriptions of blacks and Hispanophone peoples in *Mercedes* and *Jack Tier* often reflect racialist stereotypes. Cooper did not reject all elements of Hispanicism.

However, Cooper took issue with jingoistic rhetoric that blinded his countrymen to expansionism's excesses, what he believed to be its endemic corruption and violence. In the novels, Cooper thus seeks to offer a responsible, nuanced depiction of Hispanophone peoples. *Mercedes*, for instance, historicizes Spanish court intrigues as reflections of the times, rather than as evidence of innate Spanish degeneracy. Similarly, *Jack Tier*'s Mexican Juan Montefalderon exhibits a patriotism that Cooper presents as admirably rivaling that of many US Americans. US characters often come across much worse. These works' complexity and subtlety render O'Sullivan's arguments naive and banal. Cooper shows that underneath O'Sullivan's tidy narrative of national ascendency, there is a complex moral reality. Typical Hispanicist stereotypes elide the individual variability of a heterogeneous Hispanophone population. Moreover, grandiose Hispanicist assumptions regarding the necessity of US domination obscure the conflict, bloodshed, and corruption that attempting to bring such expectations to fruition will necessarily entail.

Historicization of Cooper's laudable manner of offering nuance to US-Hispanophone conflict provides insights into both the period and the ideological motivations for Cooper's art. His turn to realism aesthetically manifests the growing conservative skepticism toward liberal expansionism he felt during his late period. Cooper elaborates his conservative views in political writings such as "A Letter to His Countrymen" (1834) and *The American Democrat* (1838). His novels of this portion of his career are often didactic works meant to express the views found in these nonfiction political writings (Spiller 1965, 33, 42). Cooper viewed Manifest Destiny as a mythic narrative regarding the unstoppable extension of US empire and democracy. In his view, Manifest Destiny represented the worst excesses of liberalism, whose abstract logic failed to account for the peculiar situations and traditions of different peoples. Cooper explores such situations and traditions in what are, relatively, these novels' responsible portrayals of Hispanophone peoples. The works make a variety of other related critiques of liberalism, such as in *Jack Tier*'s skeptical portrayal of the appeals Stephen Spike makes to "free trade" as he defends his treasonous dealings with Mexico. Cooper's realism, finally, favors restraint and nuance in the face of liberal abstractions.

Antiliberal Conservatism

Considering the loose manner in which the term "conservative" (to which I will frequently refer in this chapter, chapter 5, and the coda) is often used in both scholarly and popular venues, a working definition is needed. British philosopher Anthony Quinton defines "conservatism" as "a conviction of the radical intellectual imperfection of the human individual, as contrasted with the historically accumulated political wisdom of the community, as embodied in its customs and institutions. This conviction is associated with a parallel belief in the moral imperfection of mankind" (Quinton 1978, 11–12). For the conservative, he explains, "The consequence of men's intellectual imperfection is that they should not conduct their political affairs under the impulsion of large, abstract projects of change arrived at by individual thinkers working in isolation from the practical realities of political life. . . . The consequences of men's moral imperfection is that men . . . will on the whole act badly. . . . They need . . . the restraint of customary and established laws and institutions" (13). Quinton elaborates that conservatism's more particular qualities are its commitment to "traditionalism . . . [which refers to] the conservative's attachment to, or reverence for, established customs and institutions . . . organicism, which takes a society to be a unitary, natural growth, an organized, living whole, not a mechanical aggregate . . . [and] political scepticism, the belief that political wisdom, the kind of knowledge that is needed for the successful management of human affairs, is not to be found in the theoretical speculations of isolated thinkers but in the historically accumulated social experience of the community as a whole" (16). Although individual conservative thinkers may express distinct positions, the beliefs in man's intellectual and moral imperfection and consequent traditionalism, organicism, and political skepticism compose conservatism's doctrinal glue.

As it manifested itself in response to the Enlightenment, modern conservatism is a reactionary, oppositional political philosophy that sees itself as the voice of common sense amid the rampant spread of dogmatic, excessive forms of liberalism. Enlightenment-influenced liberals subject traditional beliefs to scrutiny, they believe that market laissez-faire-ism produces innovation and wealth, and they encourage policies that enable people of all classes to seek social mobility. Against the conception of man's innate rationality and perfectibility that liberal ideas are based on, conservatives—soberly, in their view—argue for man's moral and intellectual imperfection. They rail against what they view as the hubris of basing politics and social organization on abstract, humanistic, universal theories such as those proposed by John Locke, Adam Smith, Jean-Jacques Rousseau, and the French philosophes. These theories are, according to conservative doctrine, bound to fail because they were developed by individual thinkers working in isolation from political exigencies. Similarly, they are founded upon rationalistic principles that neglect to account for man's intellectual imperfection. Conservatism, in this respect, is deeply antihumanist. As opposed to the liberal idea that intellectual, Cartesian man possesses the agency necessary to build a better world, conservatives construe man as radically overdetermined by social forces that are beyond his control. According to conservatives, these forces are to be trusted, not challenged. Only the collective wisdom of organically constituted beliefs, institutions, and governmental forms can provide a reliable guide for humanity. Universalist humanism is based on what conservatives view as false pride in man's rationality, but collective wisdom, although not fail proof, has a trial-and-error credibility.

Traditional conservatism must be distinguished from "conservatism" as we colloquially understand it. In today's US parlance, the terms "liberal" and "conservative" are commonly used to describe, respectively, the Democratic and Republican parties. Although it may seem surprising considering the vitriolic tenor of US politics and, particularly, the intensely pejorative way the right uses the term "liberal," both of these parties could be generally described as liberal. Both are dedicated, for instance, to cultivating the operation of the Smithean "invisible hand," or to maintaining a market system they believe will create the conditions for the greatest individual liberty and happiness for the most people. The difference between the two is not over the validity of liberal tenets but rather over how best to provide for their operation. Generally, in recent years, most mainstream Republicans have promoted a radical conception of individual liberty, neoliberal market deregulations, and an aggressive foreign policy. Democrats typically have contended that state-enforced egalitarianism through labor regulations and a robust social safety net made up of initiatives such as universal state-supported health care are necessary to create opportunities for individual advancement. That stated, even this distinction may be eroding due to the breakdown of the welfare state and the increasing corporatist neoliberal orthodoxy. These shifts reveal that a corporatist form of classically liberal values is at the heart of mainstream politics and governance. (It remains to be seen whether a potentially unconventional Trump presidency will spur deep party realignment.) Classical conservatism, though, is an approach outside the political philosophies occupied by these two parties. Its emphasis on tradition and its skeptical impulses are foreign to both. For instance, although libertarianism is frequently described as "conservative," the utopianism inherent in its raptures over the "free" market's capacity to alleviate misery could not be further from traditionally conservative skeptical restraint. Moreover, libertarianism acknowledges no traditional order other than individual rights and market rationality, which again differentiates it from the conservatism Quinton (1978) describes.

Despite its reactionary roots, traditional conservatism often manifests itself in hybrid, partially liberal forms. This has been true both today and during the eighteenth and nineteenth centuries. Strictly dichotomizing conservatism and liberalism obscures the complexity observed in actual historical actors. Indeed, that purely conservative positions are rare reflects the traditional conservative's skeptical resistance to systems. For instance, particularly in his reaction to the French Revolution (1790), Edmund Burke is oftentimes considered the archetypal antiliberal and the father of modern conservatism. The challenge Burke poses to the regnant political and economic order, his aversion to political theory, and his promotion of Christian natural law all suggest his adherence to Quintonian conservative values of traditionalism and his belief in man's intellectual imperfection. Burke's position, though, is consonant with liberalism in that it accepts the capitalist idea that the drive to accumulate wealth is utilitarian and will contribute not simply to individual happiness but also to social progress. His distrust of social mobility puts a decidedly conservative cast on his version of capitalism, but the ambiguity is worth noting (Macpherson 1980, 37, 40, 53, 58, 61, 69). Similarly, although the term "conservative" is often misleading when applied to today's Republican Party, its religious branch exhibits more traditionally conservative features (although often with a crusading fervor at odds with conservative restraint), which again demonstrates the difficulty of applying these terms precisely to particular political actors.

Cooper as Liberal Conservative

Cooper is illustrative of these classificatory difficulties. He vocally supported US democracy (as he believed it should operate), and he staunchly defended individual liberties. In these respects, his thought was classically liberal; he was not a simple reactionary. Cooper, though, had a conservative spin on liberalism, writing in "A Letter to His Countrymen" that "here [in the United States], the democrat is the conservative, and, thank God, he has something worth preserving" (Cooper 2000b, 343). This insistence on conservation rather than progress comprises the antiliberal conservatism that emerges in his later political thought. "Through many of [Cooper's] books," comments conservative philosopher Russell Kirk, "runs a pervading distrust of America's anarchic temper, her appetite which respects no prescription, her intolerance that scowls from behind a bombastic affirmation of absolute liberty" (Kirk 2001, 198). Cooper's *American Democrat*, Kirk explains, promotes reigning in these tendencies "to strengthen democracy by marking out its natural bounds" (200). *The American Democrat* particularly advocates for strict adherence to the Constitution as the institutional glue that can contain the centrifugal tendencies inherent in US democracy. Cooper believed the document's genius resided in its restraints against excessive democratic impulses, restraints without which Cooper believed the US system would tend dangerously toward leveling.

As part of this defense of his interpretation of the Constitution, Cooper expresses his belief that nationalist sentiments led many US Americans to develop misleading ideas regarding equality. Cooper chides his readers to remember that the US system has flaws, praising it "on account of its comparative advantages [especially its elevation of the people], and not on account of its perfection" (Cooper 2000a, 364). Among these imperfections, he proceeds to discuss erroneous views regarding democracy and equality. Intoxicated by a culture that celebrates natural rights, radical egalitarians may dream of perfect equality. Cooper insists that although democracies support some degree of civil and political equality ("equality of rights," that is, the franchise), "equality of condition is incompatible with civilization, and is found only to exist in those communities that are but slightly removed from the savage state. In practice, it can only mean a common misery" (392). Even with "equality of rights," "there is no more a literal universal suffrage, than a literal equality. All these terms must be received in a limited sense, their meaning amounting merely to a comparison with other and older conditions of society" (460). As Cooper strikingly sums up this point, "The celebrated proposition contained in the declaration of independence is not to be understood literally. All men are not 'created equal,' in a physical, or even in a moral sense" (395). Cooper's wary emphasis on recognizing complexities lying beneath misleading nationalist abstractions comprises a persistent rhetorical strategy in the work (Birzer and Willson 2000, xxiv).

Cooper's comments regarding why inequality of condition is necessary exhibit a characteristic mood of conservative restraint and prudence. Cooper emphasizes that there are imperfections in all human institutions. He thus advocates that the nation keep in mind the "possible" just as much as the "best" when seeking the best possible way. As he applies this notion to the issue of inequality, "There are numerous instances in which the social inequality of America may do violence to our notions of abstract justice, but the compromise of interests under which all civilized society must exist, renders this unavoidable" (Cooper 2000a, 396). Inequality is, quite frequently, unjust in Cooper's view, but it must be allowed to encourage the individual pursuit of excellence and to empower those most capable of leadership to influence society. Without financial independence, the gentry would not have the freedom from constantly thinking about self-interest to be disinterested and objective in political matters. They need intellectual space to contemplate philosophy and government and the freedom to gather and to share ideas with other similarly blessed individuals. Only with such privileges can they work to maintain social stability. Because hierarchy is necessary for maintaining constitutional safeguards, it is of the utmost importance for property to be protected by rule of law (Ewart 1977, 72–75). Radical egalitarian demagogues and their social speculation threaten this hierarchy; Cooper's views on their agenda reflect Quinton's comments regarding political theorists working in isolation from political realities. US practices may not be perfect, Cooper suggests, but some sacrifice of equality is necessary for the greater good of society.

Conjointly with this perspective on rights and equality, Cooper expresses suspicion toward public opinion. He feared that many were coming to believe that shifts in public opinion were sufficient to warrant legislation against sacredly protected rights, even property, regardless of constitutionally established governmental processes. As Cooper explains, "The pretence that the publick has a right to extend its jurisdiction beyond the reach of the laws, and without regard to the principles and restraints of the fundamental compact that binds society together, is, indeed, to verify the common accusation of the enemies of democracy, who affirm that, by substituting this form of government for that of a despotism, people are only replacing one tyrant by many" (Cooper 2000a, 465–66). This tyranny of public opinion, Cooper contended, was easily manipulated by a demagogic US press whose radical reformist political arguments were little more than cover for attempts to acquire power and monetary gain. Such editors and writers, in Cooper's view, manipulate their readers' willingness to rally around social and political chimeras such as jingoistic nationalism and absolute equality.

A final notable aspect of Cooper's conservatism that emerges in *The American Democrat* is a distrust of commerce. The contemporary right rallies behind market rationality as the ultimate arbiter of social value, touting the "businessman" as the quintessential national type and a worthy political leader. This view had roots in nineteenth-century arguments that the market was the ultimate arbiter of the good, making the businessman who was adept in satisfying its needs an ideal leader. This libertarian view holds an equivocal place in the conservative tradition, and Cooper resembles classical republicans in his ambivalence toward possessive individualism and the profit motive. Merchants, Cooper writes, are disposed "to sacrifice all governing rules, to protect the interests of the day." "It follows," he continues, "that a community governed by men in trade, or which is materially influenced by men in trade, is governed without any fixed principles, every thing being made to yield to the passing interests of the hour, those interests being too engrossing to admit of neglect, or postponement" (Cooper 2000a, 478). Cooper zealously defended the claims of private property. In his view, private interests must always be balanced with public duty. The merchant's activities could easily spiral into the unbridled pursuit of gain, which would corrupt the moral fiber. Such pursuit encourages fidelity to individual profit rather than a sense of duty to improve the community. The profit motive can become so strong that merchants are willing to corrupt the market by averting taxes, cheating their fellow citizens, and infringing upon the rights of individuals who play by the rules. Cooper thus actively defends those rules. Because of their financial independence from the morally enervating market, gentlemen rather than merchants were more likely to be able to maintain a balanced view of the relationship between individual interest and the public good. They thus ought to be accorded prerogative in making political decisions and reminding those less privileged of their duties. Here, again, Cooper's conservatism is apparent. The right to pursue individual gain and elevation is an intrinsic good in the US system, but that right can be easily abused. Strong restraints in the form of a well-regulated economic system and a social order that defers to the gentry's views are needed to check a commercial society's harmful tendencies.

The Historicism of *Mercedes of Castile*

In the novel's preface Cooper sarcastically contrasts *Mercedes of Castile* to other works "with the trifling difference that we state truths, with a profession of fiction, while the great moral caterers of the age state fiction with the profession of truth" (Cooper 1840, 1: x). The assertion immediately calls attention to the novel's purported truth-value while also positioning the work in the wider context of commentary that is written "with the profession of truth" despite being, Cooper contends, more fanciful. Given that Cooper is writing about the Hispanophone world, it makes sense to include expansionist commentary on that world among the work Cooper is criticizing. Cooper's response is his attempt at a responsible account of the actions surrounding Columbus's first voyage. His approach contrasts with the Whig history of much early US discussion of Columbus and Spanish colonialism. Such discussion was consistent with the Black Legend. According to the Black Legend's historical logic, Spanish colonialism was a mere stumbling block to the Anglo-American establishment of a more morally benevolent civilization in the New World. For his part, Cooper depicts the Spanish culture and political institutions of the late fifteenth century as reflections of a historically specific society that was much different from his own, not exhibitions of a transhistorical Spanish depravity. His work thus resembles what Eileen Ka-May Cheng describes as the attempt of a number of US historians of this era to attempt to divest themselves of biases and to empathize with their subjects before making historical judgments (Cheng 2008, 2, 9–10). US Americans should understand early modern Spain, Cooper contends, on its own terms before passing judgment. He suggests that if US Americans insist on comparing nations and do so without prejudice, they might be disappointed to learn that the nineteenth-century United States is not always as superior to fifteenth-century Spain as US Americans think. His principal point, though, is simply that the heroes-villains historical logic that construes colonial-era Spain as a backward nation in contrast to northern Europe and especially England ignores the period's messier moral and technological reality.

For instance, Cooper emphasizes that the Iberian Peninsula was ahead of the game in the exploration of the Western Hemisphere. Although this would seem a common-sense point, given Portugal's success in exploration and Spain's initial dominance of the Americas, it could be easily lost in the Hispanicist atmosphere. In one passage in which Luis and a priest discuss whether the earth is round (despite his historicism Cooper voices the spurious notion that Columbus's principal challenge in attaining funding for his expedition was combating the flat-earth myth), the priest asks why sailors can see distant sails before they see the rest of the craft, intending to illustrate the round-earth theory to the doubting Luis. Using an English boat as an example, the priest asks, "Do the English put the largest of their sails uppermost on the masts?" Luis replies, "They would be fools if they did. Though no great navigators—our neighbors the Portuguese, and the people of Genoa, exceeding all others in that craft—though no great navigators, the English are not so surpassingly stupid. Thou wilt remember the force of the winds, and understand that the larger the sail the lower should be its position" (Cooper 1840, 1: 59). In this offhand fashion Cooper reminds his readers that southern Europe in many respects boasted the most advanced European societies at the turn of the fifteenth and sixteenth centuries.

More pointedly taking issue with stock Hispanicist accounts of Spanish antiquity, in his characterization of Luis, Cooper historicizes Spanish military culture. As Cooper writes of Luis, "Martial qualities, in that age in particular, redeemed a thousand faults; and Don Luis had even been known to unhorse, in the tourney, Alonzo de Ojeda, then the most expert lance in Spain. Such a man could not be despised, though he might be distrusted" (Cooper 1840, 1: 74). In Hispanicist accounts the Spanish passion for demonstrating honor through knightly sports and war was viewed as exhibits in Spanish bloodlust. For Cooper, though, these pursuits represent a cultural paradigm that, although it had become antiquated by the nineteenth century, was once shared across medieval Europe. Medieval Spain should not be scrutinized, Cooper implies, because it did not see such activities as barbaric, no European nations yet doing so.

Cooper's comments on Spanish religion, similarly, undermine typical Hispanicist accounts of Catholic depravity and duplicity. In a passage that illustrates his historicist approach, Cooper writes, "At that day, churchmen enjoyed a species of exclusive favor, mingling with all the concerns of life, and not unfrequently controlling them." Cooper points out that many US Americans criticize this influence within Roman Catholic nations; however, he also insists that "no people afford stronger evidences of the existence of this control, than the people of the United States, more especially that portion of them who dwell in places that were originally settled by religionists, and which still continue under the influence of the particular sects that first prevailed." Cooper ties this influence to US Americans' unfortunate tendency to seek "to extend the control of society beyond the limits set by the institutions and the laws, under the taking and plausible appellation of Public Opinion." He concludes with a defense of the Catholic Church's role within his novel's world, writing that "there is no question of the ascendency of the Catholic priesthood throughout Christendom, previously to the reformation; and Isabella was too sincerely devout, too unostentatiously pious, not to allow them every indulgence that comported with her own sense of right, and among others, that of a free access to her presence, and an influence on all her measures" (Cooper 1840, 1: 90–91). Many Hispanicist accounts descried Catholic influence on the Spanish state, considering the religion itself a mishmash of mystifications that hindered the advance of reason in Hispanophone communities and that provided cover for iniquitous actions. Cooper, though, contends that although there may be some truth to such perceptions, it must be remembered that Catholicism was ascendant throughout medieval Europe. Its influence in Spain reflected not so much a particular failing on the part of the Spanish as a historically specific European attitude toward religion and politics, one whose validity was being debated in nineteenth-century Spain just as in other parts of the West. What is more, he emphasizes that many US Americans have little grounds for condemning Spain on account of its failure to separate church and state. Cooper, ever suspicious of anything Puritan, reminds his readers that many within the United States supported national policy institutionalizing their religious beliefs. As Cooper knew, antebellum anti-Catholicism emerged from evangelical groups that decried "popish" political influence while seeking to mobilize public opinion in favor of policies supporting their own views. US critics of Spanish religion should look in the mirror, Cooper suggests.

Cooper's comments regarding Spanish religion respond not just to popular nativist attacks on Catholicism but also to erudite perspectives voiced by New England's liberal Christians. Such writers were generally more muted in their advocacy against Catholicism. Moreover, whereas nativists feared Catholic influence in US society, liberal Christians feared both nativist sectarians and Spanish Catholicism. For these thinkers, the presence in Catholicism and sectarianism of corruption, resistance to the separation of church and state, and superstition exemplified rational spirituality's superiority. These liberal Christians were particularly fond of condemning sectarianism by comparing its zealotry to the Inquisition. They feared that US democracy would allow either sectarianism or Catholicism to infiltrate US government (Jakšić 2007, 3). Cooper, working from his interpretation of the Constitution, recognized the dangers of merging church and state. Yet these New England writers, like the zealous nativists they opposed, based their image of Spain not on an intrinsic identity, as they thought, but on specific moments in the nation's development. Neglecting the presence of vigorous nineteenth-century debate within Spain and other traditionally Catholic countries regarding relations between church and state, this group misleadingly used the phantasm of Spanish Catholicism as a political cudgel.

On historicist grounds Cooper also excuses Spanish seizure of natives. After the explorers arrive in the West Indies, Cooper writes that "it is true that violence had been done, in a few instances, by seizing half a dozen individuals in order to carry them to Spain, as offerings to Doña Isabella; but this act was easily reconcilable to usage in that age, equally on account of the deference that was paid to the kingly authority, and on the ground that the seizures were for the good of the captives' souls" (Cooper 1840, 2: 92). The point flies in the face of the mystifications of the Black Legend, accordingly to which Spanish treatment of the Indians manifested a transhistorical Spanish cruelty and despotism. The genocide of Native Americans was typical of European colonialism, and Cooper points out that Columbus's actions in seizing natives, although unjust, reflect the "usage in that age," not Hispanic bloodlust.

Cooper's historicization exhibits his conservative outlook in that it takes societies to be organically constituted wholes that must be understood from within. This outlook leads him to conclusions that may come across, to many contemporary readers, as insightful, such as his points regarding church and state. As seen in the discussion of the slaughter of natives, though, his historicization elsewhere leads him to more obviously reactionary conclusions. For instance, in one passage he praises Queen Isabella's pursuit of traditionally feminine domestic duties despite being an immensely powerful monarch, writing "Isabella, herself, was seated at a little table, where she was employed with her needle, the subject of her toil being a task as homely as a shirt for the king, it being a part of her womanly propensities to acquit herself of this humble duty, as scrupulously as if she had been the wife of a common tradesman of her own capital. This was one of the habits of the age." Cooper then decries the fact that modern US women "condescend to touch any thing as useful as the garment that occupied the needle of Isabella of Castile" (Cooper 1840, 1: 91). The passage conservatively suggests that shifting nineteenth-century gender standards, such as greater freedom among private women to pursue intellectual and leisure activities instead of domestic responsibilities, should not be viewed as progress. Rather, women should adhere to gendered traditions because doing so cultivates personal discipline and commitment to family, values conservatives continue to bemoan the loss of today.

Sexism of this sort comes across as reactionary even to today's moderates. It may also seem a small excuse for the violent actions of Columbus and the Spanish colonists that those deeds were generally acceptable within the culture. However, the Hispanicist context in which Cooper was writing must be remembered. Negative depictions of Spanish colonialism on the part of US Americans were not honest appraisals of the period's horrors but rather exercises in national identity formation and imperial fantasy. When US Americans such as O'Sullivan depicted Hispanophone peoples as unsuited for modern life in a liberal democracy, they construed US Americans as, by contrast, peculiarly fitted for such a role. Given that they viewed liberal democracy as the most appropriate form of government, they believed that US Americans deserved a leadership capacity in world affairs. Hispanophone peoples, US Americans thought, were unsuited for self-governance. Ideologues such as O'Sullivan held that US Americans had a responsibility to spread liberalism to these Hispanophone peoples and thus to open constrained economies. US expansion was the only thing that could encourage Hispanophone peoples to cultivate the personal political responsibility and individual acquisitiveness that, expansionists argued, would facilitate greater contributions on the part of these peoples to the world economy. For Cooper, in their self-interested drive to find a historical basis for their ideological position, Hispanicist ideologues ignore the fact that medieval Spanish customs do not illustrate Spain's incapability to undertake life in a liberal democracy. Rather, they exhibit a historically characteristic European way of life that has little bearing on contemporary debates regarding the appropriateness of US expansion into the Hispanophone world.

The question of how self-interest can obscure the true nature of one's actions is important to Cooper. This preoccupation informs conservative positions of his that seem less reactionary. For instance, in another passage in which medieval Spanish traits are touted over nineteenth-century practices and philosophies, Cooper negatively depicts Sancho Mundo's unfair trade with the natives, which Sancho attempts to defend by appeal to the philosophy of "free trade." As Cooper writes, Sancho "had decorated the persons of many of [the natives] with hawk's-bells, and had contrived to abstract from them, in return, every ornament that resembled the precious metal [gold], which they possessed. This transfer, no doubt, was honestly effected, however, having been made on that favorite principle of the free trade theorists, which maintains that trade is merely an exchange of equivalents; overlooking all the adverse circumstances which may happen, just at the moment, to determine the standard of value." Cooper then depicts Sancho's views on trade through a dialogue between Sancho and Luis. Sancho defends free trade, arguing that, "Is not the value of a thing to be settled by what it will bring in the market?" He receives the following skeptical reply: "'If it be honest to profit by the ignorance of another,' answered Luis, who had a nobleman's contempt for commerce, 'then it is just to deceive the child and the idiot.'" Sancho, though, cautions that Luis's views might "unsettle trade, which ought to be as free and unencumbered as possible." Cooper concludes the conversation by observing that "Sancho was thus occupied in explaining his notions of free trade—the great mystification of modern philanthropists" (Cooper 1840, 2: 107–9). For Cooper, appeals to the importance of maintaining free trade, that sine qua non of neoliberalism, are easily deployed by self-interested merchants and financiers to put a face of philosophical legitimacy on acts that harm the community. Cooper here exhibits the classically republican view, which defended individual liberty but suspiciously viewed the unbridled pursuit of personal gain as potentially undermining the long-term good of the community and instead benefiting the individual immediately. Cooper's point reflects the Smithean precept that whereas legitimately competitive markets benefit society, unregulated markets are not truly free. A few influential merchants/traders can corrupt competition by engineering trade to their benefit, hurting the community in the process. Cooper points to a similarly unfair power dynamic in Sancho's trade with the natives, which is not truly "free" given that the natives are unaware of the European value of the commodity they give up.

Cooper's perspective on Hispanicism is analogous. Just as appeals to "free trade" can seemingly legitimize rapacious commercial activities, typical Hispanicist accounts of Spanish antiquity put a face of legitimacy on chauvinistic, imperialistic attitudes toward Spanish America. In doing so, free trade and Hispanicism function as discursive constructs that mediate power relations.

Cooper did not achieve a perspective outside dominant prejudice toward Hispanophone peoples. In some respects, he keeps step with Hispanicist attitudes. For instance, Cooper frequently appeals to race by referring to "warm Castilian blood" (Cooper 1840, 1: 30) and the like as a regulating factor in the fiery, honor-obsessed Spanish character. Cooper apparently agreed with the notion, increasingly popular during the antebellum period, that Spanish difference is racially determined.

Despite his acceptance of this aspect of Hispanicism, however, Cooper's perspective in *Mercedes of Castile* must be distinguished from the more excited versions of the discourse propagated by Barlow and then, in a more intense and racialized form, the antebellum expansionist press. Operating from selective histories of Spain and its conquests in the New World, such views were characterized by hyperbolic claims that Hispanophone peoples were irredeemably degenerate, US American expansion into Spanish America the providential harbinger of liberal-democratic freedoms and modernization for a hopelessly backward people. Cooper advocates a more moderate view. Whatever Spain or its New World legacy might be in the present, Cooper suggests, there was much to admire in Spanish antiquity. The regrettable aspects of Spain's history could just as much be evidence of historically specific attitudes as of something rooted in the Spanish character. Ideologues who forsake integrity by perverting history via their attempts to order history's complexities according to simplistic, nationalist narratives regarding what they would like to believe about the present delegitimize their causes in the eyes of the discerning.

Jack Tier: The Patriotic Mexican Gentleman as the True American?

Cooper's comments in *Mercedes* regarding Spaniards' warlike disposition assume additional significance when considered in the light of 1840's jingoistic support for a US invasion of Mexico. Not only does the US perception of medieval Spanish love for martial practices show ignorance of these pursuits' typicality in the era; US Americans, Cooper suggests, should be more interested in recognizing their countrymen's own bellicosity and corruption. Cooper's position, to an extent, reflects the New England scholars' criticisms of the expansionist press. According to these scholars, a persisting Spanish national character devoted to religion and chivalry emerged due to the pressures of the Reconquista, when Spain expelled Muslims from the Iberian Peninsula. Yet when Spaniards lost their common enemy after nobly liberating their homeland, this national character devolved into a cruel desire to conquer (Jakšić 2007, 2). These scholars sought to define an ideal US national identity against this religious and martial Spanish character. They, for instance, feared that in becoming an imperial nation, the United States was repeating Spain's errors. Although Cooper was not opposed to expansion per se, he also was concerned about the jingoistic manner in which it was defended and how that jingoism might be used to support destructive policies. He thus hesitated at the Democratic press's enthusiasm. Although I focus on that immediate hesitation, Cooper's position also contrasts with that of New England intellectuals in an important respect. Like the enthusiasts, these scholars base their perspective on distinctions between the United States and the Hispanophone world. The two differ on this matter merely in that whereas the enthusiasts see Mexico as a debased nation that needs conquest, the intellectuals see the enthusiasts as devolving into Spanish tendencies of excessive violence. Cooper was not opposed to making such national distinctions, but he cautions that they can obscure matters.

Cooper takes up these issues in his US-Mexican War novel, *Jack Tier*. The narrative centers on an exchange of gunpowder between treasonous US American merchant captain Stephen Spike and Mexican patriot Don Juan Montefalderon. At the novel's opening, Spike sets sail on the *Molly Swash* for the Caribbean, where he states that he intends to sell flour at Key West. Spike is assisted by his more honorable first mate Harry Mulford. Mulford is initially unaware of Spike's intentions, although he is vaguely suspicious of his captain's character. Also aboard the *Swash* are the beautiful Rose Budd and her widowed aunt. Spike, who plots to force marriage upon the minor heiress Rose, has tricked Rose's simpleminded aunt into believing that Rose should sail for the sake of Rose's actually robust health. Rose's affections are reserved for her suitor Harry. Also accompanying the voyage is the titular Jack Tier, who convinces Spike to allow him to join the voyage at the last minute. Tier has an observable interest in Spike that remains unexplained until the novel's conclusion. On the voyage, Spike frequently eludes federal craft that seek to inspect his cargo. The *Swash* successfully arrives in the Dry Tortugas and rendezvous with Montefalderon. Although to Cooper's readers

Montefalderon represented the enemy in this wartime novel, Cooper depicts Montefalderon as an honorable, selfless gentleman patriot whose unalterable purpose is to aid his country's fortunes. During the gunpowder transfer the Mexican schooner capsizes, with many Mexicans dying and the gunpowder and a bag of doubloons sinking to the ocean floor. Spike seeks to recover the schooner, but, while doing so, a US naval cruiser, suspicious of Spike, attacks. During the fracas, Mulford, Rose, her aunt, the aunt's Irish servant, and Tier escape to a nearby island. However, after he eludes the cruiser, Spike captures the escapees, taking the two women and Tier back on the ship while leaving Mulford to die on a small key. Tier and Rose, however, save Mulford while Spike and Montefalderon are occupied with determining how to recover the sunken schooner. In the novel's climax, Mulford assists the naval cruiser in capturing Spike, although not before Spike sacrifices many lives, including those of Aunt Budd and Montefalderon. The reader is finally apprised that the mysterious Tier is actually Molly Swash, Spike's wife whom Spike had many years prior abandoned at a foreign port. Tier/Swash had since lived as a male sailor, eventually seeking again to sail with her husband with conflicting desires for vengeance and reunion. Tier/Swash lives out her days with Mulford and Rose, who are now married.

In *Jack Tier* Cooper continues to refine a realist mode. The narrative does, it must be said, involve sensational and arguably ridiculous elements such as piracy, close escapes from death, and cross-dressing. Moreover, like *Mercedes*, most of its characters are predictable, two-dimensional heroes or villains. The work lacks high realism's psychological individualization. However, its fixation on the lower classes, on the mundane details of nautical life and especially nautical crime, and its demystification of press rhetoric lend it a realist air. His earlier work tends to fixate ultimately on his genteel milieu. In *Jack Tier* no such personages are found; the cast is diverse and unidealized. Although Mulford and Rose exhibit the virtues of the usual noble Cooperian male and female leads, Mulford is a low-born mate on a dilapidated merchant vessel, Rose a middling heiress. The mass of the characters are rough-and-tumble sailors, with the villain, Spike, being one of the most ignoble in Cooper's rogues' gallery. Montefalderon is the closest to a genteel character, and as a Mexican, he is not representative of the New York gentry featured in so many Cooper tales. The novel also exhibits realism in its depiction of the dialect and social life of sailors. Cooper, moreover, instructs the reader regarding sailing strategy and nautical jargon, drawing humor from Aunt Budd's misuse of such terminology. The plot itself could hardly be said to focus on the transcendent. The heroism it involves is not of world-historical import but rather involves the apprehension of an ignoble smuggler. Other plot focal points include crime and a cross-dressing vengeful wife, certainly mundane subject matter. The novel exhibits Cooper's desire to depict this material in a rational way via how Cooper lampoons what he views as the unrealistic, manipulative social foibles of the time, such as the press's tyrannical manipulation of public opinion, religious fanaticism, and the temperance movement (Cooper 1848, 1: 110; 2: 88). In sum, the novel offers an unromanticized, informative look at the maritime corruption endemic to the US-Mexican War.

A significant aspect of this realism is the demystification of liberal nationalism. Cooper's turn from romance to realism represents an aesthetic manifestation of his growing conservatism during the US-Mexican War period, a conservatism insisting on restraint against liberalism's excesses. Proponents of Manifest Destiny excitedly touted Anglo-American racial superiority and the consequently unstoppable extension of US empire and democracy. In his "corrective to popular conceptions of the war and national attitudes toward Mexico" (Iglesias 2011, 184), though, Cooper interrogates binaries touting Anglo-American ascendency and Mexican degeneracy. As he writes in his preface, "We have had occasion to refer often to Mexico in these pages. It has been our aim to do so in a kind spirit; for, while we have never doubted that the factions which have possessed themselves of the government in that country have done us great wrong, wrong that would have justified a much earlier appeal to arms, we have always regarded the class of Mexicans who alone can properly be termed the 'people,' as mild, amiable, and disposed to be on friendly terms with us. Providence, however, directs all to the completion of its own wise ends. If the crust which has so long encircled that nation, enclosing it in bigotry and ignorance, shall now be irretrievably broken, letting in light, even Mexico herself may have cause hereafter to rejoice in her present disasters" (Cooper 1848, 1: iv–v). Although this passage shows a potentially insidious benevolent imperialism by legitimizing a war that was largely a pro-slavery land grab, it also shows a friendly attitude toward Mexico. Unlike O'Sullivan, Cooper focuses on Mexico's redeeming qualities and expresses sympathy for the Mexican people's struggles, struggles he views as results of poor political leadership rather than innate Mexican degeneracy. He hopes that the US-Mexican War will lead to improvements for the Mexican people, not just in that they will be exposed to US American culture, but in that their failures in the war might lead Mexicans to turn a more critical eye to their government. Jingoistic, uncharitable depictions, for Cooper, are unfriendly toward a national neighbor and reveal a hubristic belief in the United States' ability easily to correct Mexico's problems.

Cooper's insistence on the US war effort's ambiguity is made clear during a dialogue between Montefalderon and Rose. Here, Montefalderon reports on a conversation he has had with Mulford, in which Mulford states: "As for this war, I know but little about it, though I dare say the Mexican government may have been wrong in some things that it might have controlled and some that it might not—but let right be where it will, I am sorry to see a nation that has taken so firm a stand in favour of popular government, pressed upon so hard by another that is supposed to be the great support of such principles. America and Mexico are neighbours, and ought to be friends; and while I do not, cannot blame my own country for pursuing the war with vigour, nothing would please me more than to hear peace proclaimed" (Cooper 1848, 1: 142). Although Cooper, again, legitimizes the United States' actions in the war, through the admirable Mulford and Montefalderon he also acknowledges the war effort's questionable aspects. Whereas many tout the war as an expression of Manifest Destiny, the war exhibits a nation premised on self-determination "press[ing] upon" another people with similar aspirations. This point reflects Cooper's broader sense that whereas US nationalists celebrate the nation as the apotheosis of the glories of liberal democracy, the most excited advocates of that view are demagogues who manipulate public opinion against the nation's principles.

Cooper's contrasting depiction of Captain Spike and Montefalderon embodies his point that the war's reality is more complex than pro-war jingoism suggests. Spike is a specter of excessive nationalism come back to haunt the nation, a traitor who defends his actions with appeals to the liberal rhetoric used to promote unhinged expansionism. By contrast, Montefalderon is a self-effacing republican who is deeply devoted to country, a man whose leadership would be a boon to any nation. As Cooper alludes to Spike in the book's opening, "The species of treason portrayed in these pages is no uncommon occurrence; and it will often be found that the traitor is the loudest in his protestations of patriotism." That treason, Cooper argues, proceeds from Spike's particular vice. Spike clamors for "the rights of the people" but is in fact guilty of "corruption and selfishness" (Cooper 1848, 1: v). Cooper indicates that although such behaviors may shock some readers, they are not uncommon. The United States is a nation with all too many Spikes, one in which his views are all too influential.

That Spike rationalizes his actions by appeals to free trade illustrates Cooper's conservative view of how the unbridled pursuit of self-interest celebrated by liberalism is corruptive. Taking a civic-republican view, Cooper contends that duty to the national community must come before self-interest. Disavowing such duties as inimical to their right to pursue personal gain, "free trade" extremists, Cooper argues, appeal to liberalism to put a face of philosophical legitimacy on rapacious practices. Cooper, as we have seen, contended that the life of trade cultivated an amoral tendency to place making a buck before duty to the public good. The profit motive, in his view, had to be checked by the community's sympathies to benefit the public in the manner liberals believed it could. The unhinged Spike represents market self-reliance taken too far. A venal merchant whose desire for gain brooks at no qualm or law, including avoidance of treason and murder, Spike's life of trade has left him without a moral compass. As Cooper describes him, "Spike had a conscience that had become hard as iron by means of trade. He who traffics much, most especially if his dealings be on so small a scale as to render constant investigations of the minor qualities of things necessary, must be a very fortunate man, if he preserve his conscience in any better condition. . . . He saw no particular harm in making the best bargain he could; nor was it easy for him to understand why he might not dispose of anything he possessed for the highest price that was to be had" (Cooper 1848, 2: 200). Whereas liberals such as Barlow describe trade as a civilizing force, Cooper claims that it corrupts men like Spike. Even at his life's end, after his iniquity has been exposed and he has been captured, he feels little compunction for his treasonous actions. He is not a man who does evil knowingly but rather one who has come to see evil as good, good as evil. In an earlier passage in which Tier refers to the work of the US government cruiser that pursues Spike as fulfilling its "duty," Spike replies, "Duty!—You little scamp, do you call tormenting honest traders in this fashion the duty of any man?" (177). Spike's self-deceived description of himself as "honest" illustrates his blindness to what for Cooper is precisely the problem: Spike is unable to balance his pursuit of self-interest with his duty, duty being central to the civic-republican view. His loyalty is to himself, with no thought for the ramifications of his actions to the larger community. Cooper thought that men such as Spike were common in the United States, that their perspectives were too powerful, and that their behavior was merely an extreme manifestation of the liberalism many believed was what was best about the United States and what the nation might offer Mexico. Cooper implicitly asks whether a United States in which Spike represents "national overreaching" (145) is really what excited nationalists suggest the nation to be?

The novel's genteel representative of Mexico, Montefalderon, acts out of duty to country. Cooper develops a contrast between Spike and Montefalderon during passages following the capsizing of the Mexican schooner. This contrast is consistent with his view that too much involvement in trade often corrupts individuals, whereas the gentry's independence engendered disinterestedness. During a dialogue between the two characters, Cooper writes,

> "I had forgotten," [Spike] at length answered. "The gold must have all gone down in the schooner, along with the powder!"
>
> "And the poor men!"

> "Why, as for the men, Señor, more may be had for the asking; but powder and doubloons will be hard to find, when most wanted. Then the men were poor men, accordin' to my idees of what an able seaman should be, or they never would have let their schooner turn turtle with them as she did."
>
> "We will talk of the money, Don Esteban, if you please," said the Mexican, with reserve.
>
> "With all my heart, Don Wan—nothing is more agreeable to me than money. How many of them doubloons shall fall to my share, if I raise the schooner and put you in possession of your craft again?" (Cooper 1848, 1: 139–40)

Cooper here contrasts Montefalderon's disinterested concern for his fallen compatriots and his country more generally with Spike's single-minded obsession with money. Montefalderon shows himself to be a man who has taken advantage of his privileges by cultivating humanity and sympathy; Spike shows himself to be one who believes men are more replaceable than money and commodities. Spike values sailors solely on the basis of their seamanship, viewing them as means instead of ends. His statement to this effect draws a rebuke from Montefalderon, although the socially obtuse Spike does not notice the judgment.

After having exhibited these differences through dialogue, Cooper elaborates the contrast. He emphasizes that despite his sorrow over the loss of his countrymen, "the late catastrophe did not in the least unman" Montefalderon. Hardly a representative of a "degraded race," as a San Francisco *Herald* editorial described Californio Mexicans in 1859 (quoted in Pitt 1966, 205–6), Montefalderon's perseverance in the face of adversity might surprise some US American readers because "it is too much the habit of the American people to receive their impressions from newspapers," from which "the opinions . . . obtained are very much on a level, in value, with the thoughts of those who are said to think aloud, and who give utterance to all the crudities and trivial rumours that may happen to reach their ears." The newspapers give "very false notions of our neighbours of Mexico." Cooper concedes that the Mexicans are largely "a mixed race [with] the various characteristics of such an origin." Mexico, he laments, "is unfortunately little influenced by the diffusion of intelligence which certainly exists here." However, he insists "that even Mexico has her redeeming points. Anglo-Saxons as we are, we have no desire unnecessarily to illustrate that very marked feature in the Anglo-Saxon character, which prompts the mother stock to calumniate all who oppose it, but would rather adopt some of that chivalrous courtesy of which so much that is lofty and commendable is to be found among the descendants of Old Spain." Getting to the point of this lengthy introduction to his contrast between Spike and Montefalderon, Cooper describes the pure Castilian creole Montefalderon as an ideal patriotic gentleman. Unlike Spike, Montefalderon is exactly the kind of individual Cooper thought was a fitting leader for a nation: "The Señor Montefalderon was earnestly engaged in what he conceived to be the cause of his country. It was scarcely possible to bring together two men impelled by motives more distinct than Spike and this gentleman." Whereas Spike "was acting under impulses of the lowest and most grovelling nature," Montefalderon "was influenced by motives of the highest." As Cooper continues, "He saw in the events of the day, a province wrested from his nation; and, in his reasoning on the subject, entirely overlooking the numerous occasions on which his own fluctuating government had given sufficient justification, not to say motives, to their powerful neighbours to take the law into their own hands, and redress themselves, he fancied all that has occurred was previously planned; instead of regarding it, as it truly is, as merely the result of political events that no man could have foreseen, that no man had originally imagined, or that any man could control" (Cooper 1848, 1: 151–52). In these passages Cooper does legitimize racialist, essentialist perceptions of Mexico by suggesting that the nation's large mixed-race population has "necessarily" negative effects on the country's demographic makeup. Moreover, he continues to show a lack of concern over the US-Mexican War's pro-slavery, imperialist dimensions, attributing US American actions to circumstance rather than agenda, implicitly also suggesting that US influence might benefit Mexico.

That stated, he also cautions against how the press elides individual variability within the Mexican population, pointedly suggesting that too many Anglo-Americans dichotomize the differences between the two nations instead of recognizing that both contain many races and types of individuals. O'Sullivan and other such expansionists clearly figure in the background of Cooper's concern. The passage singles out the press for deforming public opinion and urges readers to avoid relying on demagogic editors bent on misleading the public with the covert goal of benefiting particular political parties and agendas.[1] Whereas the Hispanicism such writers touted plays to US American prejudices by positing Hispanophone individuals as invariably being degenerates who are unfit for life in a modern liberal democracy, Cooper suggests that such broad generalizations fail to acknowledge that many Mexicans are better so fitted than many US Americans.[2] Cooper presents Montefalderon as evidence for his claims regarding how such discourses elide individual variability (Iglesias 2011, 186). Cooper describes Montefalderon's devotion to country as being of the "highest" nature, particularly in contrast to Spike's "grovelling" motivations. Montefalderon's gentlemanly disinterestedness makes him an ideal candidate to lead Mexico toward a better future. Spike's extreme liberalism, though, has unfitted him for life in a balanced liberal democracy. Unfortunately, demagogic celebrations of the market impulse, free trade, and the businessman as the best US American type make it more difficult for US Americans receptive to balanced views to see that a man like Spike is hardly an ideal representative of the nation. Montefalderon's devotion to country blinds him to his country's faults to some extent, but that is understandable, Cooper suggests. Given that Mexico can produce men who are so clearly superior to US Americans such as Spike, surely the view of O'Sullivan and others of Mexico must be, at best, oversimplified (Rodríguez 2010, 147).

As these passages begin to suggest, Montefalderon might be the novel's most "American" character. Particularly within the novel's publication era, which was shortly after the Age of Revolutions, one definition of "American" pertains to being willing to make sacrifices so that one's countrymen can enjoy liberty and self-determination. Cooper places a conservative spin on this definition, melding it with his insistence that the individual pursuit of gain must be balanced by duty to the community as defined by the gentry. Cooper believed that gentlemen who have sufficient wealth not to need to worry about pursuing self-interest and who can thus objectively contemplate the communal good are best suited to lead their nations, and Montefalderon has clearly taken advantage of his privileges to develop his patriotism. Cooper argues that although US Americans are "*par excellence*, Americans," "a sense of right should teach every man that what may be patriotic in an American, would be exactly the same thing in a Mexican, and that we ought to respect in others sentiments that are so much vaunted among ourselves" (Cooper 1848, 2: 50–52). In this light, Cooper suggests that Montefalderon is certainly more American than Spike, indeed more American than Mulford, who despite being virtuous is not fighting for the larger community. If the United States is to offer any sort of positive influence to Mexico, that influence must exhibit a wise balance between US liberalism and learning and Montefalderon's patriotic, gentlemanly republicanism. Cooper's representation of Montefalderon as not only his novel's ideal Mexican but also ideal American more generally was intended, simultaneously, as a caution against simplistic views of Mexico and also as an admonition that his readers not forget the gentry's priorities in determining national destinies. Cooper hoped his readers would heed this admonition rather than buying into the radical view that the Anglo-American businessman—a Spike, for instance—is necessarily best suited to lead in a liberal, market-driven world. That Mexico grants Montefalderon the prestige he deserves, whereas many US Americans would not, illustrates, for Cooper, a lesson those US Americans could learn from Mexico, one they indeed must learn to deserve the power they desire.

Ironically, Montefalderon's "Iberian blood" contributes to this gentlemanly American-ness, which Cooper admires as communally defined decorum in coherence with his skepticism toward US liberal individualism. Whereas in the just-quoted passage Cooper describes Anglo-Saxon blood as contributing to a bellicose, imperialistic individualism, he describes Montefalderon's Spanish stock as chivalrous. This racial proclivity manifests itself in Montefalderon's aristocratic, self-effacing love of country in contrast to the self-serving patriotism Cooper descries in his countrymen. Although Cooper's positive attitude toward Spanish blood reflects his more negative one toward indigenous Mexicans, it opposes popular Black Legend–informed attitudes toward Spain by valorizing Spanish chivalry as a valuable rather than an antiquated characteristic. Cooper also here opposes more totalizing views of Mexico.

In an additional conservative move, Cooper argues that conquering Mexico is impracticable, a point via which he sets up the implication that it may not even be desirable because most of the nation is far from ready for liberal democracy and is in better hands being governed in an authoritarian manner by men of Montefalderon's class. Cooper suggests through Montefalderon that even if the United States wins the conflict, Mexico will not be wholly subdued, and Mexico's peculiar culture and situation will not easily assimilate to the US way of life. As Montefalderon admonishes Mulford, "no nation of the numbers of ours can be, or ever was conquered, unless by the force of political combinations. In a certain state of society a government may be overturned, or a capital taken, and carry a whole country along with it, but our condition is one not likely to bring about such a result. We are of a race different from the Anglo-Saxon, and it will not be easy either to assimilate us to your own, or wholly to subdue us. In those parts of the country, where the population is small, in time, no doubt, the Spanish race might be absorbed, and your sway established; but ages of war would be necessary entirely to obliterate our usages, our language, and our religion from the peopled portions of Mexico." Cooper concludes that Montefalderon's judgment is "entitled to the consideration of all prudent and considerate men" (Cooper 1848, 2: 107). The use of the word "prudent" reflects Cooper's conservative insistence on restraint. In conservative parlance "prudent" signifies recognizing human fallibility and that we should focus on the possible rather than on unattainable ideals. Montefalderon emphasizes that Mexico, although a small, weak nation in contrast to the United States, is all the same too powerful and populated to be overrun. In the background of Cooper's depiction of Montefalderon's claim is O'Sullivan's argument that Mexico would eventually be forced to amalgamate or perish in the face of Anglo-American expansion. Even accounting for his acceptance of the war's role in facilitating expansion, O'Sullivan generally believed expansion should be a gradual, peaceful process. Proponents of the All of Mexico movement took the concept of Manifest Destiny a step further and argued that the United States should take the opportunity provided by having a national army mobilized and annex Mexico in its entirety. The nativist John A. Perry echoed this sentiment a few years later when he wrote in a travelogue that he "hop[ed] the Americans will pity [Mexico] and take the country and civilize and moralize the people" (Perry 1853, 69). Such ideas' feasibility must to Cooper have seemed even more preposterous than O'Sullivan's views.

Cooper, despite elsewhere pondering the potential benefits of the war to Mexico, even raises questions about O'Sullivan's idea that Mexican assimilation is necessary and desirable. Montefalderon suggests that as a product of Spanish colonialism, Mexico is not appropriate soil for the tilling of US liberal democracy. Cooper provides a conservative spin on Hispanicism here by insisting on the organic unity and inassimilability of the United States and Mexico as discrete societies. His argument resembles the racialist antiexpansionist argument that Mexico could not be assimilated to the United States due to differences between Mexico's mestizo and the United States' Anglo-American populations. This argument was popular among antiwar Whigs and moderate Democrats (Horsman 1981, 239). However, in a realist move, Cooper also places in Montefalderon's mouth sentiments that were common among elite Spanish American patriots, including Simón Bolívar. Bolívar believed that after having lived under Spanish colonial dominion, most Spanish Americans were not accustomed to the individual political participation and civic responsibility necessary for life in a US-style liberal democracy (Shepherd 1918, 272). Bolívar thus stressed that Spanish America ought to assume more centralized, authoritarian forms of republican government. These views were typical of the interpretation of the Spanish Enlightenment that was popular among the leaders of the Spanish American revolutions. This interpretation held that national liberation from colonial bonds, economic liberalization, and the encouragement of self-interest among the people was desirable but that full individual political self-determination may not be consistent with a strong republican community (Coronado 2013, 115, 137–38). Bolívar's attitude toward the United States is manifest in that of Montefalderon. Cooper's characterization of Montefalderon thus enhances a historical verisimilitude that reflects his aims of writing a realist novel through which he sought to counterpoise idealistic notions of US-Mexican relations with a more complex reality.

Conclusion

As might be expected of an author who shared in his era's racism and expansionism, two related factors blunt the revolutionary force of Cooper's challenge to Hispanicism. First of all, Cooper's Castilian Mexican gentleman Montefalderon would have been thought rare by 1840s Anglo-Americans, and Cooper's challenge to his readers' racial attitudes regarding Mexico hinges more so on reminding them that men such as Montefalderon exist rather than challenging racism per se. As many would have agreed, an editorial in the July 31, 1846, issue of the *Augusta Daily Chronicle and Sentinel* challenged the All of Mexico movement on the grounds that the United States would be burdened with "a sickening mixture, consistent of such a conglomeration of Negroes and Rancheros, Mestizoes and Indians, with but a few Castilians" (quoted in Horsman 1981, 239). Cooper makes a different argument against All of Mexico, emphasizing that it is impracticable. He also seems to imply that it is unnecessary given that men like Montefalderon may be trusted to lead the country. Whereas it might seem that Cooper's depiction of Montefalderon as a representative Mexican also challenges Anglo-American racism, what he is really doing is reminding US readers that a white gentry capable of determining Mexico's future remains in place in the country. This is not a challenge to Anglo-American racism per se, as Cooper does not question the dismal views his contemporaries had of mestizos.

Moreover, Cooper's depiction of Montefalderon is consistent with his conservative, reactionary view of class. Cooper thought that the leisure that wealth afforded the gentry enabled them to study philosophy and politics. Their views thus counted for much more than those of the less privileged, and they had special responsibilities in the protection of communal social stability. This view illuminates less apparent political ramifications of *Jack Tier*'s critique of imperialism. Montefalderon's argument that Mexico is not ready for US-style liberalism reflects what Robert Fanuzzi describes as a belief popular among the privileged in Spanish America that although the US system was admirable, Spanish American women and lower-class men were not ready for self-determination (Fanuzzi 2012, 187). Although Cooper's respect for communal values and self-sacrifice may seem admirable, Cooper is also here acceding to an elitist Spanish American view meant to maintain an inequitable social system that benefited men of Montefalderon's class. Even given the lip service Cooper pays to political equality in *The*

American Democrat, one is left wondering whether Cooper found this conservative Spanish American view more appealing for its consistency with his own reactionary perspectives on class.

However, Cooper's novel exhibits how his realist literary attitude enabled him to view the ideology of jingoistic Hispanicist expansionism in a light different from that of many of his contemporaries. As Marjorie Levinson explains, New Formalism may enable apprehension of the sophisticated means by which works of literary art challenge ideological oversimplifications (Levinson 2007, 560). For Cooper the expansionist view that it was the United States' Manifest Destiny to civilize degraded and oppressed Hispanophone peoples was such an oversimplification. Cooper shows how despite its acceptance among many US Americans, Manifest Destiny exhibited internal incoherence. Manifest Destiny, to be sure, was never completely agreed upon in the antebellum United States; it encountered resistance even within the expansionist Democratic Party and was generally very unpopular with liberal Christians and Whigs. However, if there was ever a degree of consensus on the matter, particularly within Cooper's Democratic Party, it was during the US-Mexican War years. During this period, Cooper challenged expansionist excesses with a rich realist depiction of the Hispanophone world.

3
Herman Melville's "Benito Cereno" as Critique of Hispanicist Exceptionalism
Cosmopolitanism and Ironizing Identity

Readers of Herman Melville's "Benito Cereno" who are sensitive to questions of identity and race have tended to focus on Amasa Delano's view—funneled through free-indirect discourse—of black slaves (e.g., Karcher 1980, 109–59; Tawil 2006, 191–208; Yellin 1970). Such studies are now supplemented by the acknowledgment that Delano's response to Benito Cereno reflects Anglo-American prejudices against Catholic Spain and its New World colonies (Emery 1984; DeGuzmán 2005, 47–67; Nelson 1993, esp. 112–14; Sundquist 1993, esp. 143, 148).

This chapter makes two points regarding these issues. First of all, as Allan Moore Emery and Eric Sundquist indicate, the stereotypes upon which Delano relies do not simply construe Spaniards as the Black Legend's violent despots. For Delano, Spaniards and Spanish American creoles are also languorous and inefficient (Emery 1984, 50–53; Sundquist 1993, 148). These characteristics were not as pronounced in the colonial typologies. I contend that Delano's perspective thus reflects the nineteenth-century, US Hispanicist evolution of Anglophone attitudes toward Hispanophone peoples. Through Hispanicism Delano self-reflexively imagines himself against Cereno as a US American who is well fitted for a managerial role in a capitalist, liberal-democratic world. Delano, thus, voices antebellum imperialist beliefs that Hispanophone peoples—whether "off-white" Spaniards or creoles (DeGuzmán 2005, esp. xxiv, xxvii) or Spanish Americans of mixed racial ancestry—were racially incapacitated for sovereignty's duties.

Delano's attitudes toward Spaniards and Africans are distinct but interrelated. Both views are self-reflexive. Contemplating Spanish and African difference, Delano imagines himself to be racially superior as an Anglo-American. Delano's understanding of blacks as subhuman, though, bolsters his sense of himself as possessing basic human capacities of free will, reason, and aesthetic sensibility. Such views, refracted through romantic-racialist tropes regarding blacks, reflect what Morrison terms "Africanism," the pervasive US discourse through which US Americans imagine cherished self-perceptions against a mysterious, demonized black presence (Morrison 1993, esp. 5, 17). In perceiving Spaniards and their New World brethren as despotic and inefficient, Delano views himself as a member of a benevolent racial and national community that is exceptionally endowed to forge liberal-democratic social, economic, and political institutions. He thus believes himself entitled to usurp management of Cereno's ship and slaves.[1]

My second point regards how Melville interrogates such discourses by using a sophisticated form of storytelling. Some have described Melville's approach, although good-intentioned, as overdetermined by the racialism pervading his white US American culture. Dana D. Nelson claims that whereas "Benito Cereno" subverts how Delano views blacks and Spaniards according to static types, the tale fails to imagine alternatives to these typologies (Nelson 1993, 109–30). More intent on examining the tale's depiction of the Spanish, María DeGuzmán, too, contends that although Melville denaturalizes how Delano confirms his whiteness through reflection on the "off-white" creole Cereno, this critique is undermined by what DeGuzmán reads as the tale's damnation of Cereno and Babo (DeGuzmán 2005, 47–67). These claims inform my view that by ventriloquizing Hispanicism through Delano, Melville emphasizes how it informs US exceptionalism. In doing so, Melville ironizes Delano's sense of himself as the benevolent representative of an exceptional nation. Melville reveals how Delano's perspective occludes the in fact rapacious Delano's ability to realize that he and Cereno share much in common. I also part ways with Nelson and DeGuzmán; inspired by neoformalist arguments for literature's socio-civic power, I champion Melville's efficacy in thinking beyond exceptionalism. More so than Cooper, Melville challenges Hispanicist exceptionalism per se, rather than merely arguing for restraint against the discourse's most excited versions. Proposing grounded alternatives to racist and imperialist policies was not Melville's aim, but his tale suggests formal alternatives to racialist exceptionalism by calling attention to the qualitative differences between manners of telling stories about relationships and identity. These opposed manners can be described as forms of cosmopolitanism. In contrast to the self-absorbed Spaniard Cereno, Delano self-reflexively identifies as a gregarious cosmopolitan who good-naturedly navigates the differences between cultures. Delano's cosmopolitanism, thus, reflects his Hispanicism, much as Barlow understood cosmopolitanism in contrast to Spanish-ness. However, Melville implies another, nonexceptionalist cosmopolitanism, one premised on skepticism toward identity categories; the ability to revise preconceptions about identity; and sensitivity to context. The evocation of this more rigorous cosmopolitanism is a major achievement of the tale.

Putnam's Monthly, "Benito Cereno," and Hispanicism

The Hispanicist contexts Melville commented upon through his depiction of Delano are exhibited in articles about Spain and Spanish America appearing in *Putnam's Monthly* around the time of the journal's 1855 publication of "Benito Cereno." Such articles exhibited fascination with and prejudice against Hispanophone peoples. Melville's engagement with *Putnam's* is well documented, particularly regarding the journal's slavery politics (Post-Lauria 1995; Robbins 1997, 547–59). His interest in the material on Spain and Spanish America has also been noted (Emery 1984, esp. 50; Post-Lauria 1995, 5). Whereas scholarship attests to the *Putnam's* articles' broadly imperialist dimensions, I here emphasize their reflection of nineteenth-century, US American views about Spanish-ness. In the *Putnam's* pieces (typically ethnographies or travelogues reporting on Hispanophone locales' landscape, customs, politics, and wealth), Hispanophone peoples are not only vicious and despotic but also lazy and lacking in possessive individualism. This characterization contrasts with the author's identification with what he construes as the modern, US American values of entrepreneurship that are necessary for success in a liberal-democratic, capitalist world. These stock Hispanicist tropes inform what Sarah Robbins describes as the general nationalism of *Putnam's* (Robbins 1997, 548–51).

Articles such as "Annexation" (Anonymous 1854), which favorably compares US expansionism to prior forms of empire building, attest to the demonization of Spanish colonialism. Two other texts, though, illustrate nineteenth-century, US views of Hispanophone peoples. The second issue of *Putnam's* includes "A Glance at Havana." In this unsigned travelogue, the author narrates his trip into the exotic Cuban port city, reporting on his entrance into the harbor on board a steamer and his experiences after landfall. He writes in the first-person plural, evoking identification with his readers. The article reflects how these texts construe consensus between author and US reading public regarding a Hispanophone world whose difference confirms the author's sense of US superiority. The writer focuses on the inefficient management of human and natural resources in Cuba, a flaw construed as a product of the Spanish economic and political aversion to liberalism and the concomitant backwardness of its people. Upon arriving in the harbor, the author is immediately approached by a lethargic pilot, even though "the entrance to the harbor of Havana is the plainest possible sailing." "Were it an American or an English port," he continues, "the offer to pilot a vessel into it would be regarded as a patent swindle." In Havana, though, things work differently, as "a corps of pilots has been established by the Spanish government, and a neglect to employ one is sure to be resented as a slight offered to the authorities" (Anonymous 1853b, 186). He explains that "the Captain of the Port . . . has absolute power over every vessel that enters it. . . . The vessel, therefore, which should enter the harbor unpiloted would be pretty sure to find herself ordered into the most inconvenient position which his ingenuity could possibly discover" (186). The forced usage of unnecessary pilotage affronts the author's free-market sensibilities. Moreover, he views the captain's ability arbitrarily to make life difficult for those who resist the Cuban economic scheme as indicative of the invisible operation of power in Cuba. This operation contrasts to the transparency favored by US liberal democracy.

This piece continues in the following issue under the title "How They Live in Havana," in which the (presumably same) author walks the reader through Havana. The article describes Havanese social and domestic customs—what the hotels and food are like, what the inhabitants do at their leisure, what social etiquette is expected, and so on. Although not explicitly focused on economic and political matters, the discussion, again, self-reflexively represents Cubans as less fitted for life in a liberal democracy than US Americans. Nineteenth-century US liberal discourse assumed a separate-spheres model in which the wife, hearth, and home provided moral suasion. This moral suasion was necessary to cultivate men's virtuous behavior in a market-driven public sphere that encouraged cutthroat behavior. The article is at pains to show that this does not happen in Cuba. The hotels are "nothing more or less than . . . boardinghouse[s]"; the author puns that in them, "bed and board" become one, "the bed being in fact a board" (Anonymous 1853c, 288). He more pointedly comments that in Havana, "the man whose *volante* and harness have a thousand dollars' worth of silver worked into their decorations, and whose *calesero* (coachman) carries enough of bullion about him to purchase his freedom, will not have so much, or so expensive furniture in his house as the New-Yorker who considers himself in very moderate circumstances" (289). The passages ridicule the contrast between exterior and interior, construing a telling inversion between the customs of Havana and the United States. In the States the home space welcomes and refreshes, whereas the exterior is rugged, enterprising, and productive; in Havana, the exterior is foppish and wasteful, the interior inhospitable and enervating. A similar equation is implied in passages noting the lack of privacy in Havana (290). Privacy might seem a simple matter of etiquette, but separate-spheres ideology accorded it great importance, positing that a safe haven from the outside world was necessary for the moral suasion offered by the private sphere. The author's perception of Cuba's failure to maintain this necessary division further suggests his view of Cuba's illiberality.

"Benito Cereno" as Metafictional Commentary on Hispanicist Inconsistency

These and similar *Putnam's* articles offer warrant for a discourse of US imperial management that "Benito Cereno" examines. As Nelson explains, Delano seeks recognition of his prerogative as a white, managerial man through identification with fellow captain Cereno. When Cereno does not provide that recognition (Nelson 1998, 2), Delano becomes suspicious that Cereno is an imposter to his captaincy and decides to appropriate Cereno's ship (16). Delano fails to recognize the true state of affairs—black revolt—because he blindly believes that white managerial men monopolize power. As Nelson briefly acknowledges elsewhere, Delano's perception is complicated by his sense that Cereno is not exactly white (Nelson 1993, 112). Cereno is a Spanish creole, an important distinction given that Melville added many details playing up Delano's attitudes regarding Spaniards to the real-life Delano's account, which says little about such attitudes (Emery 1984, 51–52, 53, 57–59, 61, 66; Newman 1986, 98–100). As DeGuzmán (2005) elaborates, Delano's ambivalence toward Cereno reflects Spanish-ness's equivocal place in Delano's Anglo-American perspective. White and not white, modern and medieval, representing a nation that tried to build an empire in the New World but failed, the Spaniard functions as a test case in exceptionalist Anglo-American self-construction. For these reasons, Cereno's behavior triggers Delano's wariness about Spaniards (Nelson 1993, 112). Indeed, Delano has as much riding on believing that Cereno is *not* of his caste as he does on believing that Cereno is—if, per Nelson, Delano confirms his managerial aptitude when he condescends toward blacks, he also does so through interactions with Cereno.

Although Delano typically refers to Cereno as "the Spaniard," Cereno is a creole native of Chile. Early in his interactions with Delano, Cereno declares that he is "a native and resident of Chili" (Melville 1987, 57). He confirms this declaration in the concluding deposition, when he expresses his intention "not [to] return home to Chili, but betake himself to the monastery on Mount Agonia" in Peru after the conclusion of the legal proceedings against the revolted slaves (114). The distinction between peninsular and creole Spaniards is important. Notably, Amasa Delano's source text (Delano 1970, chapter 18, 318–53) does not note Cereno's Chilean nativity, which suggests that Melville had particular reasons for inventing a creole origin for his character. I argue that the emphasis on Cereno's origin points toward

Delano's ambivalence regarding Cereno. In describing Cereno as a "Spaniard" rather than a "Chilean" or a "creole," Delano signals his desire to establish identification with Cereno as a fellow white man of the managerial class. Delano's usage is consistent with a long-standing Anglo-American practice of referring to white Spanish Americans as "Spaniards" rather than as "Mexicans," "Peruvians," "Chileans," and such, to differentiate them from people of color living in these nations. This usage was adopted from that of the creoles themselves. Although peninsular Spaniards often looked down upon creoles, provoking the creoles' ire, the creoles were eager to identify with peninsulars to enforce racial hierarchies in their nations.[2]

However, as John J. Johnson explains, Anglo-Americans held particular negative prejudices against creoles that could be described as intensifications of prejudices held against peninsular Spaniards. The Black Legend established that peninsulars were cruel religious zealots. Moreover, as seen in Barlow, what was thought to be the eighteenth-century decline in Spanish fortunes planted the idea that Spaniards were decadent, backward, and improvident. As the creoles established Spanish American republics in the early nineteenth century, Anglo-Americans developed particular views regarding Spain's New World legacy. First of all, given the perception of lingering preferences for autocratic government and attendant political instability in these republics, Anglo-Americans viewed creole political and intellectual elites as ideologically inept. Second of all, the creoles' tolerance for peoples of color and willingness in many cases to abolish slavery before emancipation was enacted in the United States inspired Anglo-American distaste for the perceived social naïveté of the creoles. Lastly, Anglo-Americans came to view creoles as even more economically improvident than peninsular Spaniards (Johnson 1993, 11–12). Some of these views are attested in *Putnam's*, and they are evident in Delano's perception of Cereno.

Melville begins to reveal Delano's Hispanicist perspective from the moment Delano sees the ship. The sight reminds him of "the lawlessness and loneliness of the spot, and the sort of stories, at that day, associated with those seas" (Melville 1987, 47). The stories inflecting Delano's perspective here may be romances of Spanish pirates, narratives commonly associated in the Anglo-American imagination with the seas off South America even though pirates were typically northern Europeans plundering Spanish gold. These associations trigger Delano's apprehension, although he characteristically sheds his fears by power of his "good nature." As he gets a closer look at the boat, he continues to view it in light of his attitude toward Spain. Emery describes the boat as "symboliz[ing] . . . a 'tottering' Spain" and "stand[ing] . . . for Spain's Western empire" (1984, 52). The boat's decrepit appearance stirs Delano to imagine what he takes to be its romantic, illustrious past. Delano sees in it what was "in its time, a very fine vessel" that "under a decline of masters, preserved signs of former state" (Melville 1987, 48). He fixates on an exotic "stern-piece, intricately carved with the arms of Castile and Leon, medallioned about by groups of mythological or symbolical devices; uppermost and central of which was a dark satyr in a mask, holding his foot on the prostrate neck of a writhing figure, likewise masked" (49). Here, Spanish and gothic figures articulate in Delano's eyes: "the arms of Castile and Leon" are juxtaposed with a frightening mythological image. These impressions color Delano's engagement with the *San Dominick*. What emerges is a metafictional demonstration of how such stories shape experience.

As should already be clear, in addition to Spanish piracy, tropes regarding Spanish aristocratic languor also underpin Delano's perspective. (Although these tropes are conjoined, an analytic distinction will prove useful.) As Delano offers assistance to Cereno, he notes Cereno's "grave and ceremonious . . . national formality[, which was] dusked by the saturnine mood of ill health" (Melville 1987, 51). Delano further perceives a "sour and gloomy disdain . . . not unlike . . . his imperial countryman's, Charles V" (52–53). Delano's attitude toward Cereno, here, hearkens back to the traveler's appraisal of the inefficiency of Havanese aristocratic trappings in *Putnam's*. To Delano, Cereno's "ill-health" marks Cereno's incapability to command, which Delano generally associates with Cereno's Spanish identity. Viewing Cereno as "at once a genteel courtier . . . and an impotent master" (Sundquist 1993, 148), Delano, while contemplating "Don Benito's small, yellow hands" (note the perception of racial difference), "easily inferred that the young captain had not got into command at the hawsehole, but the cabin-window; and if so, why wonder at incompetence, in youth, sickness, and gentility united" (Melville 1987, 58). This ready inference reflects Hispanicist perceptions of creole aristocratic languor. Delano eventually becomes preoccupied with the notion that Cereno is a poor manager. Delano's particular concern is the apparent disorder of the blacks, which he ascribes to Cereno's "strengthless style of command" (Emery 1984, 52) but which, of course, reflects successful mutiny. Although Delano acknowledges that "long-continued suffering seemed to have brought out the less good-natured qualities of the Negroes" (Melville 1987, 51), he believes the central problem is that the "San Dominick wanted . . . stern superior officers," as "not so much as a fourth mate was to be seen" (54). Delano thus frequently patronizes Cereno with advice regarding proper command, for instance, suggesting that Cereno "keep all [his] blacks employed, especially the younger ones, no matter at what useless task" (59) after witnessing a black boy attack a white one.

Melville uses Hispanicism as an aesthetic mechanism to produce the suspense experienced both by Delano and by the first-time reader who sees through Delano's eyes without knowing the tale's conclusion. (Accounts of this suspense, such as that of Edward S. Grejda [1974, 136], typically neglect Hispanicism.) Delano eventually becomes uncertain regarding what is happening on the *San Dominick*, sensing that something is amiss but unable to discern what. As he regards a seemingly stereotypical Spanish ship, Delano perceives himself to be embroiled in a gothic romance with an ambiguous captain and crew. Rather than recognizing black rebellion, Delano, as Sundquist explains, "vacillates between dark suspicion and paternalistic disdain for the Spaniard" (Sundquist 1993, 148). Is Cereno the piratical Spaniard of the Black Legend who will betray Delano, or a languorous, inefficient creole who needs direction?

It must here be mentioned that Delano is blind to black rebellion partly because he sees blacks as inevitable servants. As Nelson observes, Delano persistently "denies the slaves Subjectivity" (Nelson 1993, 112)—he is unable to recognize their desire for freedom. Delano, after all, takes "to negroes . . . genially, just as other men to Newfoundland dogs" (Melville 1987, 84); this human-animal analogy (one of many Delano makes) betrays Delano's belief in innate African childishness and fawning subhumanity. His view's impact on his perception is frequently apparent. For instance, in one passage, Delano contemplates a Spanish sailor's attempt to give Delano a hint about the mutiny, an attempt that Delano mistakes as a possible sign about Cereno's treachery. Delano speculates that Cereno and the blacks are working together, but he quickly concludes, "But they were too stupid. Besides, who ever heard of a white so far a renegade as to apostatize from his very species almost, by leaguing in against it with negroes?" (75). Here, Delano's racist view of black intelligence (note the polygeneticist reference to "species") makes it impossible for him correctly to read the sailor's attempted signal. The state of affairs on the boat—a brilliantly orchestrated slave mutiny—is, indeed, unfathomable to him.

Compounding his inability to recognize black rebellion, Delano finds the interpretations suggested by Hispanicist tropes preferable to what he views as the impossibility of black humanity. As Sundquist puts it, when Delano confronts black revolution, that reality is "conceal[ed] . . . behind the shadow play of the contest between the American and the European" (Sundquist 1993, 151); Delano imagines different possible roles for Cereno and the Hispanic crew but has a more static view of the blacks (Fiedler 1997, 400). For instance, in the well-known Gordian knot scene, when the sailor gives Delano the knot, one of the blacks comes to them, tells Delano the sailor is a fool, and takes the knot and inspects it, clearly suspicious (Melville 1987, 76). Despite witnessing this evidence of black rebellion, Delano ponders Hispanicist alternatives. Upon seeing his whale boat returning to the *San*

Dominick, he complacently says to himself, "I to be murdered here at the ends of the earth, on board a haunted pirate-ship by a horrible Spaniard?—Too nonsensical to think of!" (77). Shortly afterward, Babo returns and bids Delano go to speak with Cereno, who has recovered from a coughing fit. Delano decides he has been mistaken in his suspicions, laughingly thinking to himself, "What a donkey I was. This kind gentleman who here sends me his compliments, he, but ten minutes ago, dark-lantern in hand, was dodging round some old grind-stone in the hold, sharpening a hatchet for me" (77). In rejecting the signs of black rebellion because of his Africanism, Delano first decides that Cereno is not the piratical, vicious Spaniard. Then, given evidence by Babo that Cereno was simply ill, Delano comforts himself in the belief that Cereno is a "kind gentleman" who is physically incapacitated to manage a ship. Robert S. Levine claims that Delano ascribes the ship's disorder to how Cereno is "deficient as a leader because he is not 'Spanish' enough" (Levine 1989, 204). Delano is certainly preoccupied with Cereno's managerial capacity, but the despotic Spaniard is not the only Hispanicist trope available to Delano. That of the languorous, inefficient Spaniard is just as, if not more, appealing to him. That trope coheres with general Hispanicist attitudes toward creoles. He prefers both options, in any event, to the *San Dominick*'s reality.

In the deposition readers learn that Babo orchestrated affairs on the *San Dominick* to deceive Delano (Melville 1987, 109). Babo does so, in part, by playing upon Delano's Hispanicism. Babo also relies on Delano's Africanism by acting the part of the faithful, submissive servant that Delano finds appealing and by correctly gambling on Delano's inability to see black capability (Nelson 1993, 111). Babo also, though, stages the inefficient Spanish ship to Delano. Babo has instructed the Spanish sailors to occupy themselves with odd, useless tasks, oftentimes undertaken by more men than necessary. He has also apparently instructed Cereno to fake sick anytime there is a need for Cereno and Babo to conference privately, playing to Delano's proclivity to believe that Cereno is not fit for the hardships that have supposedly occurred. (Certainly, Cereno's actual fear and debility figure here, too.) Particularly telling is how Babo has Cereno dress in a gaudy outfit that Delano perceives as typical of South American aristocratic, despotic trappings (Melville 1987, 57). In the conclusion it is revealed that Cereno finds it particularly distressing that this "dress . . . had not willingly been put on. And that silver-mounted sword, apparent symbol of despotic command, was not, indeed, a sword, but the ghost of one. The scabbard, artificially stiffened, was empty" (116). Cereno is horrified at the memory partly because Babo has made a "travesty of Don Benito's former Subject-status by *forcing* him to assume the role he once *commanded*" (Nelson 1993, 120). Cereno's feelings likely also reflect his recognition of having been forced to lower himself in Delano's sight by performing a stereotypical form of creole mastery. Delano views the scabbard as a sign of lawless creole despotism, but Babo has made Cereno simulate this form of virility while symbolically castrating him.

That Delano holds tightly to his views until the truth is forced upon him during the tale's climax reflects those perceptions' centrality to his sense of self. Crucial to that self-perception is the difference between how Delano understands blacks and Spaniards. When observing blacks, Delano confirms what he perceives as the humanity that undergirds his "singularly undistrustful good nature" (Melville 1987, 47). In one illustrative example, Delano, during one of Cereno's absences, comes upon "a slumbering negress . . . lying . . . like a doe in the shade of a woodland rock"; upon waking, the woman "delightedly . . . caught [her] child up, with maternal transports, covering it with kisses." The "sunny sight" pleases Delano, and he thinks to himself, "There's naked nature, now; pure tenderness and love" (73). This passage does not appear in the real-life Delano's narrative; Melville invented it to exhibit Delano's racial views. Coming shortly after Delano has had an equivocal encounter with a sailor that has aroused his suspicions, the sight helps Delano conjure up his "undistrustful good nature" and to become confident in his safety. As Andrew Delbanco explains, "Melville knew that in America the dignity of whites depended on the degradation of the blacks" (Delbanco 2005, 156). Delano's perception of the woman through an animalistic simile to a "doe" reflects Delbanco's insight. Melville associates Delano with antebellum romantic racialism. This view construes blacks as embodying positive natural forces, whereas more virulent racisms emphasized black savagery. However, romantic racialism still construed blacks as less human than whites (Robbins 1997, esp. 531–59; Tawil 2006, 191–208). In finding something beautiful and "pure" in her "naked nature," Delano exercises an intellectual, aesthetic capacity through which he elevates himself above the woman, who is figured as part of nature (Nelson 1993, 124). Once he is satisfied in this capacity, he complacently dismisses the notion that anything unfavorable might happen to him.

Delano's Hispanicism informs his self-conception differently. A commonality must first be noted: Delano is comforted whenever the blacks and Cereno conform to his preconceptions. For instance, in an early passage in which Delano and Cereno pace the deck, "Don Benito, with Castilian bows, solemnly insisted upon his guest's preceding him up the ladder leading to the elevation." Delano experiences a twinge of fear as he ascends the ladder after seeing that "two of the ominous file [of blacks,] . . . one on each side of the last step, sat for armorial supporters and sentries." However, "when, facing about, he saw the whole file, like so many organ-grinders, still stupidly intent on their work, unmindful of everything beside, he could not but smile at his late fidgety panic" (Melville 1987, 59). Here, Delano's fear of a potentially treacherous Cereno and crew, which he figures as medieval "armorial supporters" and "sentries," is assuaged as he comes to believe that the two blacks are "stupidly intent on their work." Delano is calmed by what he perceives as characteristic black intellectual inferiority combined with the typical inefficiency of Hispanic management; his recognition of "stupidity" in the work the blacks perform registers both stereotypes. Such moments that adhere to his prejudices bolster his sense of security as a man who controls his situation.

The difference between the roles Hispanicism and Africanism play is that whereas Delano confirms his humanity through Africanism, he confirms his aptitude for liberal management through Hispanicism. In viewing Cereno as nationally incapacitated to lead his ship and slaves, Delano projects his own capacity to do so. Melville emphasizes this point by portraying Cereno as Chilean and thus gesturing toward Anglo-American stereotypes regarding not just Spaniards in general but creoles in particular as ideologically and entrepreneurially unsophisticated and thus unfit to manage. An especially illustrative passage occurs shortly after Cereno asks Delano how well armed Delano's ship is. Babo has put Cereno to this task in consideration of possibly overtaking the *Bachelor's Delight*, and it puts Delano on guard. Delano, though, decides the questions are just further evidence of Cereno's weakened mind, "good-naturedly explain[ing] away [his fears with] the thought that, for the most part, the poor invalid scarcely knew what he was about." This realization convinces Delano that "for the present, the man was not fit to be entrusted with the ship. On some benevolent plea withdrawing the command from him, Captain Delano would yet have to send her to Conception." Delano believes that "the sick man, under the good nursing of his servant, would probably, by the end of the passage, be in a measure restored to health and with that he should also be restored to authority." Musing upon the wisdom of this "tranquillizing" plan, Delano self-congratulates himself with the thought that "there was a difference between the idea of Don Benito's darkly preordaining Captain Delano's fate, and Captain Delano's lightly arranging Don Benito's" (Melville 1987, 69–70). Delano's decision that Cereno's odd behavior is a product of Cereno's incapacitation coheres with the general tenor of Delano's Hispanicism. Delano believes that Cereno's ostensibly aristocratic, Spanish initiation into his captaincy has not prepared Cereno for his voyage's hardships. This decision prompts Delano's perception of prerogative as a man upholding liberal, capitalist values, feelings through which he presumes the duty to commandeer the *San Dominick* until Cereno can do so himself.

Just as Delano considers undertaking this duty, "'with pleasure' would Melville's confident countrymen have similarly taken upon themselves the responsibility for a 'spellbound' Spanish America" (Emery 1984, 53). Delano's Hispanicist assumption of prerogative embodies the nationalist imperialism of *Putnam's*, which construed self-interested imperialism as beneficence. As Louis A. Pérez Jr. explains, the United States "was singular in the degree to which it so thoroughly obscured the distinction between selfless purpose and self-interest" (Pérez 2008, 174). Cohering with Pérez's claim, *Putnam's* articles such as "Annexation" suggested that due to political and economic illiberality, Spanish America was incapable of achieving on its own the modernization the United States could bring. For these reasons, US Americans should feel not shame but pride in their imperial ambitions. US imperial discourse thus provided cover for the territorial and pecuniary benefits produced by US expansion and the concomitant terror experienced by Spanish America.

Melville scrutinizes the Hispanicism of *Putnam's* by revealing Delano's motivations to be equivocal, despite his sense of innocence and entitlement.[3] Although Delano thinks of himself as altruistically arranging the *San Dominick*'s affairs, his offer of assistance is after all a "business transaction" (Melville 1987, 91), and the final counterrevolt "is prompted not by any wish to 'redeem' the oppressed but by a simple desire for material gain" (Emery 1984, 54). After deciding in light of his officers' advice that he should not personally participate in the attack, Delano appoints his chief mate to lead the charge, and "the more to encourage the sailors, they were told, that the Spanish captain considered his ship as good as lost; that she and her cargo, including some gold and silver, were worth more than a thousand doubloons. Take her, and no small part should be theirs" (Melville 1987, 100–101). Far from being disinterested, Delano and crew are willing to make capital of their deeds, significantly on pretext of a self-interested interpretation of Cereno's plea that they leave the ship to its fate (Nelson 1993, 116–17).

These passages suggest another inconsistency: Hispanicism construes the United States as exceptional to Hispanophone nations when that exceptionality is equivocal. Delano understands his managerial aptitude against that of Cereno, but Melville not only shows that Delano is not exactly what he thinks he is but also that Delano is much like what he views Cereno to be. As Delano commands his men to retake the *San Dominick*, he "appoint[s] his chief mate—an athletic and resolute man, who had been a privateer's-man, and, as his enemies whispered, a pirate—to head the party" (Melville 1987, 101). The mention of piracy recalls that Delano's perspective on Spain is conditioned by tales of the Spanish Main. Confirming this point, at the narrative's climax when Cereno desperately leaps into Delano's whale boat, a frenzied Delano, still unaware of what is actually happening, yells to his men to "give way for your lives . . . this plotting pirate means murder!" (98). Through his Hispanicist lens, Delano misinterprets Cereno's actions as piracy in contrast to his own self-conception as a benevolent captain. Yet Delano's chief mate is a reputed pirate, a fact that undermines Delano's self-differentiation from Cereno. Delano's failure to disarticulate himself from Cereno suggests their shared guilt as exploitative, violent, racist captains. More broadly, as Emery explains, Melville "was . . . conscious of America's mimicry of Spain" as a nation that sought through appeals to religious and racial hierarchy to impose a moral order on the Western hemisphere (Emery 1984, 56). What Delano and the US Americans Delano represents take to be different and particular to Spain is, in fact, common to both the United States and Spain.

Irony, Cosmopolitanism, and "Benito Cereno"

Melville's depiction of Delano serves to comment not only on how imperialists constructed US national identity as liberal and managerial but also as cosmopolitan. What did "cosmopolitanism" mean in Melville's world? The *Oxford English Dictionary* defines "cosmopolitan" in its adjective form as follows: "1. Belonging to all parts of the world; not restricted to any one country or its inhabitants. 2. Having the characteristics which arise from, or are suited to, a range over many different countries; free from national limitations or attachments." These definitions were established by the antebellum period. As John Bryant explains, in Melville's day, the cosmopolitan was "an easily recognizable cultural type. For eighteenth-century European *philosophes*, the cosmopolitan ideal had expressed the liberal longing for a political, economic, and spiritual communion of all races and nations. Thus, the true cosmopolite was 'at home' wherever he traveled—London, Paris, Rome, Leipzig, even Philadelphia" (Bryant 1987, 21). The cosmopolitan, Bryant writes elsewhere, "is a 'man of feeling,' a humorist, a gentleman traveler and a 'citizen of the world'" (Bryant 1984, 276). As Bryant elaborates, this figure was at times viewed suspiciously in the antebellum United States. The line between a genial cosmopolitan and a rootless confidence man appeared narrow; a cosmopolitan might seem more a "chameleon than a gentleman, more a satirist than a humorist" (279). For the moment, I work with the first sense in which Bryant discusses the concept, but I return to the latter.

Although cosmopolitanism ostensibly promoted questioning national traditions and identities, some US nationalists paradoxically figured the United States as an exceptionally cosmopolitan nation. We have seen this figuration in Barlow. The second *Oxford* definition listed before gives another example, a quotation from Ralph Waldo Emerson. In "The Young American" Emerson states that, considering the influx of immigrants into the United States and their dispersal over the nation's expanses, "it cannot be doubted that the legislation of this country should become more catholic and cosmopolitan than that of any other. It seems so easy for America to inspire and express the most expansive and humane spirit; new-born, free, healthful, strong, the land of the laborer, of the democrat, of the philanthropist, of the believer, of the saint, she should speak for the human race" (Emerson 1983b, 217). Emerson, elsewhere, expresses qualms about cosmopolitanism, for instance in his contrast between traveling and self-culture in "Self-Reliance" (Emerson 1983a, 277–79). In "The Young American," though, he calls for his listeners to build a cosmopolitan nation with the most "generous sentiment, whose eminent citizens [are] willing to stand for the interests of general justice and humanity" (Emerson 1983b, 226). Emerson's exhortation reflects a broader nationalistic view of a progressive, inclusive United States. In Hispanicist texts this cosmopolitan national identity was celebrated against what was perceived to be a provincial, exclusive Spanish identity. For instance, the *Putnam's* articles "Cuba" and "Annexation" posit that the United States, in contrast to Spain and Spanish America, offers benevolence to all, regardless of identity and history. "Cuba" states that US "nationality" is "the practical realization of cosmopolitanism" (Anonymous 1853a, 16). The US empire-building projects such as the annexation of Cuba promise a time when "all the nations of the earth shall be as one people" (16), a utopia in which petty prejudices will no longer impede the individual's pursuit of happiness.

Several aspects of Melville's characterization of Delano signal Delano's self-understanding as a cosmopolitan. Delano exhibits bourgeois sympathy and racialist benevolence in his reaction to the *San Dominick*, expressing paternalistic concern for those he perceives to be his inferiors. These attitudes intersect with cosmopolitanism as forms of cross-difference sentiment. What particularly distinguishes Delano as a self-imagined cosmopolitan, though, is his sense of himself as a congenial man of the world who is at home anywhere he goes. He takes heart in his "singularly undistrustful good-nature" (Melville 1987, 47) and sees himself as "benevolent" (47) and "humane" (52). He is "genial," with a "good, blithe heart" (84). Delano views himself as well traveled, as revealed by the confidence he feels at being able to "converse with some freedom" in Spanish, and more generally by his assumption of familiarity with African and Spanish natures. He is a man of ready "sympathies" (51) and "charity" (53) toward members of cultures other than his own. He even makes an effort to see himself in Cereno;

while pondering how "the very word Spaniard has a curious, conspirator, Guy-Fawkish twang to it," he concludes that "Spaniards in the main are as good folks as any in Duxbury, Massachusetts" (79).

As his associations with the term "Spaniard" suggest, though, Delano construes his cosmopolitanism not only through fellow feeling for but also through self-differentiation against Cereno. A man who enjoys making "gay and humorous expression[s]" (Melville 1987, 67), Delano frequently takes offense to what he views as Cereno's unfriendly reactions to Delano's own gregariousness. Delano's resentment is most evident after Cereno refuses to join Delano for a pleasant visit aboard the *Bachelor's Delight* shortly before the tale's climax (94). Earlier, Delano perceives in Cereno an "unhealthy climax" of the need for captains to at times manage their ships with a cold lack of "sociality" toward their crews (53). Delano, in turn, thinks of himself as having balanced sociability and authority. Delano's assumption of a sympathetic outlook also reflects this tendency to construe his cosmopolitanism against Cereno. He frequently expresses pity for Babo, whom he believes Cereno does not properly appreciate. Delano, here, takes pride in extending his sympathy to the downtrodden slave (Tawil 2006, 200). What becomes apparent is that Delano's cosmopolitanism takes shape within the Anglo-Hispanic-African triangle that informs Delano's perspective. The power relationships he perceives in that triangle limit his cosmopolitanism; identities are not truly level in his view. Delano's benevolence toward Babo only persists while Delano believes Babo is a willing slave. Once that belief has been exploded, Delano loses all good will toward Babo, leading a brutal counterrevolt. Delano's cosmopolitanism does not go so far as including a willingness to empathize with Babo's desire for freedom. Delano's cosmopolitanism is hierarchical, too, in that Delano defines himself as a cosmopolitan in contrast to Cereno. His sociable regard for Cereno is counterbalanced by his sense of superiority. As we have seen, though, Delano's sense of difference is mistaken.

Here, again, Delano's disavowal of Spanish identity blinds Delano to his failure to measure up to the standards he sets for himself. Delano, thus, exemplifies what Donald E. Pease terms the "structures of disavowal" of US exceptionalism. As Pease writes, "the relations between U.S. citizens' belief in U.S. exceptionalism and the state's production of exceptions to its core tenets might be best described in psychosocial terms as structures of disavowal." The US exceptionalism, Pease argues, "enabl[es] U.S. citizens to disavow . . . measures . . . which violated the anti-imperialist norms that were embedded within the discourse of American exceptionalism" (Pease 2009, 19). In exceptionalists' view, the United States is on the one hand exceptionally benevolent, on the other the bearer of exceptional duties. Because of these duties, when US Americans violate national norms, it is different from when others do so. Accordingly, through Hispanicist- and Africanist-funded exceptionalism, Delano disavows his actions' rapacity and confirms his identity as a benevolent American. Delano represents a US type whose chief characteristic is his reflexive ability to employ exceptionalism to refashion questionable actions as innocent, his opportunism as disinterestedly volunteering his managerial expertise. Like Pease, Melville suggests that exceptionalism makes it difficult for US citizens to admit the nation's guilt.

DeGuzmán and Nelson express dissatisfaction with the tale as a critique. Although Nelson acknowledges the work's subversive insight into racism's "dehumanizing force" (Nelson 1993, 110), she points out that it offers "neither explicit criticism nor alternative action" (128). She further argues that "the narrator *participates* in the sentence and the gaze of the Lima Court at the same time he makes it possible for his readers to do the same" (128)—as DeGuzmán summarizes Nelson's point, "the narrator dehumanizingly turns Babo into an art object" (DeGuzmán 2005, 50). Despite its seemingly good intentions, the tale's irony is an end in itself rather than a means of change, a phenomenon Nelson finds typical of socially engaged writing by authors from privileged backgrounds (Nelson 1993, 127–28). DeGuzmán echoes Nelson. Melville has a "keen sense of the inhumanity of monomaniacal whiteness," she explains, but "the fact that all the characters are typed (and most definitely in a racializing, if not overtly racist, manner) and that the typing is configured in . . . a way . . . that . . . leads to not only re-cognizable but pre-cognizable doom for certain characters [Babo and Cereno] and, if not salvation, then survival for others [Delano] constitutes the real . . . dead end of the story" (DeGuzmán 2005, 52). The tale presents no "serious critique" of racism or imperialism (52).

There is a basis for such arguments. Melville was not particularly concerned with advocating specific policy proposals such as anti-imperial foreign relations (Delbanco 2005, 155). His concerns are intertwiningly epistemological and literary as opposed to political per se. Hispanicism and Africanism interest Melville, in part, as fertile aesthetic grounds, as the blinding quality of such discourses offers an engine for suspense. To the extent that his work has an ideological import, I would describe that import as prepolitical. Melville focuses on the preproposal frame as much as on the content, on how stories told about political issues are structured by assumptions about identity as opposed to what such stories tell regarding how to judge specific political programs.[4] He asks readers to engage political questions with an attitude between reflection and activity. Instead of answering political questions related to liberalism and imperialism, Melville's ironic, perspectival commentary on how imperial sociopolitical forms structure (and obscure) Delano's perception is an injunction to slow down and linger on how such questions are approached.

To say that the tale engages the prepolitical, though, is not to say that it is not politically valuable. In subverting Delano's perceived certainties, the tale opens a space for discussing political alternatives. "Benito Cereno" highlights how Hispanicism convinced the US expansionist that his imperialism was just, the chauvinist that he was cosmopolitan, the exploitative manager of his benevolent liberality. In a milieu in which such discourses seemed natural, it was difficult to judge the relative validity of political proposals because assumptions about identity clouded discussion. How could a proposal be assessed when the evidence in favor of it was an obfuscating notion of US-Hispanic hierarchy? Focusing on the prepolitical, in such contexts, is of as much political importance as evaluating specific policy options. Sacvan Bercovitch illustrates this challenge when he explains how when writing *The American Jeremiad*, he was motivated by his sense that in American traditions of dissent, "the remedy for American abuses was the American promise." The problem here is that "nay-saying . . . framed within the America-story . . . close[s] out alternatives to the culture" (Bercovitch 2012, xix). Options outside the consensus around liberal democracy are off the table. Therefore, recognizing one's entrapment within the culture is "the indispensable first step in opening vistas of political transformation" (xxiii). Melville may not advocate for the radical, non-liberal-democratic measures Bercovitch ponders, but the two concur in suggesting that political dialogue is limited if structured around questions of what is most American.

In this context, Melville's artistry is a powerful tool. One senses in dismissals of Melville's politics a dissatisfaction with high literature's distanced complexity. "Benito Cereno," indeed, exhibits memorable literary complexity by raising perspective to the level of a multilayered, ironized verbal texture. However, the way Melville constructs literature out of how political questions are framed by perspectives comprises his tale's prepolitical import. It is as a complex literary work of art that "Benito Cereno" devastatingly defamiliarizes Hispanicist exceptionalism. What is more, just as Bercovitch calls for "a scholarly-critical enterprise that might eventuate in a different framestory for the national narrative" (Bercovitch 2012, xxxiii), Melville, while offering no policy alternatives, provides alternative narrative frames, alternatives premised on the kind of literary complexity valued by perceptive critics. Revealingly, T. Walter Herbert claims that in *Typee*, "Melville's treatment . . . preserves critical ambivalences that draw him into deeper and deeper efforts to fathom what his own position truly is. . . . [H]e finds the concept of civilization coming to pieces in his hands; yet he has no alternative concept with which to replace it" (Herbert 1980, 156). An analogous point can be made for "Benito Cereno"; in examining Delano's viewpoint, Melville draws attention to US exceptionalism's instabilities and misperceptions. Yet in "Benito Cereno," a mature Melville offers a radical reconception of how stories about identity and relationships can be told, of how answers to such questions can be approached. This reconception is seen in the prepolitical, literary aspects of the tale, which are distinguished from the simplicity of the stock narratives upon which Delano's self-conception relies.

This alternative frame is cosmopolitan, but not Delano's blinding, exceptionalist cosmopolitanism. Another, nonhierarchical cosmopolitan manner of describing relationships among identities is available, one that contests how identity-based discourses violently sever human commonality in their construction of types that are, in the end, fictions, although fictions that tangibly affect our world. This more rigorous cosmopolitanism is premised on a sense for irony, here understood as the ability to denaturalize identity. As Bryant elaborates, Melville's texts and his writing process exhibit a "cosmopolitical awareness" that entails using writing to put identities into play against one another. Using writing in this manner cultivates awareness that there are multiple perspectives (Bryant 2009, 122). With such awareness one recognizes that identity may be viewed differently by each individual. This recognition comprises a nose for irony. Although such an ironic attitude might seem to threaten an anarchic groundlessness, it in fact grounds a revolutionary process of identity constitution. In this process rigorously considered change and revision are always on the table when interactions suggest that one's identity does not work. As Bryant writes, cosmopolitical awareness "is a form of critical thinking designed to familiarize ourselves with three fundamentals: 1) identities evolve . . . 2) texts also evolve because writers and readers revise them; they are fluid texts; and 3) we revise cultural identities as we revise textual identities" (124). "Revision," here, is key. For the skilled writer, a text is never final, as another perspective can always provide a fresh view on the writing. Similarly, for the Melvillian cosmopolitan, identity is conditional; frictions of identity can demonstrate the need for reflection on one's beliefs, customs, and attitudes toward others, potentially demonstrating that one's ways of engaging others need alteration (Herbert 1980, 179).

To many antebellum US Americans, a radical cosmopolitan seemed suspiciously rootless, perhaps because such an individual's orientation to the world upset stock perceptions of US superiority. Melville, though, found this aspect of radical cosmopolitanism appealing. He perceived that a cosmopolitan in this sense "challenges our apathetic being. . . . He confronts us with an invitation to trust and yet reminds us of the necessity to doubt" (Bryant 1987, 30). The cosmopolitan, in this sense, is a far cry from Delano, whose "singular guilelessness" (Melville 1987, 47) makes him "a man of such native simplicity as to be incapable of satire or irony" (63). Delano has abundant evidence that suggests that his perspectives on identity—his belief in inefficient Spanish despotism, black irrationality and servility, and his own benevolence—warrant doubt. For instance, Delano often nearly recognizes that the roles of master and slave have been reversed with Cereno and Babo. Yet Delano is unable to think outside his stereotypes. So inured is he in his self-understanding that he is "oblivious to the end of the meaning of Babo's terror and to the murderous satire contained in Melville's symbolic gesture" (Sundquist 1993, 137). In his final exhortation to Cereno, he brushes off his experience with clichés: "the past is passed; why moralize upon it? Forget it. See, yon bright sun has forgotten it all, and the blue sea, and the blue sky; these have turned over new leaves" (Melville 1987, 116). Such failures to learn from experience exemplify a complacency that is antithetical to cosmopolitical awareness.

A major aspect of cosmopolitical awareness is skepticism. Some discussions of skepticism and "Benito Cereno" suggest that through Delano, Melville thematizes humanity's inability to escape its intellectual benightedness (Arsić 2007, esp. 9; Halpern 2008, 559, 561). Does Melville present cosmopolitical awareness as a pretense? If such awareness involves recognizing the flexibility of identity, skepticism may deny the possibility of recognition per se. However, "Benito Cereno" presents skepticism not as an aspect of the human condition embodied in Delano but as an orientation to the world opposed to that of Delano. A man whom Melville implies has less "than ordinary quickness and accuracy of intellectual perception" (Melville 1987, 47), Delano is characterized by a Hispanicist- and Africanist-funded complacency at odds with the skeptic's rigorous attention to context and contingency. If Delano was less self-satisfied and had more of the skeptic's drive to self-question, he might have reacted differently while on board the *San Dominick*. The falsity of his self-understanding as cosmopolitan is cast against a skepticism that shares much with cosmopolitical awareness. Far from being paralyzed by epistemological limitations, the Melvillian skeptic can put her/his acknowledgment of those limitations to work. That self-awareness can lead to a willingness to revise one's identity and one's conceptions about others (Herbert 1980, 207–8).

The relevance to "Benito Cereno" of this more rigorous, skeptical cosmopolitanism is exhibited by the fact that the narrative relies on its existence. Delano's Hispanicist- and Africanist-funded complacency in his self-conception as a benevolent, optimistic cosmopolitan propels the suspense that forms part of the tale's aesthetic interest by keeping him from seeing what has happened on the *San Dominick*. In that "Benito Cereno" more concerns a man with such an incapacity than it does slave mutiny, per se (Tawil 2006, 197), there would be no "Benito Cereno" if Delano were capable of cosmopolitical perception. The tale, thus, highlights such perception's relevance to Delano's experience.

Here, Melville's literary, prepolitical approach becomes most meaningful. Uncomfortably experiencing suspense while inhabiting Delano's perspective, readers are invited to realize that perspective's dangers by comparing what the story is to what it might have been. In tethering US exceptionalism to Delano's point of view and questioning that perspective's interpretative validity, Melville promotes cosmopolitical awareness as a manner of interacting with the world that is qualitatively superior to exceptionalism. Skeptical cosmopolitanism is more practical than Delano's complacency. The reader is apprised of the usefulness of being the absent skeptical cosmopolitan in a "perpetually immigrant world" (Bryant 2009, 120). The ability to rethink one's self and how one relates with others would likely have served Delano well aboard the *San Dominick*. Being willing to see Cereno as something other than a despotic, inefficient manager and to see Babo as something other than an abject slave might have helped Delano understand what had happened aboard the ship before that knowledge is forced upon him. Of course, Cereno has reason to suggest that more precise knowledge would have killed Delano (Melville 1987, 115), but perhaps the inability to revise preconceptions is more dangerous. Delano nearly dies many times while on the *San Dominick*—for instance, when he threatens discipline to the unruly blacks as they attempt to take the food that Delano's crew has brought aboard. Both Africanism and Hispanicism inform how Delano reacts to this situation; both suggest to him that the blacks need the discipline he threatens, his Africanism because they are infantile servants, his Hispanicism because of Cereno's failures in management. Luckily for Delano, his preconceptions do not result in his death, but cosmopolitical awareness might have braced him with the wariness necessary not to leave his life to chance.

In highlighting how Delano might have taken a more active role in protecting himself in the tale, Melville may be warning his audience about the dangers of Delano's imperialistic attitudes. DeGuzmán suggests that as a "morality tale" regarding what Melville "envisioned as the potentially horrific consequences of becoming an empire," the tale emphasizes in particular "the part played by slavery as a stain on the aspirations of Anglo-American manifest destiny" (DeGuzmán 2005, 66). Yet whereas DeGuzmán sees a US American author fretting over whether US imperialism is sufficiently exceptional, I would suggest that the tale's prepolitical, cosmopolitical aspects comprise a critique of US imperial attitudes per se. Melville shows how complacent manners of understanding identity hinder recognition of "the unoriginality of American expansionism" that portends "its nonsuccess" (Emery 1984, 63). His cosmopolitical frame is an alternative to thinking about questions of empire that suggests not that US Americans seek to build an exceptional empire but rather that they recognize the distorting, insidious nature of seductive calls to do so.

The most salient value of cosmopolitical awareness, though, is that it is just. Delano's misconceptions regarding US liberality and benevolence, Hispanic despotism, and African servility inhibit his ability to treat others justly. Here, Babo's role is illustrative. Babo may seem to pose a problem for my reading. If Melville is touting an identity of nonidentity, an identity in which identities are always at play against one another, is Babo not the limit case of this logic in that he is void of identity? And is a silenced slave really what Melville wants to propose as a model? I contend, though, that rather than presenting Babo as a model for what an identity of nonidentity looks like, what is most notable about Babo's identity is how he serves as a blank slate against which Delano can self-construct his cherished fantasies about what it means to be a cosmopolitan, managerial US American. Through paternalistic sympathy for Babo, Delano imagines himself as a man of feeling in contrast to what he views as the heartless, despotic Cereno. Through suppression of the slave revolt, Delano leagues with Cereno against Babo to act out his self-conception as a stern, although genial, commander against savage disorder. In both cases Delano interprets Babo's actions in terms of Delano's self-conceptions, misperceiving Babo by unjustly treating him as a means to an end of self-construction rather than as an end unto himself.

The fact that Babo is void of identity looms large in Nelson's reading; she suggests that the narrative "objectifies Babo as fully as the sentence of the Lima Court," offering no insights into "Babo's motives and goals, and ultimate humanity." This "necessarily limited portrayal" is a product of Melville's privileged, benighted vantage (Nelson 1993, 130). Leaving aside the fact that Melville seems to have identified with Babo as much as any character in the tale (both, after all, are storytellers), I conclude by asking, would Babo be void of identity if he were not part of a world in which rigid notions of identity played such a dominant, oppressive role? What if Delano—who treats not just Babo but everyone as a means to exceptionalist identity formation—took a more skeptical attitude toward identity categories and sought to view others outside his own cherished self-conceptions? In such a world Babo would not serve as a blank slate through which Delano could act out his desires and preferences for self-identification. Delano could offer Babo an authentic form of sympathy. Babo's identity of nonidentity is a limit case not so much in that Babo serves as a negative model, but in that this identity exemplifies the results of how Delano views others. The value of cosmopolitical awareness and skepticism toward identity categories, the tale suggests, is that such literary sensibilities provide the basis for making a different world possible.

PART II

Hispanicism and the Case of Cuba

4
Mary Peabody Mann's *Juanita*
Cuba and US National Identity

Mary Peabody Mann's *Juanita: A Romance of Real Life in Cuba Fifty Years Ago* (1887) is a sentimental, oftentimes gothic excoriation of 1830s Cuban slavery. After arriving in Cuba from her native New England, the novel's protagonist Helen Wentworth confronts Cuba's horrors. These terrors include the corruption her childhood friend Isabella Rodríguez experiences after marriage to a Cuban planter and slavery's tragic effects on the amours of Isabella's son Ludovico and the family's "Moorish" servant Juanita. With its author undergoing reassessment after long being treated as a footnote in the lives of her more famous friends and relatives (she was married to Horace Mann, sister-in-law to Nathaniel Hawthorne, and translator for and collaborator with Domingo Faustino Sarmiento) (Elbert, Hall, and Rodier 2006; Marshall 2005), *Juanita* has garnered critical attention as an intriguing domestic abolitionist novel. Much of this work, though, has neglected to examine one of the novel's more curious aspects: its unusual composition and publication history. There are only rare exceptions to this omission (e.g., Hanrahan 2013; Jakšić 2007, esp. 113; Windell 2014, 321–22). Mann conceived *Juanita* during her 1833–35 visit to Cuba, where she and her sister Sophia went to recuperate the invalid Sophia's health. During the stay, Mann took notes on Cuban slavery that she intended to use in an abolitionist novel. She began writing after she returned to the United States and largely finished *Juanita* before the Civil War. Yet according to both an 1887 letter from Mann's sister Elizabeth Palmer Peabody to Mann's publisher's wife, Harriet Mulford Stone Lothrop, as well as Elizabeth's explanatory afterword to the novel, Mann delayed publication because she feared that the novel's unflattering portrayal of Cuba would offend her former hosts. After the hosts' deaths, she planned for publication. *Juanita* was in press when she died in 1887, and Elizabeth saw it to publication later that year.[1] Its appearance after both US and Cuban emancipation seemingly makes it an abolitionist novel without a purpose. It thus contains awkward anachronisms and narratorial tensions. Its sentimental and gothic literary conventions and abolitionism reflect antebellum sensibilities and concerns, whereas its title and some of its narratorial commentary look back on these issues from the late nineteenth century.[2] How are we to contextualize and make sense of the purpose of such a novel?

Elizabeth's afterword provides some ultimately unsatisfying answers. Explaining her sister's choice to publish the novel, she writes, "The death of the last member of the family of her host, a few years since, left her free to publish what she had seen and known of real life in Cuba, woven into a work of art of her own imagining. She thought it would be felt to be a timely publication, coming out so hard upon the time of the emancipation of the slaves of Cuba" (Peabody 2000, 222). (Cuba's gradual emancipation process, which began in 1880 with the slaves' indenture, ended with their freedom in the latter part of the decade.) The death of the family member who would have been offended by the novel's unflattering portrayal of Cuba explains why Mann might have no longer felt compelled to keep the novel under wraps, but it does not provide a positive explanation for why she might have felt it valuable to publish. Such an explanation is necessary because a solely negative one is insufficient to explain the anachronism of a postbellum abolitionist novel. More intriguing is the idea that the novel commemorated Cuban abolition. Yet how would an abolitionist novel do so, considering that it excoriates the evils of slaveholding society? A proper commemoration would turn from the past to celebrate a brighter future.

Placing the novel in the context of US-Cuban relations as they evolved during the nineteenth century proves more satisfactory. Although its abolitionism seems out of place in the late nineteenth century, its representation of Cuba registers issues spanning its antebellum composition and postbellum revision and publication. Mann likely thought the novel could speak to these issues both when she began writing and when she returned to it. During the antebellum period the United States frequently sought to annex Cuba. Such projects were generally spearheaded by Southerners eager to increase the number of slave states. In its representation of such proposals, *Juanita*'s criticisms of Cuban society often suggest the benefits Cuba might experience from union with the United States; the novel, though, rejects antebellum annexationism on antislavery grounds. Still, the United States continued to entertain annexationist proposals and imperial ambitions after slavery's demise. These ambitions culminated in the Spanish-American War, when the United States' expansionist ideologues successfully argued that the nation should become an overseas imperial power by wresting colonies from Spain. Mann's novel was published shortly before this climax. She likely returned to *Juanita* because she believed it lent clarity to developing US-Cuban relations. Although she wrote most of *Juanita* before the Civil War and thus only minimally attuned the novel to postbellum concerns, she may have believed it could function as a historical narrative that would explain the foundations of Cuban society to US readers. One of its definite postbellum revisions is its subtitle, "A Romance of Real Life in Cuba Fifty Years Ago." The subtitle signals the work's generic status not as an abolitionist novel but as a romance treating characteristic romance focal points such as exotic, gothic locales and passionate, heroic love and, more to the point, as a specifically historical romance. As historical romances explore how the past constitutes the present, the subtitle signals the novel's interest in bringing the antebellum past into conversation with the postbellum present. Therefore, although one is tempted to wonder whether the novel is an antebellum or a postbellum text, that question must be answered not according to an either/or but, rather, a both/and approach. The novel is antebellum in sensibility, but it is repackaged to present that sensibility to postbellum concerns.

This chapter comprises two sections unpacking this argument. In the first I argue that *Juanita*'s relevance to US-Cuban relations must be seen in how Mann constructs national identity. National identity interested Mann, who wrote in a January 16, 1835, letter to her future husband Horace that "I think I was meant for a statesman, for there is scarcely anything so interesting to me as the destinies of nations" (Mann 1835). National identity was, moreover, a pressing concern in the context of expansion. Both during the antebellum period and leading up to the Spanish-American War, many pondered whether the United States could be an imperial democracy. Critics of imperialism presented this project as contradictory: How could a nation with origins in anticolonial revolution, one whose national ethos valorized political self-determination, become an imperial power? This seeming contradiction was particularly apparent in the case of Cuba, where by the beginning of the Spanish-American War, revolutionaries had long been fighting for their liberty. Should not such a movement be respected? Imperialists typically countered by presenting the matter as a question of national identities. Cubans, imperialists insisted, exhibited inherent proclivities toward despotic, economically inefficient political systems and institutions. They were incapable of developing liberal institutions without the tutelage of the United States, a nation that had successfully established a liberal democracy. On its face, *Juanita* confirms this argument. Its historical narrative about Cuban slaveholding society figures Cuba as constitutionally averse to liberal democracy; by various contrasting mechanisms, it represents the United States as possessing the capacity for founding liberal institutions that is necessary to tutor Cuba in liberal ways. The novel thus follows a pattern of national identity construction and engagement with imperial contexts that we began to see in Joel Barlow's work.

What is curious about *Juanita*, however, is how it so frequently questions the celebratory national narrative it seems to construct. The liberal Hispanicist tradition Barlow established projected confidence regarding the United States' world-historical role in spreading democracy and commerce in the face of Spanish resistance, but Mann is not so sure. Mann recognizes that the US South's slaveholding history renders easy distinctions between the United States and Cuba tenuous, as she is unable to represent Cuban slaveholding as a study in the island's failure to evade the vices avoided by the United States. Among their attitudes toward Hispanophone peoples, US Americans have historically developed a special fascination with Cuba in which controlling the island and assuming superiority over Cubans is essential to the US national character (Pérez 1990, xvii). As it unsettles not just general Hispanicist views but also this special attitude toward Cuba, Mann's awareness that her distinctions are tenuous troubles her novel's nationalism.

Why bother with this argument? Most specifically, despite recent attention, *Juanita* remains an understudied, only partially understood novel. I seek to provide a compelling framework for reading this fascinating text, a text that offers insights regarding US Americans' fixation on Cuba. US Americans have arguably been more concerned with establishing superiority to and dominance over Cuba than with any other Hispanophone nation, with the possible exception of Mexico. *Juanita* interestingly engages this relationship. More generally, the chapter's discussion of the novel's uncertainty regarding nationality provides a way to rethink national identity formation. Despite frequent advocacy to the contrary, scholarly approaches to this issue frequently remain committed to fixed identity categories and linear processes of identification. In *Juanita*, though, we see Mann's attempt to police these categories' boundaries break down over the transnational relationship between the US South and Cuba. The novel highlights these categories' overly reductive nature, which cannot contain the nation's diversity.

Juanita's Liberal Critique of Cuba and Its Construction of US National Identity

What occurs in this still relatively unfamiliar work? At some point in the 1830s, Helen—a stand-in for Mann—travels to the Cuban countryside to visit her childhood companion, Isabella Rodríguez. Helen finds that marriage to a Cuban sugar planter has corrupted Isabella. After the two witness several acts of slaveholding cruelty, Helen effects a change of heart in Isabella, although the episodes grate so harshly on the Cuban's nerves that her health begins suffering. Meanwhile, Isabella's eldest son, Ludovico, and the family's favored, beautiful "Moorish" servant, Juanita, develop a romantic relationship. Generically, the novel moves between gothic sentimentalism in the chapters on the horrors of slavery and romance in the sections on the young lovers (Ard 2000, xx, xxii; Lazo 2006, 188). Ludovico and Juanita have been close friends since childhood, apparently to the point that a deeper affection exists between them. However, Juanita is a slave, which makes their union unlikely. Eventually, Ludovico becomes infatuated with and marries another woman, Carolina. Carolina's misbehavior causes Isabella's health further to deteriorate until Isabella dies. Ludovico soon also loses his wife, who dies during childbirth. Shortly before the novel concludes, he and Juanita confess their mutual affection and plan to leave Cuba for New England so they can marry. However, rioters murder Juanita during a counterrevolt prompted by rumors of slave insurrection. The novel closes with Helen and the remains of Isabella's family living wholesomely in New England, far from Cuba's horrors.

Before historicizing *Juanita* in terms of annexation, it is necessary to analyze the US nationalism the novel deploys to explore that context. The novel celebrates US nationality by figuring the United States as a liberal nation in contrast to Cuba, whose people the novel represents as averse to liberal values. Most basically, *Juanita* invokes this perspective by critiquing Cuban slaveholding society for failing to give slaves their right to life, liberty, and the pursuit of happiness. It more particularly explores how Cuban slaveholders maintain the institution by erecting systems in which invisible power operates without transparency. Mann's favor for transparency over invisibility is consistent with what Nancy Ruttenberg describes as classically liberal critiques of the despotic nature of nonrepresentative and thus nonintelligible power structures (Ruttenberg 1998, 16).

When Mann examines how invisible power operates in Cuba, she does what one would expect from a sentimental novelist: She begins on the domestic, interpersonal level. Here, the novel figures such power through the culture of silence that it views as a definitive Cuban sociocultural quality. For example, as she acquaints herself with the island's social customs, Helen observes that Cuban propriety often requires silence. She learns that "it is not considered good manners to complain of one's neighbors and acquaintances" (Mann 2000, 7) and that "the decorum of Spanish society is to be quiet, instead of talkative, even in their dances, and especially when music is the entertainment" (16). Although this custom might appear an innocent matter of etiquette, Mann highlights it to evoke a gothic atmosphere of unease, distrust, and suspicion. It is not simply etiquette that necessitates the convention; rather, as Isabella says, "They [the slaves] are . . . the only persons who have the means of knowing the events of every-day life, for it is not considered etiquette to report of our neighbors' doings. In this case, it is not because people are above scandal, but because every man lives in a glass house" (148). The convention exists because it enables society's rapacious members to obscure their actions. The tense atmosphere of this world undermines Mann's characters' interrelationships, contentment, and health. For instance, after a visitor to the Rodríguez plantation named Carolina manages to woo Ludovico while the barrier of race and slavery stands between him and his true love, Juanita, Isabella becomes uncomfortable about her daughter-in-law's tacit yet never explicitly represented misbehavior. This uneasiness wreaks havoc on Isabella's health. In that she participates eagerly in the culture of silence to the point of committing unspeakable acts, Carolina epitomizes gothic Cuba. Her entrance into the Rodríguez family contributes to its ruin.

Mann figures the negative effects of suppression of voice through the separate spheres concept central to her time's sentimental liberalism. In developing this stance, Mann drew on Harriet Beecher Stowe's *Uncle Tom's Cabin* (1852). The separate spheres concept posited that the feminine domestic sphere of virtuous wives and mothers was where children could learn the affective qualities necessary to live virtuous lives once they entered a potentially corruptive outside world. Similarly, it construes the domestic sphere as a regenerative space to which husbands could retreat following their participation in the cutthroat market. Writers such as Mann believed that contaminating the domestic sphere could corrupt its educational and regenerative functions to dire effect (Mann 1874, 53; Mann 2000, 166).

As Mann understands it, Cuba's etiquette of silence has precisely such an effect. Cuban conventions deny to women their ability to speak against vice and thus to exercise moral suasion, particularly in their primary role as their children's moral educators. Cuban mores thereby corrupt the domestic sphere by preventing women from benefiting family and community. Mann's characterization of Isabella is key here; Mann figures this studiously-if-reluctantly indifferent character as typical of Cuban matrons in her failure to fulfill her domestic role. Isabella complains that "we women cannot help" the problems of slavery (Mann 2000, 34), and this statement points up what Mann represents as Isabella's failure to exercise moral suasion. Isabella does exactly the opposite, for instance, shocking Helen by refusing to remonstrate against the breakup of a family (150). Helen learns that "one of Isabella's functions for her husband is to police both visitors and family, censuring them for protesting slavery" (Ard 2000, xiii). Mann suggests that with this inversion of a corrective domestic space, the vice produced by a corrupt society—a vice embodied in Carolina—will go unchecked in Cuba.[3]

The novel further explores these issues by representing the clashes that occur when virtuous children confront their elders' corrupt restrictions. The novel's children frequently say the things their parents wish to silence. One such child is Carlito, a slave trader's son whom Helen takes under her wing upon her arrival in Havana and who later accompanies Helen to the Rodríguez estate. As he cries to his mother that he wishes Helen would take him away from Cuba, he exclaims that he "won't live in a place where people are sold!" (Mann 2000, 22). Mann here invokes a sentimental tradition that posits that children possess a natural capacity for sympathy. This move's most immediate philosophic context is the transcendentalist view on innate divinity that informed Mann's and Elizabeth Peabody's argument that kindergartens could cultivate children's innate virtues before society corrupted those virtues (Mann and Peabody 1870, 13). *Juanita* dramatizes this philosophy in frequent tableaux focused on children's education, tableaux that particularly focus on Helen's capacity to coax antislavery positions out of the children. Such passages more fundamentally signal the novel's liberal perspective. John Locke and later liberals claimed that people respect natural rights in a state of nature uncorrupted by rapacious social conventions. Locke's claim reverses Thomas Hobbes's view that war characterizes the state of nature and that people must submit to a sovereign to protect themselves from their own depravity. When Mann suggests that children would reject slavery while their elders would accept it, she takes Locke's perspective, indicating that the children's reaction results from their proximity to the Lockean state of nature. Mann suggests, though, that without the benefits of a regenerative domestic sphere, children will not maintain these virtues. Mann expressed her belief in a March 30, 1834, letter to Horace that Cuban children are as naturally good as all other children until their environment corrupts them (Mann 1834a), but in an August 6, 1834, letter from Cuba to her friend Rawlins Pickman, "in this land of bondage . . . it seems impossible that [a child's] heart should not be hardened" (Mann 1834b).

By emphasizing how Cuba's culture of silence quiets critiques of slavery, Mann suggests that the same conventions that inflect polite and familial interactions also contribute to the maintenance of slavery. Mann begins illustrating the points in her opening by informing readers that one of the West African slave trade's peculiar horrors is that when slave catchers capture their prey, they must necessarily gag them. If they do not, "some compassionate ear might hear and betray, for English vessels were occasionally nearing the coast for this very purpose" (Mann 2000, 5). Allowing the subdued Africans their voice could lead to action against slavery; the catcher thus quiets them. Similarly, during a conversation between Helen and a slave trader's daughter, Mann writes, "Tulita, with all simplicity, had revealed all the arcana, which those more conversant with non-slave-holding communities would have concealed" (9). The passage indicates that the culturally sophisticated slaveholders use silence to keep potential critics of slavery from understanding the truth about the institution.

For Mann, the need to silence forbidden knowledge about slavery indicates a key aspect of invisible power's presence in Cuba. With Cuban slavery, illegality is the rule. In 1817 England pressured Spain to abolish its Atlantic slave trade. Cubans continued to own slaves, but they could no longer legally capture and transport new ones from Africa. This treaty was unpopular among slaveholders, who needed regular imports due to the slaves' high mortality rate. The Atlantic trade thus continued illicitly, and Cuban authorities largely looked the other way. Mann represents these breaches as a corruption of law, such as when she explains that the slave traders have little to fear because "no troublesome English commissioner resided in the country, and the one in the city took no pains to inform himself of disobedience to the treaty, knowing that the Captain General received so much a head from the slaves, and was therefore specially blind and deaf upon that subject, which made his commission practically abortive" (Mann 2000, 7). As Mann points out in explaining such phenomena, "Spanish law [in Cuba is] (violated by custom)" (18). Mann sees slaveholding convention as creating a perpetual space of exception from transparent justice, one that allows vice to go unpunished; her commentary on this matter reflects her liberal tendency to criticize invisible power in Cuba.

Mann further examines the Cuban pattern of silencing slavery's horrors as the narrative brings Helen into contact with Cuban attempts to suppress those atrocities' verbalization. Helen's observations of slaveholding custom make apparent the invisible knowledge on which the system rests. For instance, in a striking passage, Helen and Isabella visit a neighboring plantation famed for its humane, efficient master, a German count. After observing some aspects of the plantation with approval, however, the ladies accidentally come across a scene that throws slavery's barbarity into utter relief: To train hounds to catch fugitives, an overseer forces a slave to teach the dogs to hate blacks by having the slave torture the dogs while allowing the dogs to taste the slave's flesh. Upon witnessing the ladies' horror, the planter states: "'I beg your pardon, ladies,' said the Count, 'but you know, my lady,' he said, apologetically addressing la Marquesa [Isabella], 'the white man is never bitten on my plantation. This training must be attended to'" (Mann 2000, 73–74). The count's phrasing invests a system of plantation discipline in the indirect phrase "the white man is never bitten on my plantation." The phrase circumambulates its true significance. The white man is not bitten because the runaway slave must be bitten. The oblique wording illustrates the tendency away from transparency so pervasive in Mann's conception of Cuban society.

These passages suggest the basis of the novel's liberal critique of Cuba. Cuba, for Mann, not only has no functional domestic sphere but also no functional public sphere, no procedural space in which the oppressed or conscientious can voice their grievances. Such resistance is hushed here, and power operates on a level that is incomprehensible to all but the privileged. Fixating upon the closed nature of a society premised on silence, Helen comes to see herself as a tool for disseminating the knowledge that Cuban culture suppresses, musing at one point to herself that "perhaps I may be a humble instrument for enlightening society upon this fearful topic" (Mann 2000, 36). Helen and Isabella's many conversations about slavery establish Helen's gadfly function. Despite her relatively humane characteristics, her partial Cuban upbringing and marriage to a planter have trained Isabella to avoid talking about slavery's horrors. Helen, though, cannot help speaking upon witnessing horrific incidents. She serves as a foil to Cuban society by revealing what that society has veiled. In this respect, she is a synecdoche for *Juanita* itself. The project she represents is intrinsically liberal because it criticizes and corrects Cuban society's lack of communicative transparency.[4]

To some extent reflecting her time's generally racialist worldview, Mann's sense of Cuba's inability to establish a liberal society reveals a quasi-racially constituted understanding of Cuban creoles. Many of the novel's statements on Cuban difference present Cubans as racially averse to liberalism due to their Spanish ancestry, as when Mann writes that "the decorum of Spanish society is to be quiet" (Mann 2000, 16) and other like statements. Although Mann is not given to comparing Cubans with peninsular Spaniards, her prejudice toward Cuban creoles may reflect the US American view that creoles were degenerate Spaniards, also seen in Amasa Delano's desire to identify with Benito Cereno as a Spaniard rather than as a Chilean. Although there is certainly racial prejudice at play here, that prejudice is not—significantly, as we will see—essentialist. The notion of "race" the novel operates with is not the blood-based form associated with the polygeneticist theories that were becoming prominent during the mid-nineteenth century. This is apparent in Mann's lack of demonstrated interest in blood-based, phenotypic explanations of Spanish difference. Moreover, in this respect consistent with the US American view that Hispanophone societies based on African slavery were more racially stratified and less given to intermixture than Mexico and Central America, she does not explain Cuban inferiority via discussion of miscegenation between Spaniards and Africans. Rather, she relies upon the environmentalist notions that had been more common in the eighteenth century. Her views are encapsulated in her statement to Sarmiento that "I believe in the indefinite improveability of human nature and the race, and that every lamb can be brought into the fold" (Mann 2001, 218). The statement came as part of a discussion regarding the potential of the Freedmen's Bureau to elevate African Americans after emancipation and of Mann's collaboration with Sarmiento to import educators from New England to train teachers in Argentina as part of an effort to establish a public-school system like that designed in Massachusetts by Horace Mann. Her support of such efforts suggests her belief in human mutability (Mann 1868, esp. iv–v; Mann 2001, esp. 130, 140–41, 184, 218, 242).

Consistently with these views, Helen often muses on the evident contrast between the beauty and luxuriance of the Cuban physical environment and the horrors of slavery that happen in proximity to that beauty. Ruminating on this divergence, she concludes that the environment must condition the difference between Cubans and the more liberal, freedom-loving people of her homeland: "Helen felt, when she looked abroad on the festal world of that fair clime, that only in such lands could this crying sin exist—that in her own wintry one, where man is condemned to pass many of his days shut up in houses, and where inclement seasons bring their own peculiar suffering, this one added to the rest would be more than poor human nature could bear, even among the spectators and perpetrators of the iniquity" (Mann 2000, 156). We see here that *Juanita* emphasizes nurture over nature as the constitutive force in the individual's potential. The pernicious physical environment fuels a similarly damaging cultural space. If environment shapes human type, human type shapes culture, which in turn cements type. As Mann writes, "Vegetation clothed the earth there [outside Cuba] as here, but here its rank luxuriance, where untamed, typified the unbridled sweep of human propensities, while the curbs and restraints that a certain measure of civilization imposed upon it only concealed the fens and marshes that were the product of a decay as pestiferous to the physical as the corruptions of the heaven-born passions are to the moral atmosphere" (49). The passage suggests an emblematic, reciprocal relationship between physical and cultural environment; nature typifies Cuban decay because it is the source of that decay, with the interplay between the two powerfully shaping those under its influence. Given Cuba's sultrier climate in contrast to that of Spain's, Mann's concept of the environmental conditioning of difference may account for any enhanced disdain she feels toward Cuban creoles as opposed to peninsular Spaniards.

Mann exhibits these ideas by showing how Cuba has corrupted several of the novel's characters. Isabella grew up and was educated in New England, having all the benefits Helen experienced. The qualities resultant from these opportunities showed strongly during her early years. (As Peabody [1984,

448] attests, the historical personages upon whom the Rodríguez family were based were transplanted New Englanders, a point to which I will return.) Yet her marriage and acculturation to her husband's way of life have made a difference for the worse. In depicting her descent into Cuban vices, despite having been given ample opportunity to adopt US values, it might seem that Mann is making an essentialist slight on her character by showing how blood eventually shows. However, other examples suggest this is not the case, such as the characterization of the German count. He has grown up and been educated in northern Europe and has Nordic blood; if the novel followed a strictly blood-based definition of race, the count would have a naturally Germanic energetic individualism and love of liberty. One is even tempted to believe that Helen has something like this in mind when she expresses her hopes that the count will be a model slaveholder. However, she bases her hope on his having been born outside slavery, an environmental reason (Mann 2000, 72). Moreover, life in Cuba has corrupted the count, suggesting that his blood is for naught here.

Although Mann thus highlights the corruptive power of Cuban society, her emphasis on human mutability rather than essential traits suggests that individual Cubans can improve if they flee Cuba. Isabella, again, is illustrative here. As Mann writes, "Isabella had brought with her, from her old New England life, impressions and principles regarding the education of children that her Cuban life had never corrupted" (Mann 2000, 41). Cuba's influence has made her domestic habits far from what Mann sees as the ideal, but she is hardly the novel's most degraded character. For instance, rather than have a slave attend to her children during their formative years' "trying scenes and precious hours" (41), she, along with her staunch New England governess, raises and teaches them herself. Thus, although she often fails to do so properly, she at the same time places relative importance on morally educating her children. She believes that she would be remiss in this duty if she were to allow untutored slaves to teach the children, a process that would, not coincidentally, more powerfully ingrain the children's sense of the master-slave differentiation. She follows this path, Mann suggests, because she has enjoyed the educational opportunities necessary to transcend typical Cuban limitations. By the same token, in its conclusion, in which Helen takes Isabella's children with her to New England to complete their education, Mann further suggests the potential for personal reformation in more benevolent climes by indicating that individual Cubans may improve if they can escape the island's influence. That influence, in Cuba and New England, remains both climatological and cultural; linking New England's cold to its virtues, Ludovico declares that "I am going to the States to live; there is one part of them at least where there is no slavery, and I will brave the cold for the sake of turning my back upon it. I would not stay here if I were you, Miss Wentworth. I know you think we are cruel and wicked people. I do" (Mann 2000, 59). The novel later suggests that the cold will benefit Ludovico and his siblings after they finally resettle.

Their transformative move to New England is significant to *Juanita*'s project. By showing how Isabella's children improve there, Mann makes clear the contrast that drives *Juanita*'s nationalism. The novel's descriptions of Cuba's oppressive climate do not solely illustrate the source of a faulty social and political system but also serve as a statement regarding the United States. Cuba is a stage where an opposition between US liberalism and Cuban despotism plays out to focalize US superiority. Helen metonymically represents US values; values Mann sees as being particularly present in New England but that more generally characterize the US national narrative the novel invokes. Mann emphasizes this function by representing Helen as a lone, vital voice of liberalism in a desert of aristocratic, slaveholding Cuban vice. Although the States themselves mostly remain outside the narrative's field of vision, Helen's presence constantly reminds us that *Juanita* functions just as much to celebrate US virtues as it does to expose Cuban vices. When Isabella's family moves to New England late in the novel, this oppositional relationship becomes most apparent. Here, Isabella's children, formerly corrupted by slaveholding society, improve in a more benevolent US space. The United States becomes Cuban vice's cure. The novel's geographical typology bears notice here. The children find themselves away from hellish Cuba and firmly in the Promised Land on their arrival in New England. This typology further confirms *Juanita*'s nationalism.

Juanita constructs the US national identity it develops through this contrast as a bound "imagined community" in the sense described by Benedict Anderson (1991 and 1998) and Ed White (2004). The novel does so not only on the level of specific content but also via the generic qualities of what Anderson describes as the national novel. Anderson argues that the nation as an experiential orientation adheres to the forms of print-capitalism. He does not define the national novel's generic characteristics, but Jonathan Culler extrapolates a definition from Anderson's writings. Culler claims that "the effect [the national novel produces] is achieved by a broad range of narratives in which the narrator is not limited to what an empirical individual might know or perceive. . . . All that is necessary is that the narrative provide a point of view exterior to and superior to that of any particular character." He furthermore explains that "the world evoked by [this sort of] novel [must] include events happening simultaneously, extend beyond the experience of particular individuals, and be conceived as geographically situated or bounded" (Culler 2007, 48–49). A narratorial viewpoint unlike the one

Culler describes would be too limited to transcend its perspective and portray the actions of characters who do not know each other but who share a national connection in homogeneous, empty time. This connection is characterized by simultaneity; as Anderson notes, the novel "is clearly a device for the presentation of simultaneity in 'homogeneous, empty time,' or a complex gloss upon the word 'meanwhile'" (Anderson 1991, 25). In other words, characters in a national novel act simultaneously along a temporally linear, calendrical continuum. This narrative mode evokes the characters' temporal connection. When such a novel thus represents characters while evoking the nation's geographical boundedness, it binds their temporal particularity to the nation by emphasizing the characters' enclosure within national borders at a verifiable point in time.

Juanita exhibits many of this genre's characteristics; its evocation of geographical boundedness is particularly typical and significant. To this end, *Juanita* uses a documentary, ethnographic approach in its observations of Cuban slaveholding custom. These observations function mimetically, which should not be surprising in a novel whose subtitle signals an interest in "Real Life in Cuba." The reader receives third-person, seemingly objective representations of interactions among slaves; of overseers' suppression tactics; and of the absence of open communication. The novel, in its project of verbalizing what is silenced by Cuban society, poses these descriptions as representative of all plantation life in Cuba. In Andersonian terminology it represents them existing in their simultaneous particularity alongside other such instances occurring across Cuba. This ethnographic method constructs Cuba as the bound geographic totality so important to Anderson, White, and Culler's account of how nationality functions. The approach represents Cuba in its national particularity.

It might seem that a novel mostly set in Cuba would not be a good place to find a representation of a geographically bound United States. However, the contrast between Cuba and the United States that *Juanita* constructs ensures that all representations of the island reflect back on Mann's nation. Therefore, when the novel develops a sense of Cuba's bound geography, it points to the geographic division between the two territories. That geographic division carries along with it a division in national identities, Cuba's committed to slavery and therefore opposed to liberalism, the United States' committed to liberalism. The typology of place established by the end of the novel, in which Isabella's children are freed from the corrupting influence of Cuba upon arrival in a beneficent United States, serves to emphasize the geographic division that Mann constructs throughout the novel through her generic use of a documentary, ethnographic register.

The novel's climatological understanding of human difference informs its US-Cuban geographic typology. In *Juanita*, the cultural differences that bind national communities against each other are cemented by the effect that environment has on custom. The novel's ethnographic register rhetorically pictures environment's effects. Fixating on Cuba's position at the mercy of the Caribbean's tropical, passion-inducing climes in contrast to the United States' enjoyment—this is especially true of New England—of more bracing yet sufficiently temperate climes, Mann invests the geographic typology her novel constructs through its ethnographic register with a deeply laid, character-defining significance. This significance bolsters the novel's nationalism. Even though *Juanita* does not see identity in terms of blood and thus construes human types as mutable, it does provide a rationale for US national superiority on the basis of the nation's peoples' residence in a land that cultivates a wholesome love of liberty rather than despotism.

Juanita: Romancing National Identity

These aspects of the novel are played up in the depiction of the amours of Ludovico and his family's "Moorish" servant Juanita. The lovers are divided by slavery until the narrative's end, when Ludovico declares his desire to marry Juanita only to see her die before the union occurs. Throughout the book's early portions, Mann subtly intertwines bits of evidence of their mutual affection into the more central focus on Helen's and Isabella's discussions of Cuban slaveholding practice. Toward the end, Mann places this narrative on the center stage, its tragedy providing the novel's climax. This melodramatic tale of doomed passion is, along with the focus on the exotic, gothic elements of the Cuban setting, among the work's characteristic romance elements. The aesthetics of melodrama have traditionally been treated dismissively by critics, and Mann's usage of melodrama informs what I describe as ideologically confused aspects of her work. However, she also cleverly draws out melodrama's connotative potential by tethering another liberal critique of Cuban society to this narrative element. That critique must be seen in terms of how Cuba's illiberal failure to give its slaves the right to life, liberty, and the pursuit of property binds the white characters, their own freedom and personal choice being constrained by their moral bondage to the vice the slave system produces. As Mann writes, "the bondage of the master is as veritable a fact as the bondage of the slave; the one being a moral bondage only, while the other is both a moral, an intellectual, and a physical one" (Mann 2000, 54). This may sound like Southern arguments that slavery is a greater burden for the master than the bondsman. It is a different point, though, one that coheres with Mann's transcendentalist, liberal outlook. Mann suggests that a member of the planter class of relatively sound morals—Isabella, for example—is bound to a system that s/he knows is morally detestable. This binding entails a loss of moral and intellectual self-reliance. Ludovico's choice to marry Juanita places him squarely against this illiberal system; with that choice, he breaks the fetters that bind even the other relatively admirable white Cuban characters. With the help of the education that his mother, the Rodríguez family's New England governess Mrs. Warwick, and Helen provide, he transcends customary restraints against equality and personal choice by following his heart. Responding to his declared engagement to Juanita, Helen says to him, "Juanita is in every way worthy of you, and you are worthy of her. You have conquered a prejudice that holds half the world in thrall,—for the prejudice of caste is the most difficult one to overcome" (213). He thus defeats the most illiberal aspect of Cuban culture, one binding not only his compatriots but also "half the world." In doing so, he atones for foolishly marrying Carolina and becomes the novel's most noble character—indeed, a liberal hero.

The typology of place informing the novel's nationalism is best displayed here. One of the principal ways the United States allows respite from Cuban illiberality is in providing a potential safe haven for the young lovers. Knowing they cannot wed in Cuba, where social opinion and especially Ludovico's father constrain them, the two leave for New England, where they begin happily planning for marriage. Here, Ludovico can carry out the liberal heroism that would ruin him in Cuba. Mann, thus, invests her nationalist typology of place with a hint of epic grandeur in the novel's closing sections. She makes her nation the locus of heroic actions, the place where the noble but downtrodden can exercise their desires.

Things predictably do not end happily for the couple, though. After spending some time in New England, Ludovico decides to return to Cuba to speak with his father, a conversation that will include, presumably, revealing his choice to marry Juanita. In an act of self-sacrifice, Juanita insists on accompanying her lover to the land of slavery. During the trip, Juanita and her brother (the brother is an implied rebel leader) are brutally killed during a reactionary counterrevolt. The tragic error of Ludovico and Juanita is that they leave New England for Cuba. The contrast informing the novel's nationalism is again held up in this passage, perhaps more strongly than anywhere else; Cuba is never shown in a harsher light than when it burns out Juanita's and Ludovico's love (I use "burn out" quite literally—Juanita and her brother die when the jail where the suspected rebels are being held is burned down), and the liberal safe haven offered by the United States is never more strikingly remembered than when Cuba is shown thus. If the couple had stayed, the ending would have been different.

The novel's two generic registers—documentary realism concerning slavery's horrors and gothic romance focused on the unfulfilled love between two of its main characters—work hand in hand to inform the novel's nationalism. The uneven balance between these two registers might seem aesthetic flaws; after all, the novel's climax swiftly unravels in only a few pages after Mann has spent over two hundred pages minutely detailing the customs of Cuban slavery. Perhaps this apparent flaw owes to the novel's uneven composition history, but there is a certain well-designed coherence here, too. After using the documentary portions to construct rudimentary national typologies, Mann puts the melodramatic romance plot to work to point up those distinctions on a powerful, emotionally gripping level. The differences become no longer the fruits of detailed observations, but rather the starkly contrasted good and evil of melodrama. Cuba's gothic horrors are more starkly depicted, the United States' heavenly qualities more laudably evoked. The differences originally constructed in the documentary vein are charged with additional significance as they are recast in light of the novel's melodramatic conclusion. If readers have yet to see the significance of the national typologies the novel develops, the conclusion forces such recognition.

Juanita and the Other within the Nation

The novel puts its conception of the liberal United States as a safe haven for Cuba's unfortunates to use in a seeming argument for annexation that coheres with other such arguments, both as they were forwarded in the antebellum period and in the politics of 1898. *Juanita*, though, frequently undercuts its celebration of the United States' ability to fix Cuba's problems by anxiously meditating on the import the US South poses for the nation. The novel figures this issue through its association of the South with Cuba. For most of the narrative, the South remains tensely on the margins of the novel's focus on Cuban slavery. It comes most squarely into view at the precise moment when one might expect the novel to express the greatest confidence about US nationality—when the characters muse on the annexation question. Here, annexationism's roots in slavery politics bring the similarities between the South and Cuba into view. The anxiety the novel evinces in these moments suggests its uncertainty regarding the United States' success in fulfilling its ideals.

Juanita complexly engages with historically specific debates on annexation, debates that roared from the antebellum period of the novel's composition to the postbellum period of its publication. Many in both the United States and Cuba favored annexation, especially from the 1830s on. The island became the most prosperous sugar colony in the New World after the Haitian Revolution ended Saint-Domingue's predominance. Many interests thus desired to free Cuban sugar markets from autarkical Spanish tariffs. US Americans, moreover, saw control of Cuba as essential to national security. They worried that an unstable Cuba could either fall prey to a rival European power or become a bloodbath of black-on-white violence like Saint-Domingue. Finally, before the Civil War, many US southerners and Cuban creoles—and this, we will see, is key for *Juanita*—agreed that the two societies were natural bedfellows because of their shared commitment to slavery. In the antebellum period, annexationist speculation ranged from the Polk administration's proposals to purchase Cuba from Spain to illicit attempts to "liberate" the island through force. The most famous such latter effort was led by Narciso López, a former Spanish military officer. Along with US filibusterers, López organized multiple failed attacks on Cuba in the early 1850s.

Annexation remained a major issue during the latter half of the nineteenth century. With its attractiveness to slaveholders no longer at issue, there was less overt desire to annex the island. During this period, the United States adopted a "no-transfer" policy, stating that it would not interfere with Cuban sovereignty as long as Spain controlled the island. This arrangement satisfied US fears of European encroachment in the hemisphere and of Cuban independence. However, many in the United States believed their nation would inevitably possess Cuba. The situation came to a head in 1898, when the United States intervened in Cuba's insurgent revolution for independence. Ostensibly acting on the revolutionaries' behalf, the United States in fact leagued with Cuban elites who feared the egalitarian Cuba libre movement; these elites supported annexation as a means to suppress the underclasses. The United States did not annex Cuba after victory against Spain, but it exercised sovereignty over the island during the early twentieth century through the Platt Amendment and other measures.

Although all of these issues inflect *Juanita*'s discussion of annexation, the most significant to this abolitionist fiction is annexationism's relation to slavery. Cuba's place in debates over slavery was fraught. Expansionists in both the free-soil and pro-slavery camps desired to control the island, and whether it would continue to maintain its slavery system after annexation was a matter of debate. However, many in the United States believed the island was more desirable to pro-slavery forces. Moreover, figures like López were pro-slavery, and the sugar planters were annexation's most vocal Cuban proponents. López and the Cuban planters were widely represented as such in the United States. Lars Schoultz identifies non-slavery-based rationales for annexation as "subterfuge for a southern effort to acquire more slave states" (Schoultz 2009, 19), and it is impossible to imagine that Cuba would not have become a slave state after US takeover.[5]

Reflecting this antebellum ideological conflict, *Juanita* displays an ambivalent stance on annexation, one that, as we will see, points to ambivalence regarding the celebrations of US national identity in which it often engages. The novel was set in the antebellum period, and several of the characters discuss the time's annexation proposals as an attractive possibility for the island. Mann's third-person narratorial commentary often supports their suggestions. Although the narrator laments the "difficulty . . . of making innovations among a people so nationally ignorant as the inhabitants of the Spanish Colonies," she concludes that such difficulties might be overcome through annexation (Mann 2000, 201). Annexation here serves as a method for solving the problems that plague Cuba. The fact that it is the heroic characters in *Juanita* such as Helen and Ludovico who support annexation and that the novel does not acknowledge continued colonial status or independence for Cuba as serious possibilities for the island (two options that were seriously considered by Cubans themselves, particularly after Cuban support for annexation waned in the postbellum period) further suggests Mann's support for a benevolent version of annexation meant not to spread but to end or at least ameliorate slavery's effects (Windell 2014, 321–23).

That Mann views as positive the effects that Cuba would experience if the United States adopted the island as its ward coheres with how the novel represents Cuban difference as a matter of environment and how it touts the beneficent change that Isabella's children undergo when they arrive in the United States. Although annexation would not alter the island's physical environment, which for Mann contributes to its despotic, vicious culture, annexation would alter Cuba's cultural and political environment; the alteration might not be perfect, but it would certainly be for the better in Mann's view. Mann analogizes the United States' broader education of Cuba to Helen's education of Isabella's children. Her representation reflects a tendency among US Americans to think of Cuba as a childlike pupil, a tendency with antebellum roots but one that would become particularly manifest in the many propagandistic cartoons published around the time of the Spanish-American War depicting Cuba as a child and the United States as an adult parent or teacher (Johnson 1993, 116–19). Just as Helen provides to Isabella's children the education in New England values necessary to subvert the children's parents' pernicious teaching of Cuban slaveholding values, so, too, does annexation facilitate a national imperial education premised on the United States succeeding where Spain failed by tutoring Cuba in maintaining liberal institutions. Annexation might play the same role for Cuba as would, via Mann's 1860's to 1870's collaboration with Argentine politician Sarmiento, importing northeastern teacher-education models to Argentina as part of an effort to acculturate Hispanic culture to a US liberal standard (Jakšić 2007, esp. 2, 111, 122). If not for Mann's environmentalist emphasis on human mutability, this imperial education would not be possible in her view. Mann's understanding of Cuban difference in terms of nurture as opposed to nature facilitates viewing Cubans as, despite their acculturated evils, having the potential to better themselves under the right conditions.

Those conditions are, necessarily, premised on annexation. Warranting particular remark in the narrator's defense of annexation is the word "innovation" (Mann 2000, 201), which trades upon a contrast between the open and the closed that the novel's liberalism often invokes. Cuba's closure to modernization, freedom, and communicative transparency, so emphasized in Mann's liberal critique of the island's culture, can only, the narrator suggests, be opened by union with what the novel has indicated to be the more liberal United States. This necessity is pointed up in a passage in which Mann writes that the Cubans desired annexation because they "were descendants of the very Spaniards who tyrannized over them, and gradually learned to hate the mother-country, which showed such rapacious greed, and so little sympathy for their true interests" (208). Mann here implicitly likens the creoles' relationship to Spain to the US Founders bristling under the illiberal English crown. The analogy is as invested in exhibiting how Cuba and the United States are different as in how they are similar, as it also suggests that Cuba cannot help itself in the same way that the young United States did. Whereas the Founding Fathers fought for their liberty, Cuba merely chafes, like a discontented child, under a tyranny that would likely continue to exist if the island attempted self-sovereignty after being freed from the Spanish yoke. Not ready for self-government, Cuba needs the United States to escape Spain and to protect itself.

In that Mann assumes that Cuba will attain freedom only through US intervention, the novel reflects what Louis A. Pérez Jr. describes as the US imperialist pattern to mask self-interested territorial motives by associating annexation with the spread of liberalism (Pérez 2008, 174). This move addressed the ideological problem of defending imperialism in an ostensibly anti-imperial nation by equating the self-interested goal of establishing US sovereignty with the rhetorically more attractive object of spreading liberty and opening constrained economies. To recognize the ideological sleight of hand here, it is worth remembering that, as the aforementioned parent-child metaphor suggests, many North American annexationists desired to cede little agency to Cuba. Cuban annexationists sought statehood and political self-determination, whereas many US Americans who supported annexation—although not necessarily the Southerners who wanted more slave states—wished to make Cuba a territory without national self-representation. The tendency to view Cuba as incapable of liberal democracy without the United States' help fueled an ideological formation that denied Cubans the right to self-government. If this view had its way, Cubans would not have attained the sovereignty they desired. We often think of how the United States viewed Cuba as a childlike ward in terms of the politics of 1898 and afterward. Anglo-American desire to dominate Cuba did intensify in the late nineteenth century, but it has antebellum roots that surface in Mann's representation of her characters' understanding of Cuban prospects in the 1830s (Pérez 2008, esp. 5, 52, 111; Pérez 1990, 1–81).

Of course, *Juanita* is not exactly an antebellum text, and readers must consider why Mann chose to revise and publish an antislavery novel so long after slavery had been abolished. Although family correspondence and other documents suggest that fear of offending her Cuban hosts while they were alive as well as wishing to commemorate the 1880's Cuban abolition of slavery prompted Mann to wait until when she did to publish the book, these reasons do not fully explain her decision. Mann's choice to publish *Juanita* in the 1880s suggests that she believed the novel had something more to say to the late-century moment. It stands to reason that her concern must have been the continuing question of US-Cuban relations, including the prospect of annexation. Mann, indeed, wrote in an 1867 letter to Sarmiento that she wished eventually to publish *Juanita* so that she could correct erroneous impressions regarding Cuba among US Americans, in particular a popular view that the island's problems could not be ameliorated through improvements in education much like those Sarmiento wished to institute in Argentina (Mann 2001, 184). Such comments suggest she believed the novel had something to say to postbellum US readers curious about Cuba.

What is more, the novel was published not many years before 1898. Its suggestions of Cuban illiberality speak to the increasing fervor with which many from the United States at the time argued for annexation as a moral imperative. Mann's indication that there was little hope for Cuban uplift without the United States' assistance resonates, for example, with essayist Edmond Wood's 1901 claims that good government had "never been successfully exercised [by] any people of Spanish origin or training" (Wood 1901, 67) and that because "every one of the fifteen Latin American republics has had many domestic revolutions, the conclusion is reasonable that Cuba is not free from the same tendency" (73). Wood makes these points, which are consistent with broader US American prejudices toward Spaniards and creoles that intensified during this time, in support of the necessity of stern imperial governance in Cuba. Much like such interventionist cries, Mann's novel introduces annexation not as a question of territorial acquisition but rather of the altruistic imperative of caring for and educating a weak, "nationally ignorant" (Mann 2000, 201) neighbor island in establishing liberal institutions.

Yet Mann is finally not so confident about annexation. In tension with her annexationist sentiment is her sense that annexation is not so much a matter of spreading liberal values as it is of capitulating to illiberal Southern interests. During a conversation about annexation between Helen and Ludovico, the narrator cynically points out that "little did the friends then know that the responsible wish for annexation, which the States had so clearly expressed, had far different objects in view in forming that wish. To extend the area of slavery was their aim at that day" (Mann 2000, 214). This passage associates annexation with Southern desire to increase the number of slaveholding states. Mann's connection of Cuba to the South reflects an antebellum cultural tendency among pro-slavery Southern annexationists to envision a shared history between themselves and Cuban creoles as being engaged in a shared effort to establish racially stratified societies based upon slave labor (Guterl 2006, 448, 457, 464). The tie between the South and Cuba is a peculiar aspect of the special attitudes US Americans have held toward Cuba, attitudes that have more typically construed Cuba as a primary national Other rather than acknowledging similarities between the United States and the island. True to the more general pattern, New Englanders were anxious about this connection for various reasons (447). As Reginald Horsman describes, New Englanders were opposed to the incorporation of territories such as Mexico and Cuba that contained large numbers of nonwhites (Horsman 1981, 245). Mann's openness to racial amalgamation, as reflected in *Juanita* by the relationship between Ludovico and Juanita and the implied affection between Helen and the Castilian Don Andres, suggests she was not motivated by this concern. However, her commentary on annexation reflects the broader New England anxiety. Far from expressing confidence about annexation's role in the nation's liberal mission, New Englanders such as Mann expressed concerns that by exacerbating a deviation from the typical US relation to Cuba, annexation might amplify illiberal tendencies within the nation.[6] Mann's sense of this connection may have been solidified by her collaboration with Sarmiento, who compared the Hispanophone locale Argentina to the US South. Sarmiento, moreover, analogized his efforts to import New England teachers to assist in Argentine educational reforms to the Freedmen's Bureau's efforts to import Northern teachers to educate emancipated slaves after the Civil War (Velleman 2001, 3–4, 6–7). Although Mann believed Spanish American locales could be improved through education, that potential must have seemed nebulous in contrast to the present realities that would be introduced into the United States if Cuba were annexed.

One might reasonably opine, though, that Mann viewed these concerns as a thing of the past when she prepared to publish the novel in the 1880s.

When she writes that "little did the friends know . . . [that t]o extend the area of slavery was [the] aim [of antebellum U.S. annexationism] at that day," we see rare explicit evidence of Mann's postbellum revisions; through the phrase "at that day," Mann looks back at antebellum annexationism from a postemancipation moment. Mann here implies that the situation is different in the 1880s from what it was in the antebellum period; the "in that day" clearly differentiates the past from the postbellum present of Mann's eventual publication of the novel. From this postbellum perspective, annexation likely seemed more appealing to Mann. Slavery was no longer at issue, so the principal impediment to Mann's vision of expansion as a liberal project was gone. It thus seems probable that Mann chose to publish the novel in the 1880s in part because she was then more confident than she formerly was that its representation of Cuba could affirm the moral necessity of annexation. In this respect, Mann resembles other antislavery liberals—Frederick Douglass, for example (Levine 2008, 179–236; Michael 2008, 201–34)—who advocated postbellum expansion after opposing it before the Civil War.

That stated, to ascribe such a direct shift to Mann's attitude regarding annexation is still to belie her novel's equivocality on the issue. Despite having the opportunity to do so while undertaking her revisions, Mann hardly evokes confidence regarding the propriety of annexation. The novel's many qualifications regarding the United States' assumption of its liberal promise and similar qualifications regarding the nation's ability to govern Cuba rightfully reveal pressing uncertainties regarding annexation. This continued ambivalence suggests that annexation still troubled Mann. The problem for Mann is that representing annexationist ideas as they manifested themselves in the antebellum period serves as a reminder of a troubling history. Considering the peculiarities of the novel's generic qualities is revealing here. Whereas Mann originally composed *Juanita* as an abolitionist fiction, its late publication makes it a historical romance, as its subtitle indicates. Therefore, the novel is an exercise in thinking about the past's influence on the present. It views history as defining the present. This might not be such a problem if the novel evoked a narrative of historical progress, but this is not the case. *Juanita*—perhaps due to its odd composition history—is not a typical historical romance. Whereas most such texts exhibit confidence in how the historical moment depicted in the work will eventually segue into the contemporary moment, this is not true in this case. Mann knew that slavery was over and could be confident in progress on that score (Jakšić 2007, 110–11), but the novel's consideration of annexation broaches issues yet to be resolved regarding whether annexation would be a national triumph or would undermine the nation. Mann attempts to transcend history by imagining how postbellum annexation may legitimately serve the United States' liberal mission. But what if the annexation of an island with an illiberal history compromises US values? What if it strengthens lingering Southern interests, inhibiting the progress the nation has made? These uncertainties complicate the novel's historical narrative, rendering the narrative of progress tenuous. The novel fails to evince closure and separation from the past, a major problem given Mann's clear desire for the nation to put the past behind it to lend coherence to her statements regarding national identity. This uncertainty constitutes enslavement to a history of sectionalism that challenges Mann's liberal conception of the nation.

Elizabeth Peabody's statement that Mann wanted to publish the novel to commemorate abolition illustrates the novel's confused relationship with history. It is tempting simply to dismiss the statement as an absurdity. How, indeed, could an abolitionist novel commemorate abolition, when the novel fixates on the brutality of a long history of slaveholding in Cuba? Would not commemoration more properly look toward a glorious future without slavery? Simply to ignore the bizarre statement would be to miss how it points toward conceptual problems the novel faces in its consideration of national identity and history. Just as Elizabeth's claim suggests confusion regarding the novel's potential function, so, too, does the work's generic status as a historical romance indicate impasse. Both elements indicate Mann's desire to make sense of the future via considering the past. In both cases, though, there is a lack of certainty regarding the future, and if anything can be said, it is that the past portends grim prospects. It might seem that Mann had every reason to look toward the future with the confidence that the nation was capable of becoming an imperial tutor to illiberal communities like Cuba now that it had solved its slavery problem. Instead of looking toward the future with confidence, though, *Juanita* is obsessed with the past's burden. As Mann's novel ruminates on a history that suggests that the US South is more like Cuba than like her ideal vision of the United States, triumphalist claims about the nation's final assumption of its liberal promise become untenable.

By considering Cuban annexation and associating Cuba with the US South, Mann undercuts the contrast by which she attempts to imagine a US national identity. Mann's denunciation of the US South becomes anxiety over the Other's presence within the nation, an uncertainty regarding who is who in the differential national schema she has constructed. Describing the United States' unique relationship with Cuba, Pérez explains, "North American resolve to control Cuba" via exportation of US liberal institutions is "part of the [US] national character" (Pérez 1990, xvii); Mann's novel registers a breakdown in this assumption of superiority. Regionalism plays a major role in this uncertainty, but it does not tell the whole story. A number of factors suggest that the novel focuses on *national* and regional difference—or, more specifically, the implications that regional difference poses for national identity. The novel develops national identity vis-à-vis one of the United States' most intensely regarded hemispheric Others, a move that casts national rather than regional differences into relief. Perhaps better stated, the work places national differences into relief until regional differences complicate the understanding of national differences procured by national contrast. In a line that sums up on a conversational level the more generally discursive tension in the novel, Helen explains that "I have often thought we Americans do not live up to the theory of our society as we ought, but since I have looked back to my own country from this, I appreciate, as I never could before, its advanced position" (Mann 2000, 164). Helen's consideration of Cuba brings national difference—significantly at a moment of doubt—to bear, just as the novel does on a larger scale. The issue with regionalism, here, is not that it negates the national as a cause for concern but rather that it complicates the novel's nationalism. Revealingly, Mann's US characters, far from taking pride in their New England superiority, often view that pride as a cause for alarm, as it reminds them that the difference between the regions damn the nation's pretensions to greatness. For instance, in one passage, Mann writes that Helen "thought she had sympathized with the oppressed of all climes and of all times; but her home had been in the freest nation of the earth, and in the most advanced portion of that nation" (14). Here and elsewhere (e.g., Mann 2000, 46), regional difference spurs Mann to qualify the nationalist notion that the United States is the "freest nation of the earth." The slippage is slight but significant, especially when one considers its ubiquity in the novel. This problem is best brought out in the association of Cuba and the South, an association that anxiously points up the failure of the United States to establish an identity premised on liberalism. This general failure is manifest in individual failures within the novel. For instance, the novel's tragic conclusion with Juanita's death emphasizes the inefficacy of Helen's efforts as an enlightened New Englander against a slave power found not only in Cuba but in Mann's nation as well; as Monika Elbert explains, the ending "is almost as if to say that the 'enlightened' North (in the shape of Helen Wentworth) can have passing moments of charity, but that in the grand scheme of things, its effect is rather trivial. Juanita cannot find a home, and she is martyred in the end; the pains of the good New England missionary, daughter of the Puritans, seem pointless and futile. . . . Miss Wentworth's New England, even as a momentary haven of refuge at the end of the novel, is powerless in changing the system of slavery (wrought by the worst aspects of Catholicism) which so dehumanizes and which Mann describes so diabolically" (Elbert 2013, 133). This ending suggests the gravity of the nation's internal Otherness.

With southern difference determined by the South's location in a pernicious, character-influencing climate, might not New England rest easy in the knowledge that it is safe from such influences? However, environment may be precisely the problem for Mann. With southern difference bound to sultry, passion-inducing climes, that portion of the nation—and Cuba, if Cuba joins the nation—may always remain problematically different from New England. The novel does not seem to see environment as an unsurpassable barrier, but it is clearly a barrier. Therefore, a nation built on union between North and South is irrevocably self-differentiated; Mann places the nation's fractured identity on a natural level.

With difference thus functioning in Mann's view as a substrate in the nation's identity, the only viable solution would be for New England to secede. It would seem that this was not an option that Mann approved of. Like many New Englanders, Mann's support for abolition intensified in the 1850s, but she opposed radical Garrisonian secessionism (Marshall 2005, 527–28). From *Juanita*'s postbellum perspective Mann does speak admiringly of Garrison's daring, suggesting some affinity for him in hindsight (Mann 2000, 9). Even if she had approved, however, secession was clearly out of the picture by the time of the novel's publication. And that, indeed, may more than anything else sum up the novel's inability to get over its antebellum concerns in the seemingly more benign postbellum period—with union irrevocably established after the Civil War, the US South has become a permanent Other within the nation. The wistful way that she reimagines Garrison may suggest nostalgia for a position she once disliked but in hindsight approved of, a nostalgia premised on uncertainty regarding the nation's postbellum state.

Yet even if environment or secession did provide Mann with a comforting solution to her concerns about the nation's failure of national identity, another factor proves similarly aggravating. Mann emphasizes that slavery is a national rather than a regional problem, and not simply in that the nation harbored a slaveholding region. As Mann's narrator points out, "the northern portion of [Helen's] country proved to have been deeply involved in the pecuniary gains of slavery, and therefore blinded to its heinousness" (Mann 2000, 26). Such statements pointing out the complicity in slavery of Northerners who should have known better are a constant refrain in the novel. The statements qualify the novel's otherwise nationalist sentiment, thus producing a constant doing and undoing of nationalism. Perhaps more than anything else, this recurring tension between a desire to proclaim New England superiority and dismay over even that favored land's failures suggests that Mann was unable to displace New England's—quite literal—investment in slavery onto the South. Mann's concerns regarding New England partly reflect impatience with abolitionism's inability to put "right feelings" into practice (Windell 2014, 308). However, there is more at stake. Mann's hosts in Cuba, the personages upon whom she based the Rodríguez family in a telling substitution, were New Englanders. As Mann would have thus found it impossible not to notice (Marshall 2005, 273–74), northerners invested in and ran Cuban plantations (Pérez 1990, 24–25). Mann acknowledges that one of the reasons that New Englanders in the early antebellum period had been hesitant to embrace Garrisonian abolitionism was that "the pecuniary interest northern people had in southern plantations—often the ownership of them—made it invidious to dwell upon the subject [abolition], and sealed the eyes of humanity" (Mann 2000, 9). Awareness of such investment would have made it impossible for her to displace concerns about the nation's illiberal investment in slavery onto the South as a distinct entity with no ties to or implications for the larger nation. This recognition would, moreover, make the presence of the Other within the nation all the more apparent, illustrating, as it does, that the nation has failed to displace Cuban difference. Northern complicity in slavery means that not only can guilt not be displaced on the South; the nation's complicity with Cuban difference cannot, either. Mann's recasting of her hosts as Cubans in and of itself suggests her inability to extricate New England from Cuba.

Juanita's obsession with the association between North and South, United States and Caribbean, constitutes a breakdown of the environmental understanding of difference upon which its national typologies rely. Whereas the novel generally ascribes difference to environmental factors, bemoaning the recalcitrance to improvement in southern regions whose environment encourages despotic vices, the presence of slaveholding interests among Northerners suggests that the problem is more pervasive. Illiberal customs may be powerful enough not only to take root in environments that are conducive to cultivating them but, additionally, in environments that would seem to dictate against such customs. The novel oftentimes suggests that environment, although a powerful force in shaping human type, is not an absolute hindrance to education and betterment; the unfortunate side to this suggestion is that beneficial environments are not enough to stay the spread of illiberal interests, a point illustrated in passages regarding northern investment in slavery. The passages thus suggest a breakdown of one final stronghold for keeping the Other out of the nation. If illiberal interests can thrive in the North, then the North's more beneficent environment is no sure safeguard against the introduction and cultivation of the illiberal character prominent in Cuba. The problem becomes not only sectionalism and the national union of environmentally opposed regions. It becomes, too, that the environmental constitution of difference, although a good guide to human variability, is no sure and final guide. For that reason, the entire nation is liable to the corruption entailed by the incorporation of Cuban characteristics.

The association between the Unites States and Cuba and how it undermines Mann's conception of national identity applies to both of the historical moments the novel speaks to. The issue may seem to be more clearly a problem in how it relates to the antebellum, slaveholding milieu of the novel's composition, but it also troubles the novel's postbellum publication context. We typically associate a more assertive, chauvinistic nationalism with hegemonic late-century liberalism, a confidence produced by the nation's ostensibly successful navigation of the challenges posed by sectionalism and Civil War and widespread (although unevenly distributed) economic prosperity. Mann, as we have seen, in some ways conforms to this paradigm. Yet her transformation of an anachronistic antislavery novel into a historical romance points to anxiety over the import of the history the novel represents, a history that implicates a supposedly liberal United States in leaguing with Cuba in slavery's defense. This anxiety amounts to an obsession with the problems history's claims pose for the United States' self-conception. History serves as a reminder that the South continued to have an ambiguous relationship to the nation after the Civil War. Despite triumphal claims regarding the Civil War's resolution of the internal contradictions the early nation faced, many Southerners still viewed themselves as a people apart from the nation. This is an age, after all, when white Southerners increasingly and successfully advocated returning to prewar social and economic norms, norms that in the guise of Jim Crow laws and slavery-like institutions such as convict leasing would predominate throughout much of the twentieth century (Blackmon 2008). White Southerners, moreover, at this time increasingly romanticized Southern difference. Northern progressives, likewise, continued to view the South's legacy and identity as troubling to aspirations to nationally universal liberalism. The South had not, in this view, successfully conformed to the paradigm liberal nationalists espoused. Mann's novel reflects these and other persistent dislocations of nationality.

The novel's romantic conclusion with Juanita's death allegorically evokes this dislocation of nationality. *Juanita* invests nationalist fervor in the notion that Ludovico and Juanita can only realize their love, expressly forbidden in Cuba, in the beneficent United States. *Juanita* represents Ludovico as a liberal hero for his attempt to pursue that love, and the United States serves as the space in which that heroism can be put into practice. This detail glorifies the United States' aspirations to liberal nationhood. However, Ludovico and Juanita's romance is never consummated, as Juanita tragically dies before that can occur. *Juanita* is another in a long line of antebellum novels to broach the issue of interracial romance only to stifle that prospect with the heroine's tragic death. (James Fenimore Cooper's 1826 *The Last of the Mohicans* is the urtext here.) Numerous scholars have argued that such melodramatic plots reveal the inability of Anglo-American culture to imagine interracial union (e.g., Rosenthal 2004, 122–23; Wardrop 1997, esp. 62–63). This may well be the case in *Juanita*. It bears notice that given the book's sense of the nation's failures to live up to its liberal ideals, *Juanita* is unable to imagine a happy ending for the couple. The novel may displace its concerns over whether the couple could succeed in the United States by killing Juanita off in Cuba, where the death can be blamed on Cuban illiberality. After all, interracial marriages were hardly smiled upon more in the United States, whether New England or the South, than in Cuba. Juanita's death might, thus, be understood as a mercy killing. Mann, to save herself from representing the coup de grâce to her liberal nationalism that would occur if she were to return the characters to an illiberal United States, kills Juanita off before that happens. The death provides the cover needed to take the focus off what would happen to the couple in New England. Lurking beneath the surface here is intense uncertainty regarding whether the nation can serve as the locus for liberal heroism. If the relationship functions to place the novel's nationalism on the allegorical level of the characters' romance, then their failure to consummate their relationship constitutes the breakdown of the allegory supporting that nationalism.

5

José Antonio Saco's Antiannexationist Essays

Cuba, Hispanicism, and National Identity

In antebellum US culture, Anglo-American nationalists constructed US identity as devoted to the related ideals of cosmopolitanism and liberalism. They often understood these qualities as white, US American ways of approaching the world, and they figured racial and national Others as constitutionally averse to cosmopolitanism and liberal democracy and thus as foils to US identity. Hispanicism provided such an Other, suggesting that Hispanophone peoples were incapable of liberal-democratic self-government. US identity formation was an imperialist discourse. For expansionists who equated the right to territorial sovereignty with the ability to maintain liberal-democratic institutions, Hispanicism provided the evidence necessary to defend appropriating Hispanophone territories from peoples thought incapable of self-government.

These discourses have been taken to task by traditionally canonical writers such as Cooper and Melville and, even more so, by writers from the margins who wrote in the name of dispossessed peoples. These writers critiqued the identity-fixated and imperialist strain of national identity construction, suggesting that cosmopolitan liberalism's universalist foundations had become corrupted by their articulation to particular identities. Some such criticisms stress that resolving these problems requires rededication to universals and resistance to racialism and nationalism. In his *Joaquín Murieta*, for example, John Rollin Ridge demonstrates the incoherence of the Hispanicist-driven understanding of national identity by showing how Euro-American settlers use Hispanicism to deny Murieta's right to become a self-made man in California. The Cherokee Ridge analogizes Murieta's plight to that of Ridge's nation in the era of the Indian Removal Act and the Trail of Tears. For Ridge, national identity was a means for taking what should be a universal individual right and limiting it to particular identities in a conquered territory. He held that remedying these problems required returning to the universalist sensibilities supposedly at the liberal project's heart. Through his negative characterization of the Euro-American settlers' inability to sympathize with Mexicans such as Murieta, Ridge calls for a cosmopolitan sensibility that enables cross-racial identification (Havard 2015, 333–43). Ridge would agree with Stephen Holmes that failures of liberal societies exhibit not liberalism's philosophical infelicities but, rather, how particular societies fail to live up to liberal ideals (Holmes 1993, xiv–xv). The prevalence of this approach among writers contesting how Anglo-Americans tethered cosmopolitan-liberal values to US identity attests to liberalism's centrality to nineteenth-century US emancipatory discourses. Certainly there was also a powerful tradition of conservative critique of imperialism. However, what came to be recognized as the reformist US thought of the period generally pushed for more universal extension of market-based individual rights, although there was often disagreement about just how universal those rights should be. Participants in the discussion did not so much question the liberal project's validity but ask how best to complete it.

In the Hispanophone world, though, the understandings of universal political self-determination and possessive individualism that formed US liberalism's core were less accepted. To be sure, a vibrant Enlightenment movement occurred in the Spanish-speaking world during the eighteenth and nineteenth centuries. The movement saw the growth of what Raúl Coronado terms "disenchantment" regarding what had formerly been understood as the transcendental authority of the crown and church. It called for economic liberalization via reconsidering mercantile policies as well as some degree of political liberalization by establishing legislative branches and limiting monarchical and clerical power. However, these reformers generally defended their arguments not via the language of the rights of man and possessive individualism popular in Anglo-American discourse but rather via promotion of the good of the *patria* (homeland), *nación* (nation), and *pueblo* (people) (Coronado 2013, 25, 106–7, 113–15, 124, 137–38). The thinkers rejected radical individualism, instead emphasizing that maintaining continuity with communally inherited norms is necessary to maintain the *felicidad pública* (public happiness). Many were skeptical of democracy and thought that the privileged classes knew best how to determine the felicidad pública, largely because the movement's leaders were generally enlightened aristocrats or bureaucratic elites rather than members of the bourgeoisie (114–15). Their ideas exhibited the focus on traditionalism and organicism that I described as conservative in chapter 2. Spanish Enlightenment could be described as modernization with what would be considered in the Anglophone world an anti-individualist, classically conservative spin. However, describing the Spanish Enlightenment in this manner risks confusing distinct intellectual traditions, as "conservative" in the Hispanophone tradition connotes not skepticism toward possessive individualism but rather adherence to monarchical autocracy and clerical influence on the state, views that were largely unfathomable in the nineteenth-century United States. Although the movement exhibited what might seem reactionary elements from an outside perspective, its focus on the felicidad pública provides a meaningful corrective to the individualist excesses of liberalism.

Cuban intellectual José Antonio Saco (1797–1879) formulated a response to Hispanicism along these lines. Saco was an expatriate who is known for provocative and complex literary essays that presaged the conflicts over Cuban sovereignty that would come to a head in the late nineteenth century. He is often considered to be a radical due to his opposition to both slavery and annexation. However, I read his denunciation of US imperialism as being underpinned by what may seem, comparably to Cooper, a conservative critique of liberalism and Hispanicism. This critique ought more properly to be understood as consistent with Spanish Enlightenment precept, in the context of which it would not be considered more radical than other examples in the tradition but also would not be considered conservative. However, I will use the term "conservative" at times in this chapter to emphasize how Saco moderated his views over the course of his career and to imply comparisons to other writers I have discussed in this study to sketch out Saco's positioning vis-à-vis those writers. Saco's Hispanic response to Hispanicism, characterized by what I will refer to as his "Hispanism," seems to reflect Hispanicism by positing that Cubans possess organically constituted, traditional identities that are intrinsically different from those of North Americans. However, rather than arguing that Cuba's identity entails an incapacity for self-determination, Saco appeals for Cuban self-determination precisely through the maintenance of Cuban identity.

In discussing this Cuban who wrote back to US liberal Hispanicist imperialism, I elaborate not only on liberal-conservative political debates as they focalized around Hispanicism but, more particularly, as they emerged around the special relationship between Cuba and the United States. The vigorous nature of the debate Saco engaged reflects the unique place of the Cuba-US relationship in the national imagination of both US Americans and Cubans. Both peoples have imagined this relationship as crucial to their identities as collective peoples. Historically, US Americans have arguably been more concerned with establishing superiority to and dominance over Cuba than with any other Hispanophone nation, with the possible exception of Mexico depending on era. Cubans have likewise varyingly looked to the United States as a savior from Spain and as a threat to their autonomy. Mary Peabody Mann and Saco reflect this dynamic. Whereas in *Juanita* Mann defines US identity as liberal in contradistinction to Cuban despotism and agonizes over US failure to maintain that distinction, Saco insists that Cuban cultural difference must be protected against intense US desires for incursion into Cuba. In doing so, he renders absurd Mann's annexationist fantasy of US benevolence toward the island.

José Antonio Saco, Hispanicism, and *Nacionalidad*

Although Saco exhibits some views that could be described as conservative from an Anglophone point of view, many of those views are consistent with liberalism as it was understood in Spanish Enlightenment thought. Some of Saco's views are unequivocally liberal when viewed from any perspective. He favored modernizing, industrializing reforms that he believed would diversify Cuba's economy, such as business-friendly tax reform, freedom of the press, and expanded public education. He hoped these policies would increase Cuban autonomy from Spain (Ortiz 1928, lxi). He argued against the illegal slave trade. He also opposed the US annexation movement, popular both in the United States and among his countrymen. As an early Cuban critic of US imperialism, he presaged José Martí and Fidel Castro. Generations of Cuban radicals have embraced him as a forerunner of the *Cuba libre* movement and the Communist revolution. Finally, Saco often self-identified as liberal (e.g., Ortiz 1928, liv, xxx). Naturally, many critics and historians have accepted this self-identification (Gutiérrez de la Solana 1988, 99). This hagiographic view does not fully encapsulate his views' subtleties though.

Understanding Saco's response to Hispanicism requires considering how his political thought evolved over the course of his career. His early work comprised a more radically liberal interpretation of Enlightenment thought. As a student, he was a disciple of the notable Cuban reformer Padre Félix Varela, who vociferously criticized the colonial authorities who carried out Spain's increasingly mercantile and repressive policies. These policies reacted to the recent democratic revolutions on mainland Spanish America. Varela was an early Cuban advocate for liberalizing trade and instituting civil reforms. Saco, too, wrote to support such reforms during the 1820s and early 1830s. He argued for increased Cuban autonomy from Spain. Saco never supported what he viewed as impractical plans for a revolution for independence, but he did harbor hopes that one day independence would be possible (Navarro García 1994, 136, 144). He also frequently spoke against the slaveholding establishment. Although the slave trade had been long abolished, Cuban planters believed that the explosive growth of Cuba's sugarcane exportation during this period required that the trade continue unabated. The government tended to league with the sugarocracy in winking at the trade. Saco opposed the administration's tolerance, and although he stopped short of radical abolitionism, he often expressed his belief that slavery would not survive the nineteenth century. Although, as we will see, his motivations for attacking slavery were ambiguous, Saco's criticisms in all of these regards evidenced a strongly liberal thrust. This fact was not lost upon the antiliberal regime, which, led by Captain General Miguel Tacón, exiled Saco to Spain in 1834. Although Saco generally favored practical compromises, Tacón and other power brokers on the island viewed him as a seditionist. They also feared Saco's profound influence on younger Cuban intellectuals.

After being exiled from Cuba, Saco spent much of the remainder of his life expatriated in Europe. During this period, his idealism gave way to other concerns. As Josef Opatrný writes, "Saco, working since the 1820s for reforms to lead Cuba toward prosperity and enlightenment, now doubted whether such reforms might not also lead to a loss of Cuban identity. Without ever explaining the reasons, he changed his priorities from political and economic freedoms for Cuba to a 'Cuban, not an Anglo-Saxon, Cuba'" (Opatrný 1994, 49). What prompted this shift to being concerned with the organic integrity of Cubans as a people was the question of Cuban annexation to the United States. This matter increasingly preoccupied Saco over the course of the late 1830s, '40s, and '50s, when he penned a series of complex essays on Cuban nationality (39). Although his early statements on the issue seemed to suggest the contrary, Saco became a staunch critic of annexation, premising his resistance on the importance of maintaining Cuba's national identity. In articulating this argument, Saco shifts from his earlier radicalism toward his relatively "conservative" (I place the term in scare quotes as a reminder that it is being used out of context as a heuristic) interpretation of Spanish Enlightenment views as they relate to Cuba.

Further context is needed before elaborating this point. Many of Saco's circle, such as Gaspar Betancourt Cisneros, were among annexation's most vocal proponents. Cuban annexationist arguments hinged on two related issues: firstly, achieving greater political and economic national self-determination by escaping Spanish colonial sway and, secondly, the slavery question. Annexationists believed that the United States' liberal-democratic government and free-market economy offered Cuba more self-determination than it enjoyed under Spanish despotism and mercantilism. Moreover, although independence might have seemed preferable in terms of providing for a purer sovereignty than what would be enjoyed under the United States, many annexationists—as did Saco—viewed Cuban independence as an impossibility. They feared the depredations of large imperial powers like England on their small island community. They were also concerned that their African slaves would revolt if they were no longer deterred by the mother country's army. Slavery's relationship to the annexation debates was complex. Most annexationist creoles were enlightened liberals who favored loosening the traditional order's grip, but they were often slaveholders, too. Their views on slavery bespeak the competing allegiances to theory and practice inherent in their position, much as was the case for US slaveholding patriots such as Thomas Jefferson. Some viewed slavery as an evil, but they at the same time saw it as essential to Cuba's economic prosperity, which was almost totally based on sugarcane production. They moreover feared that Cuba could become a second Saint-Domingue and generally believed that lessening slavery's yoke would invite revolt. Most annexationists, therefore, were motivated by the desire to procure the US South's protection for Cuban slaveholding (Cruz-Taura 1997, 92). By the same token, the most vocal US proponents of annexation were southerners who saw annexation as an opportunity to extend the slave power.

When he engaged this polemic, Saco's contemporaries initially believed he favored annexation. In his 1837 essay "Paralelo entre la isla de Cuba y algunas colonias inglesas" ("Parallel between the Island of Cuba and Some English Colonies"),[1] Saco made comments that annexationists construed as favoring their position. He begins this essay by praising the decentralized, unobtrusive manner in which the English colonial regime governed Canada in contrast to Spain's mercantilist approach to Cuba. He argues that it would be in both Spain's and Cuba's interests for Spain to follow the English model, as this approach would secure greater liberty and economic prosperity for Cuba and increased Cuban fidelity for Spain. If Spain were to fail to follow this model, however, Saco proposes an alternative:

> Darle [Cuba] entonces una existencia propia, una existencia independiente, y si es posible tan aislada en lo político como lo está en la naturaleza; he aquí cual sería en mi humilde opinión el blanco a donde debieran dirigirse los esfuerzos de todo buen cubano. Pero si arrastrada por las circunstancias tuviera que arrojarse en brazos extraños, en ningunos podría caer con más honor ni con más gloria que en los de la gran Confederación Norteamericana. En ellos encontraría paz y consuelo, fuerza y protección, justicia y libertad, y apoyándose sobre tan sólidas bases, en breve exhibiría al mundo el portentoso abatimiento se levanta y pasa con la velocidad del relámpago al más alto punto de grandeza.

> To give her [Cuba] an existence of her own, an independent existence, and if it is possible one as isolated in political as in natural terms; this is the goal to which every good Cuban ought to strive. However, if forced by circumstance to seek the arms of a foreign nation, in none could we fall with more honor nor more glory than in those of the great North

> American Confederation. In these we would find peace, consolation, power and protection, justice and liberty, and supporting ourselves on such solid foundations, in no time at all we would exhibit to the world that we could elude failure and rise with the speed of lightning to the highest point of grandeur. (Saco 1928e, 6)

Although Saco prefers independence if Spain drives Cuba to reject the colonial bond, he sees the United States as a viable alternative.[2] The Lockean move Saco makes here reflects his radical early liberalism. The Cuban people may reject their covenant with the mother country and seek their own master if Spain fails to support Cuban interests. This notion appealed to Cuba's annexationists, who cited the respected author in their support.

In the 1840s though, Saco claimed that he had been misread. In a response to V. Vásquez Queipo, he writes that he only favored annexation in the case of the direst necessity, if, for instance, Spain proved an absolutely intolerable master or unable to stay a slave revolt. Claiming that this was not the case at the moment, Saco denies his support in no uncertain terms, claiming that he would prefer anything—whether it be independence or the status quo—to union with the United States (Saco 1928f, 15). As Saco later restates the point,

> Lo primero que deseo es que Cuba, libre y justamente gobernada, viva unida a España. Lo segundo, que disuelta esta union, ora por la madre, ora por la hija, Cuba trate de conservar su nacionalidad, y de constituirse en estado completamente independiente. Lo tercero, que si las circunstancias le fueran tan adversas, que no pueda existir por sí sola, ni salvarse de su total ruina sino arrojandose en los brazos de los Estados Unidos, entonces y sólo entonces lo haga como la única tabla a que pueda asirse en su naufragio.
>
> My first desire is that Cuba, free and justly governed, remains united to Spain. The second is that, if this union is dissolved, whether by the mother or by the daughter, Cuba attempts to conserve its nationality and to become a completely independent state. The third is that, if circumstances are so extremely adverse that Cuba cannot exist independently nor save herself from total ruin without throwing herself into the arms of the United States, then and then only shall she do it as her only recourse from shipwreck. (Saco 1928d, 25)

The idea that annexation could only be a last-ditch exit strategy signals a decided change in Saco's approach. Whereas he had also qualified his support for annexation in the 1837 essay, the tone here is entirely different; in the early work, he seems open to the possibility, which is not the case in the later essays. Saco is being a bit disingenuous in his disavowals of his previous support. His position on annexation had shifted.

Expounding on these initial statements, over a series of subsequent essays Saco provided a critical response to annexationism that interrogated the movement's tenets one by one. One of his most striking formulations came in "Ideas sobre la incorporación de Cuba en los Estados Unidos" (1848). Perhaps not coincidentally, this essay was published at the time of the US-Mexican War, and the derogatory references to the Spanish-speaking world found in the US press at the time could not have failed to impress Saco. In this essay, Saco forwards two antiannexationist arguments. First of all, he recognizes the problems of the annexation movement's relationship to Cuban slavery. He emphasizes the movement's incoherence, claiming that it is inconsistent for annexationists to promote the expansion of liberal freedoms because many of the movement's partisans viewed annexation as a way to maintain slavery in the face of English and Spanish abolitionist pressure. Saco also insists that an annexationist war would precipitate precisely the apocalyptic slave revolt annexationists so feared. The desperate slaves, recognizing annexation as the pro-slavery movement it was, would see their chance in the unrest the revolution caused and would themselves revolt (Saco 1928a, 46). Haiti, Saco argued elsewhere, revealed the dangers of unrest (Saco 1928g, 72, 129). Saco's detractors, most of whom supported annexation in part because they viewed it as a necessity for maintaining slavery, often impugned Saco as an abolitionist for these views. Although Saco claimed that slavery would one day end (he was a gradualist abolitionist [103]), he vigorously denied that he was motivated primarily by abolitionism. Instead, he claimed that he opposed annexation from a desire to protect the creoles from the slaves (Ortiz 1928, xli; Schmidt-Nowara 2001, 96).

Saco's second argument in the essay is that whereas annexationists despaired of Spain's ever enacting the liberal political and economic reforms they believed the United States would provide, Saco, despite his negative experience with the mother country's colonial government, places some faith in Spain. He is moreover skeptical of the United States' motives, writing that "desde que se sienta con fuerzas para balancear el número de cubanos, aspirará a la dirección política de los negocios de Cuba; y la conseguirá, no sólo por su fuerza numérica, sino porque se considerará como nuestra protectora o tutora y mucho más adelantada que nosotros en materias de gobierno" / "because they would feel that their forces would outbalance the number of Cubans, they will aspire to the direction of Cuban business; and they will direct it, not only by virtue of their strength in numbers, but because they will consider themselves as our protector or tutor and much more advanced than us in matters of governance" (Saco 1928a, 36). Saco expresses his doubts that the United States intends to grant Cuban creoles the political and economic autonomy they desire, instead governing Cuba paternalistically. Saco was not mistaken; whereas Cuban annexationists believed Cuba would achieve US statehood and thus the same self-determination and place in governance enjoyed by the US states, many US annexationists lacked confidence in Cuba's capacity for self-determination and desired the island to be a territory rather than a state, much like Puerto Rico and the Philippines would become after the Spanish-American War. This lack of confidence was a product of Anglo-American prejudice against a society thought to be led by inferior creoles and to be mostly composed of even more inferior mulattoes and Africans. Even if Cuba was granted representation in the federal government, its population dictated that it would not wield much power in contrast to the other states and their Anglo-American populations, which would place more of its leaders in powerful positions and easily forward their interests over Cuba's (Saco 1928b, 12). If the Cuban creole population were larger, annexation might pose less threat (Pérez 1990, 53).

Saco's most serious charge against annexation is that it would prove fatal to Cuba's *nacionalidad* ("nationality"). It is here that his emphasis on what Russell Kirk describes as conservatism's traditionalist, organicist conception of the felicidad pública as peculiar to the needs and customs of particular societies is most apparent (Kirk 1982, xv). His other claims all on some level service this multivalent argument. In an essay responding to the angry criticism prompted by his "Ideas sobre la incorporación de Cuba en los Estados Unidos," Saco claims that what most distresses him about annexation is that the evils attendant to it—particularly, black revolt and Anglo-American dominance—"mataría infaliblemente dentro de pocos años la nacionalidad cubana" / "would infallibly eradicate Cuban nationality within only a few years" (1928g, 71–72). "La nacionalidad cubana," Saco writes, "perecerá con la incorporación de Cuba a los Estados Unidos, sea cual fuera el modo con que se haga . . . en nuestro estado actual, la guerra civil por la anexión sería muy fatal a los cubanos y provechoso solo a los extranjeros." / "Cuban nationality will perish with the incorporation of Cuba to the United States, whatever might be the mode with which it is achieved . . . in our current state, civil war for purposes of annexation would be extremely fatal to Cubans and fruitful only for foreigners" (74).

A war over annexation, Saco claims, would result in extreme loss of creole life and wealth. The creoles will lose all when caught between the Spanish military, their own uprising slaves, and an ostensibly benevolent but in fact imperialist United States. Creole losses would include their way of life. The United States, dismissive toward Spanish institutions and cultural norms, would move to replace those institutions and force Cubans to assimilate to Anglo-American culture after having moved in upon the ashes of a once-prosperous society. Saco analogizes this turn of events to the plight of Louisiana creoles under US rule after the Louisiana Purchase, creoles who, as Saco points out, were slowly losing their community's distinctive qualities under force of US intrusion (Saco 1928g, 219–20).

When his respondents claimed that nothing of the sort would occur, Saco argued that in addition to failing to understand that the United States would reorganize Cuban society in its own image, his enemies had misunderstood the nature of nationality. Here, Saco devotes a great deal of attention to developing a traditionalist definition of "nationality," writing,

> Para disipar la confusión en que mis impugnadores han envuelto esta materia, es preciso que antes sepamos lo que es *nacionalidad*. Confieso que no es fácil definir claramente esta palabra: porque consistiendo la nacionalidad en un sentimiento, los sentimientos se sienten, pero nunca se explican bien. Así en vez de valerme de definiciones imperfectas y obscuras, me serviré de ejemplos y diré: que todo pueblo que habita un mismo suelo, y tiene un mismo origen, una misma lengua, y unos mismos usos y costumbres, ese pueblo tiene una *nacionalidad*.
>
> To dispel the confusion in which my critics have enveloped this issue, it is first necessary to know what "nationality" is. I confess that it is not easy to define this word clearly: Nationality consists in a feeling, and feelings are felt but rarely explained well. Therefore, instead of availing myself of imperfect and obscure definitions, I will bring forth examples; let us say that every people that inhabits the same ground, has the same origin, the same tongue, the same usages and customs, that people has a nationality. (Saco 1928g, 196)

Saco's definition emphasizes the inherited communal norms that shape Cuban society, the cultural qualities that differentiate Cubans from other national communities. Saco's emphasis on examples instead of theory suggests that his understanding of nationality was more interested in the concrete than the abstract. He was more invested in the stuff of Cuban community and tradition than in idealism or universal standards.

Saco's point depends on a distinction between nacionalidad and *nación* ("nation"). He argues that when his enemies take issue with his position on nacionalidad, they have in mind nación and mistake the crucial distinction between the two. Analyzing this mistake, Saco quotes one disputant, who pseudonymously refers to himself as Saco's "Discípulo." This interlocutor wrote, "Nación no es otra cosa que la reunión de varias provincias y pueblos con derechos y obligaciones recíprocas, regidos por un gobierno común y propio" / "Nation is nothing other than the conglomeration of various provinces and peoples with rights and reciprocal obligations, ruled by a shared government of their own" (Saco 1928g, 196–97). He continues that Cuba as a colony of Spain lacks nationhood in this sense, which leads him to suggest that Saco mistakenly argues for maintaining something that Cuba does not possess in the first place. This interlocutor's definition of nation largely comprised abstract (the operative term here) political entities and processes: provincial divisions, reciprocal obligations among subjects, national self-government, and so on. It may be true, Saco cedes, that annexation would not negatively affect Cuba's nación in this sense, Cuba not possessing this sort of nationhood by virtue of its colonial status. Saco even acknowledges that Cuba might enjoy greater political and economic self-determination as part of the United States than it does under Spain, even if that self-determination may not be such as the annexationists hoped. Consistent with Spanish Enlightenment preference for the felicidad pública over possessive individualism, though, political nationhood is a secondary issue for Saco, as it is distinct from and of inferior significance to nationality. As he writes, "Nada entiendo de nacionalidad política; lo que sí entiendo es que la política influye en reanimar, comprimir o sofocar las nacionalidades existentes" / "Political nationality means nothing at all; rather, politics influences nationalities to reanimate, compromise, or suffocate themselves" (203). For Saco, nación as the "Discípulo" understands it merely refers to procedural relationships and policies. Nación is thus important only in so much as it enables a nacionalidad to maintain its traditions. The danger of annexation is that it might do the opposite.

Not recognizing this distinction between nacionalidad and nación leads, Saco observes, to a mistaken sense that nacionalidad is a small hurdle in the race for progress. Saco quotes one of his disputants as suggesting in this regard that "Las tendencias del siglo borran las nacionalidades" / "The tendencies of the century are erasing nationalities" (Saco 1928g, 227). Saco disagrees with this remarkable, cosmopolitan statement with a striking formulation of his own, writing, "Cabalmente se observa todo el contrario. Desenvolverse las nacionalidades, luchar por separarse unas de otras y adquirir una existencia soberana, he aquí la gran verdad que proclama el siglo XIX" / "The absolute opposite is in fact the case. The untangling of nationalities, fighting to separate one from the other and for the acquisition of a sovereign existence, here we have the great truth of the nineteenth century" (227). Modernity is a mixed blessing for Saco, as it signals the challenge of maintaining one's nationality in this primordial, existential sense, and it is this that Saco feared annexation threatened. The nación might thrive under US rule, but Saco expresses his desire that "Cuba no solo fuese rica, ilustrada, moral y poderosa, sino que fuese Cuba *cubana* y no *angloamericana*" / "Cuba not only become rich, enlightened, moral, and powerful, but that Cuba remains *Cuban* and not *Anglo-American*" (Saco 1928a, 36). Saco, in other words, feared that annexation threatened nacionalidad.

Saco's belief that annexation would have tragic effects on Cuban nationality is informed by his sense that annexation is premised on Hispanicist conceptions of nation that would not encourage respect for Cuban prerogative. Saco asks his countrymen to entrench themselves along the lines of their Cuban difference from the United States. His response to Hispanicism oftentimes seems like a form of Hispanicism. Hispanicism posited an essential difference between the two peoples by suggesting US Americans to be more adept in maintaining liberal institutions than Hispanophone peoples construed as committed to traditional, despotic political forms. Saco agrees that these two peoples are far too different to be appropriate bedfellows. Just as Hispanicism decried Hispanophone peoples for an antiliberal, conservative commitment to tradition, Saco argues that it is precisely tradition that constitutes Cuba's nacionalidad. This nacionalidad must be protected to maintain Cuban self-determination. Yet his defense of Cuban sovereignty marks his departure from Hispanicist logics. Hispanicism, after all, construed Hispanophone peoples as incapable of self-government without assimilation to US culture. Saco's conservative defense of nacionalidad—his insistence on living by the code of Cuban tradition—is aimed to protect Cuban communal self-determination against a Hispanicism that denies that self-determination in a bid for territorial expansion.

Saco and Hispanicism: Cultural Autonomy and Anticosmopolitanism

Similar to Cooper, Saco's "conservative" insistence on maintaining Cuban difference is premised on his critique of excessive forms of liberalism, forms Saco viewed as threats to Cuba. One is reasonably tempted to view Saco's antiannexationist arguments as simply concerned with expediency and feasibility. Yet expedience's philosophic currency in conservative perspectives points to deeper differences with his enemies. Their reactions are illustrative. For instance, Cisneros wrote in an 1849 letter to Saco, "aquí tengo que sacar el machete a cada rato que estos malditos Calaveras que te tratan de vejestorio, retrógrado, y dicen que estás tocando el violón, y que lo que quieres es lucírtela en la tribuna de las Cortes de España y otras tonterías por este estilo" / "I have to take out the machete each time these damned numbskulls impugn you as an old crank, a reactionary, and say that you are talking nonsense, that what you truly desire is to look good for the tribunal of the Spanish Cortes and other foolish things of this sort" (Cisneros 1928, 50). Cisneros's letter reveals that Saco's enemies viewed his criticisms of annexation as those of a backward conservative and an obsequious tool of the Spanish. This should not be surprising, considering the dispute's philosophical import. When Saco attacks his interlocutors' claim that nationality is an inconvenient distraction from their goals, he particularly takes issue with what in the context of the Spanish Enlightenment would have been viewed as more radically liberal elements. Their belief in the relative unimportance of nationality and identity indicates their debt to Enlightenment cosmopolitanism. For these writers, a people's attachment to their nationality's inherited cultural norms is an impediment to social and economic progress. They view liberal democracy—what George M. Frederickson describes as the *herrenvolk* variety (Frederickson 1987, 61–68)—as the governmental form most likely to ensure fiscal and political self-determination, to ensure, in short, possessive individualism. They favor abstraction and theory over the concrete particularities of experience. They prefer to emphasize the rights of the abstract political and economic actor rather than those of the national actor. They offer theories regarding the benefits Cuba would experience under what they view to be a rational, just governmental system rather than accepting what they know and are familiar with. They are, lastly, willing to undertake a violent break with the past to experiment with implementing these projects.

Although he recognized the need for reform, Saco viewed the more radical elements of these arguments as dangerous wishful thinking. In a condemnatory response, Saco writes, "sólo en la embriaguez de su liberalismo ha podido escribir que a permanecer un día más como estamos en Cuba, es preferible que '*perezcamos todos, hombres, mujeres y niños en el campo de batalla*'" / "solely owing to his inebriated liberalism has he been able to write that to remain a single day more as we are in Cuba is it preferable that '*we all perish, men, women,* and *children in the field of battle*'" (Saco 1928g, 131). The striking formulation "embriaguez de su liberalismo" is telling. Despite his Enlightenment ethos, there was something about the idea of making a too-dramatic break with Cuba's inherited sociocultural ties with Spain that Saco viewed as akin to drunkenness.

Maintaining Cuban nationality against what he viewed as fanatics was important to Saco because he believed that freedom in any form not including the free exercise of Cuban cultural identity as traditionally understood was not freedom at all. Saco viewed the matter in this manner because the preservation of cultural autonomy rather than political freedom gives shape to his conception of the relationship between nation and self-determination. Without cultural autonomy, Cubans would lose what defines them as a people, including traditional aspects of their culture such as their religious beliefs, language, and mores. If they lose these characteristics, Saco maintains, Cubans will retain no agency in determining their nation's future. Any model for change that fails to recognize the importance of tradition threatens that agency. In contrast to the annexationist insistence on Cuba's freedom to break with the past and to adopt preferable political arrangements, Saco argues for a more moderate understanding of agency. This understanding begins with the idea that any viable reforms must be in dialogue with and protect cultural autonomy.

For Saco, if profound changes in Cuba's sociopolitical situation are to occur in a beneficial manner, it will not be by means of a sudden, revolutionary imposition of foreign models that are, for Cubans, abstractions with which they have little experience. Instead, a process of carefully considering alternatives would need to occur. Independence might one day be possible, but for the time being change would require working for beneficial reforms within the confines of attachment to Spain and its traditional political avenues. Doing so would be the best way to ensure Cuban cultural autonomy and would serve as a strong grounding for ethical behavior in Cuban life. As Saco writes, "El patriotismo, el puro e ilustrado patriotismo debe consistir en Cuba, no en desear imposibles, ni en precipitar el país a una revolución prematura, sino en sufrir con resignación y grandeza de ánimo los ultrajes de la fortuna, procurando siempre enderezar a buena parte los destinos de nuestra patria" / "Patriotism, pure and enlightened patriotism, should in Cuba consist not in desiring impossibilities nor in precipitating the country in a premature rebellion but, rather, in suffering with resignation and grandeur of spirit the outrages of fortune, always endeavoring to direct the destiny of our nation wisely" (Saco 1928a, 47). As Saco immediately emphasizes, this was not an "apática y cobarde resignación" / "apathetic and cowardly resignation"; clearly, the enlightened, politically active Saco advocates an approach that can hardly be so characterized. However, Saco assumes that historically inherited political complexities place limitations on human action. Saco thus argues for striking a balance between prudential recognition of the historical inheritance and proactively trusting in the hand of providence. This is a sense of change in keeping with a more moderate interpretation of the Spanish Enlightenment than that championed by the radical liberals. The position reflects Anthony Quinton's analysis of the roles of traditionalism and organicism in conservatism, as it argues against attempting to make a striking break with the organically constituted traditions that characterize Cuban life (Quinton 1978).

Saco's sense of exactly what constitutes Cuban nationality further confirms his conservatism. Saco's twentieth-century admirers remember him as a prototypical Cuban nationalist who provided an early articulation of a unique Cuban nationality. This move inhibits recognizing Saco's "conservatism" by painting him as a revolutionary advocate for rejecting the past and foreseeing a new future in which Cuba has a place in the scale of nations. Saco was indeed an early advocate of the idea that Cuba possessed a distinct national identity, but his sense of what that identity comprised more so emphasized Cuba's dialectical relationship to its Spanish heritage than would later views. Saco, thus, was invested in the claims history places upon identity. As Luis Navarro García claims, "La excepcionalidad del pensamiento de Saco estriba . . . en el hecho de que se esforzase por compatibilizar su patriotismo cubano con un indudable hispanismo" / "The exceptionality of Saco's thought lies . . . in the fact that he exerts himself to make his patriotism compatible with his undoubtable Hispanism" (Navarro García 1994, 139). Navarro García explains that Cuban national identity is based on the Spanish heritage, and it is this heritage that Saco wishes to protect from annexation (140). This aspect of Saco's conception of Cuban nationality explains his desire that Cuba remain politically connected to Spain. Not only had an opportunity for Cuba to break its bonds with Spain yet to present itself; Saco feared the consequences severance would entail, as he perceived an ineluctable moral and cultural tie between the island and the mother country. Saco's Hispanism, thus, reflects the traditionalism evident in his conception of nationality; national identity, for Saco, is a tradition going back far beyond the island's short history as a Spanish colony and into the more distant annals of continental Spain.

We here perhaps most clearly see the divide between how Saco's work reflects and differs from Hispanicism. Saco is not far from the Hispanicist argument that a transhistorical Hispanic identity exists that differentiates Spain and Spanish America from the United States, although as an advocate for reform, Saco more subtly views this identity as historically conditioned. However, Hispanicism posits that this identity entails an inability to self-determine due to enslavement to pernicious traditions, an inability to self-determine without incorporation into a liberal-democratic United States. In Saco's Hispanist alternative to Hispanicist imperialism, it is precisely by holding on to Hispanic traditions that Cuba can determine her future as a culturally autonomous nation.

The contours of this commitment to identity as freedom become clearer in light of Saco's position on the place of Afro-Cubans in the nation. Reflecting the US American view that I have discussed of Cuba as a racially stratified society in which creoles were less open to racial mixture than in Mexico and Central America, Saco views blacks and whites as mutually exclusive populations and argues for the incoherence of a racially diverse nation. Saco's position stems from his belief in essential black racial difference and inferiority; he viewed blacks as inferior not due to environment but rather to nature (Camacho 2007, 30; Naranjo Orovio 2001–3, 15–16). For Saco, the essentially distinct white and black populations constituted two nationalities (Navarro García 1994, 140). When Saco speaks of preserving Cuban nationality from annexation, he refers to the white, Spanish population. For Saco, these two nationalities' coexistence on the island is a constant source of anxiety, particularly because he sees African culture as profoundly influencing Cuban culture. According to Saco this is a corruptive influence, one that belies the mutual exclusivity of the two peoples and their inability to coexist peacefully. This set of beliefs crystallizes in his fears of an apocalyptic slave revolt that he believes may occur if the black population becomes too large; these beliefs lay the foundation for his arguments for the cessation of the African slave trade and his support for colonization. These reforms, according to Saco, were needed to maintain white supremacy. To this end, Saco also supported white immigration. He believed that a white majority was necessary for national progress and that active measures should be taken to encourage such a majority (Duno Gottberg 2003, 71; Naranjo Orovio 2001–3, 15–17; Ortiz 1928, xcii). Saco's critique of slavery is, thus, predicated upon his hopes for a white Cuba. This view was consistent with those of other Cuban abolitionists (Duno Gottberg 2003, 35). This throws his claims that the nineteenth century is an abolitionist century—"No se me tache, pues, de abolicionista, porque no lo soy: yo no soy más que un mensajero del tiempo, un mensajero pacífico del siglo XIX, que es el único abolicionista" / "Do not insult me, then, by calling me an abolitionist, because that I am not: I am nothing more than a messenger of the times, a peaceful messenger of the nineteenth century, which is the only abolitionist" (Saco 1928a, 53)—and that the century is the age of the nation in a light much different from that found in celebratory accounts of Saco's life (e.g., Codina Carreira 1967, 89). The claims for abolition and racial nationalism are one and the same. The nineteenth century is, for Saco, the age in which nationalities must be consolidated against the rising tide of racial cosmopolitanism, which requires the reduction of interracial mingling and thus slavery's eventual eradication (Naranjo Orovio 2001–3, 16).

Although Saco's work exhibits a cosmopolitan sensibility in rejecting traditionally accepted, absolutist political forms and a contrary favor for modern representative government, it is strikingly anticosmopolitan in its views on the relationship between race and nation. Without maintaining a healthy respect for discrete identities, Saco suggests, the nation will lose the organically constituted communal traditions that guide its members' actions.

This anticosmopolitanism again attests to Saco's capitulation to Hispanicism. The Black Legend narrative that predates and informs Hispanicism construed the Spanish heritage as deplorable in its fixation on identity and its violent intolerance for difference. Undoubtedly, Saco was aware that Hispanicist accounts of this difference obscured the United States' own histories of race-based expropriation and violence—his response to annexation, after all, is premised on his desire that Cuba not become a footnote in these histories. All the same, Saco's anticosmopolitanism reveals that his commitment to the Spanish tradition certainly entailed the discursive violence required to posit one's countrymen as unique and distinct, even though Saco did not promote the violence deplored in Black Legend accounts.

Conclusion

Although Saco is often considered the most important liberal thinker of his Cuba, his work continually indicates a "conservative" thrust. This tension seems to have structural roots. When one observes Saco's most liberal positions, one also approaches him at his most conservative. Traditionalism becomes evident in a critique of US imperialism, racism-infused anticosmopolitanism during an argument against the slave trade. One might even argue that Hispanicism is apparent in an argument against Hispanicism. It might seem that in Saco we see another example of a liberal thinker betraying liberalism's ostensible tenets, another example of nineteenth-century liberalism's distance from contemporary liberal norms. Although elements of Saco's thought (his racism, especially) indeed give pause, to describe that thought as a false liberalism is insufficient. Although the approach may yield illustrative contrasts, judging the work in light of contemporary US ideological tendencies leads to both presentist and ethnocentric misreadings. First of all, his views are consistent with a Spanish interpretation of Enlightenment thought that must be viewed on its own terms to be properly assessed. Moreover, his "conservatism" comprises a focused attempt to provide a viable alternative to what he recognized as liberalism's dangers. After he was confronted with a liberal annexationism that would attempt to impose a political paradigm on Cuba without regard for Cuba's particular history and situation, Saco reassessed his position, arriving at a more moderate reformulation.

Perhaps most strikingly, Saco recognized that the universalist platitudes of the antebellum United States—platitudes seen in Barlow and, more anxiously, in Mann—often served as smoke screens for national prerogatives. Saco reacted to how nationalist claims that the United States presented a special promise of liberty to the world belied derogatory condescension to Hispanophone nations. This pattern in US interaction with the Hispanophone world has been particularly apparent in the United States' long history of interest in Cuba. Cuba's liberal supporters of annexation were, for Saco, sadly duped in their zeal to establish shared liberal institutions with their neighbor to the north, as that zeal ignored the dangers of US universalist rhetoric. As Saco would have agreed, Donald E. Pease, in his discussions of the United States' "structures of disavowal," explains that although US Americans have often acted contrary to their nation's anti-imperial, benevolent stance, US ideologues have disavowed these exceptions' rapacity through appeals to exceptional national-racial duty (Pease 2009, 19). For Saco, annexation will entail the loss of not only Cuban territorial and economic but also cultural sovereignty due to the United States' refusal to countenance Cuban self-determination. This insidious form of exceptionalism—not the United States as an exceptionally liberal nation, but the United States as a nation that treats other peoples as exceptions to its liberalism—is for Saco what the United States has to offer Cuba. Against his compatriots' deluded adoption of universalist rhetoric, Saco offers the common-sense point that nations are traditions and histories. The traditions the United States espouses, which include expropriation and anti-Hispanic feeling just as much as liberal institutions, are threats. Saco, presciently anticipating the Spanish-American War, argues that annexation will entail the loss of not only Cuban territorial but also cultural sovereignty due to the United States' refusal to countenance Cuban self-determination. Even continued subjugation to Spain was preferable, given that Spain, at least, was part of the Cuban heritage. Saco thus asks his countrymen to reject annexation to preserve their nacionalidad; to be sure, this was a moderate move as he understood it, but it was not mistaken in its assessment of the imperial ambitions that underlaid US liberal rhetoric.

Epilogue

The Hispanicist Forebears of 1898

This book primarily examines Hispanicism's manifestations in the early national and antebellum periods. Would it have been more fitting to have wrestled more closely with 1898 and the Spanish-American War? In the late nineteenth century, US imperialists desiring control of Hispanophone nations articulated a powerful guiding ideology, challenging isolationist and humanitarian opposition by claiming that it was the United States' responsibility to improve the lot of those illiberal nations' peoples. Such peoples, the argument went, needed Anglo-Saxon guidance to develop the liberal-democratic institutions and productive economies that had flourished in the United States. Although not new, these arguments became more effective in 1898. For that reason, 1898 presents a likely place to study them. Up until then the question of empire had always been hotly debated in the United States, with moderate positions often winning. This ceased to be true at the nineteenth century's end. Historical contingencies, such as the media's misrepresentation of the sinking of the USS *Maine*, partly account for this change in public opinion. Going much further, though, are increasingly confident, aggressive, and racial attitudes regarding the nation's global mission. These changes had profound material consequences. The United States successfully undertook its most comprehensive imperial projects in the Hispanophone world, routing Spain in the war; acquiring Puerto Rico, Guam, and the Philippines; and setting up a puppet administration in Cuba. This turn of events presaged an early twentieth century marked by many direct military interventions in Latin America. The era was punctuated by US acquisition of the Panama Canal project via gunboat diplomacy during the Theodore Roosevelt administration.

For many historians and literary critics, 1898 is thus an exceptional moment. The general gist of such arguments is that 1898 and the successful cultural construction of an effective imperial ideology represent something unprecedented in US history.[1] In recent years, though, literary scholars have questioned this claim. Among them, John Carlos Rowe, Amy Kaplan, and Shelley Streeby have shown, in various ways, how imperialism and Hispanophobic feeling have deep roots in US history and culture, roots that predate and transcend 1898 (Kaplan 1993a, 231–32; Kaplan 2002, 13, 17, 94, 99, 120, 389; Rowe 2000, 14–15, 54). These are compelling arguments. It is no doubt crucial to recognize 1898's particularity; for instance, one must acknowledge analytic distinctions between types of imperialism and attend to how literary culture reflects and informs those distinctions. However, such distinctions may also obscure the significant continuities between the expansionist views of various periods. Charting such continuities, Streeby argues that presenting 1898 as exceptional risks making a false distinction between 1898 as authentically imperial because it marked the United States' first full-fledged foray into overseas expansion, and 1848 as an inauthentic-because-continental imperial moment (Streeby 2002). Such arguments, firstly, belie the presence of earlier overseas expansionism, as the United States, although less stridently than in 1898, in the years surrounding 1848 sought territory in Cuba, Nicaragua, the Dominican Republic, and elsewhere. Secondly, distinctions between 1848 and 1898 risk naturalizing the post-1848 borders of the nation, thus capitulating to the notion that those borders were a national destiny, a notion that promoted the fiction that the United States was not an imperial nation by presenting formerly Mexican lands as naturally part of the United States' domestic space as opposed to acknowledging that those lands were only gained by imperial warfare. Thus, Streeby asks us to recognize the significance of the American 1848 in US imperial history (Streeby 2002, 9–10). One could go back further, too. As soon as the Revolution ended, the United States began expanding, yet early national US imperialism is a neglected field of study due to the long history of viewing 1898 as special. This tendency is ideological. It makes imperialism difficult to recognize and thus contributes to the maintenance of imperial agendas by neglecting to acknowledge their existence as anything more than a temporary aberration in US history. Moreover, even granting that it is often useful to emphasize distinctions over continuities, it is necessary to recognize the significant role culture and text have played in laying the rhetorical and emotional groundwork of imperial agendas. Even if 1898 is exceptional, it is impossible to conceive its emergence without placing it in a cultural history that explains how arguments for imperialism became culturally viable.

In this coda, I argue that when considered in terms of Hispanicism, national identity, liberalism, and nationalist anxiety, 1898 is not so much a point of origins or an exception as, rather, a maturation. Hispanicism is overtly manifest in and might be said to have become more popular in 1898, but the construction of the grammar, so to speak, of that manifestation is to be found far earlier. I illustrate this claim via analysis of William Graham Sumner's 1898 essay "The Conquest of the United States by Spain." This Hispanicist tour de force reveals that although imperialism became increasingly popular during this period, it was not universally accepted. Sumner claims that in becoming imperial, the United States was, in effect, becoming Spain—the United States risked corrupting its morals and forsaking its economic prosperity. For Sumner, differentiation from Spain is the measure of the United States' fulfillment of the promise of its founding in liberal-democratic thought; failure, similarly, is figured as Hispanicization of the nation. This manner of defining US greatness was used by liberal imperialists who argued that the United States must intervene in Latin America to adopt a tutelary role in leading constrained economies toward greater productivity and by conservative anti-imperialists such as Sumner who for various reasons feared that the United States risked losing its distinctiveness vis-à-vis the Hispanophone world by engaging in imperialism. As we have seen, these different versions of Hispanicism emerged in the early national and antebellum periods. Sumner's essay reflects not the appearance but the crystallization of the discourse.

Sumner: Liberalism and the Failure of US National Identity

In 1872, the Yale-educated Sumner became the first US professor of sociology, a position he held for many years at his alma mater. His work is typically understood, largely due to Richard Hofstadter's influence, as a conservative US manifestation of Herbert Spencer's Social Darwinism. However, certain qualifications are necessary, as Sumner's work resists systematization. His thought in fact uses Social Darwinism in service of a classically liberal perspective. Sumner presents undeniably conservative views in his critiques of reformism (Sumner 1992a; Hoftstadter 1941, 470; Bannister 1992, xxx) and natural rights (Hofstadter 1941, 468; Notestein 1955, 392; Sumner 1913, 234; Sumner 1992b, 290–91), the latter of which he saw as a mythological social construction. In these respects, he rejected liberal universalism and contractualism. A more liberal premise underlies his thought, though. Sumner championed the capitalist, possessive-individualist view that the individual's pecuniary pursuits are the foundation of progress (Notestein 1955, 396). This argument followed from Sumner's Darwinism; whereas he saw natural rights as constructions, he believed that competition facilitated survival. Although Sumner repudiates the transcendental existence of natural rights, the virtue inherent in the individual's pursuit of material gain is a natural law (Bannister 1992, xxviii; Hofstadter 1941, 473). Working from this assumption, Sumner became one of the Gilded Age's foremost theorizers of laissez-faire, vociferating frequently against government regulation. However, he did not view himself as a defender of corporate interests. He believed that laissez-faire's ultimate beneficiary was what he referred to as the "forgotten man"—the hard-working middle-class artisan who asks nothing of the government but sufficient space in which to operate. For Sumner, the "forgotten man" all too often sees governmental plutocracy rob him of the fruits of his labor and either keep those earnings for itself or redistribute it to the undeserving (Sumner 1992d, esp. 209–10).[2]

Consistent with this Darwinist background, Sumner's opposition to the Spanish-American War is not driven by the humanitarian concern characteristic of much twentieth-century anti-imperialism. Race was relatively unimportant to him, though. With racism nearly ubiquitous among the time's Anglo-Americans, one predominant form of anti-imperialism was based on concerns over whether the United States could incorporate peoples of color. Racism spurred other Social Darwinists to argue for prompting evolution either through exterminating undesirables via imperial warfare or by managing the labor of peoples supposed to be incapable of self-government. Sumner shows little interests in these debates, although he undoubtedly held racist beliefs.[3]

Whereas many used race as a subterfuge to mask economic motivations, Sumner forefronts economics, basing his anti-imperialism on laissez-faire principles. He laid out his general case in "The Fallacy of Territorial Extension" (1896), arguing that expansion is a plutocratic scheme that infringes upon the rights of the "forgotten men" who do not consent to it. Sumner thus subjects arguments for the "white man's burden" to the same criticism with which he attacks market regulation. As he explains, "If the United States should admit Hawaii to the Union, the Fiscus of the former state would collect more taxes and incur more expenses. The circumstances are such that the latter would probably be the greater" (Sumner 1992c, 267). These expenses would fall upon the continental US citizenry, who would benefit nothing by Hawaii; rather, plutocrats with various interests in Hawaii would profit (266). The continued maintenance of underdeveloped imperial hinterlands would involve expenses such as responding to rebellions. This effort would strain the national treasury, leading to further taxation and diversion of resources. US Americans could alternatively use these resources for their own benefit. The increase in lands abroad thus corresponds to a decrease in liberty at home. Imperialism would compromise what Sumner understands as the United States' liberal institutions (270).

The general argument that Sumner makes in "The Fallacy of Territorial Extension" is the basis for the more particular claims he makes in "The Conquest of the United States by Spain" (1898). Sumner argues in the latter essay that in becoming an imperial nation, the United States is becoming Spain. If Sumner's barometer for a healthy commonwealth is the extent to which it protects the liberty of the "forgotten man," then for Sumner Spain exemplifies poor civic and economic health. Spain, as was thought to be clear from the United States' quick victory in the Spanish-American War, was not viewed as a bastion of geopolitical or economic prosperity by the late nineteenth century. For Sumner, the problem was that through imperialist, mercantile projects that merely filled the coffers of the crown, aristocracy, and clergy, Spain sapped resources that could otherwise be used by its producing classes, thus failing to ensure long-term financial vitality.

Sumner particularly insists that imperialism entails diverting national resources to combat the incursion of rival powers. After quoting a US official on the necessity of enforcing a mercantile policy against colonial ports, Sumner writes, "This is exactly the view which was held in Spain, France, Holland, and England in the eighteenth century, and upon which the navigation system, against which our fathers revolted, was founded. If we adopt this view we may count upon it that we shall be embroiled in constant wars with other nations, which will not consent that we should shut them out of parts of the earth's surface until we prove that we can do it by force. Then we shall be parties to a renewal of all the eighteenth century wars for colonies, for supremacy on the sea, for 'trade,' as the term is used, for world supremacy, and for all the rest of the heavy follies from which our fathers fought to free themselves. That is the policy of Russia and France at the present time, and we have before our eyes proofs of its effect on the peace and welfare of mankind" (Sumner 1992b, 287–88). In addition to such difficulties, empire would require quelling the rebellions of colonized peoples, as Sumner repeatedly points out in reference to anti-US backlash in the Philippines. For Sumner, the folly of this approach is that US imperial ideologues fail to note that similar necessities had strained Spain's treasury. According to Sumner this strain had a considerable role in making Spain the vulnerable nation it had become by 1898. His argument is premised on a bitter irony: In militarily defeating a Spain that cannot defend itself because of overreaches in its acquisition of colonial territories, the United States was inevitably setting itself up to suffer the same fate once it had wasted its own resources.

Sumner gives urgency to his claims by appealing to his countrymen's sense of national identity. In doing so, he does not look away from economic arguments; his arguments related to national identity are highly tied to his economic theories. The United States, in his view, is a nation that should pride itself on its commitment to the liberal values of economic self-determination and possessive individualism. However, Sumner does shift at points to speaking of this issue less in terms of logic and economic analysis than pathos and nationalism. These arguments make up the essay's most significant portions. Although Sumner was generally less interested in these issues than hard economic analysis because he believed that identity was a product of economic circumstance, he constructed his essay for an audience that responded strongly to nationalism. He opens the essay as follows:

> During the last year the public has been familiarized with descriptions of Spain and of Spanish methods of doing things until the name of Spain has become a symbol for a certain well-defined set of notions and policies. On the other hand, the name of the United States has always been, for all of us, a symbol for a state of things, a set of ideas and traditions, a group of views about social and political affairs. Spain was the first, for a long time the greatest, of the modern imperialistic states. The United States, by its historical origin, its traditions, and its principles, is the chief representative of the revolt and reaction against that kind of a state. I intend to show that, by the line of action now proposed to us, which we call expansion and imperialism, we are throwing away some of the most important elements of the American symbol and are adopting some of the most important elements of the Spanish symbol. We have beaten Spain in a military conflict, but we are submitting to be conquered by her on the field of ideas and policies. (Sumner 1992b, 272)

Why does becoming an imperial nation entail adopting the Spanish symbol? "Expansionism and imperialism," Sumner continues, "are nothing but the old philosophies of national prosperity which have brought Spain to where she now is. Those philosophies appeal to national vanity and national cupidity. They are seductive, especially upon the first view and the most superficial judgment, and therefore it cannot be denied that they are very strong for popular effect" (272). The language of "symbols" signals a shift in register from the economic analysis of "The Fallacy of Territorial Extension" and some of the less accentuated passages of "The Conquest of the United States by Spain" to an appeal to national mission. Throughout the portions of the essay dealing with these issues, Sumner invokes his audience's sense of what the United States signifies, his audience's sense of national type. Sumner assumes that this identity resides in the United States' mission of protecting the interests of liberal democracy, economic self-determination, and the "forgotten man" by opposing imperial ventures. The United States' mission is vulnerable during the Spanish-American War. Sumner uses dizzying series of ironic turns and substitutions to illustrate how close he believes the current crisis has brought the United States to ruinously "adopting the Spanish symbol."

One of Sumner's particular strategies is to appeal to his countrymen's sense that the US national past is fundamentally opposed to Spain's; the move coheres with Benedict Anderson's dictum that although the nation is a modern "invention," national communities always conceive their identities through reference to an idealized, primordial collective history (Anderson 1991, 11). Reflected in this claim is the idea that the United States originated in anticolonial revolution, as the following passage exemplifies:

> Our historians and publicists have taught us that the position of the colonists was right and heroic, and the only one worthy of freemen. The revolt was made on the *principle* of no taxation, not on the size of the tax. The colonists would not pay a penny. Since that is so, we cannot get a penny of revenue from the dependencies, even for their fair share of imperial expenditures, without burning up all our histories, revising all the great principles of our heroic period, repudiating our great men of that period, and going over to the Spanish doctrine of taxing dependencies at the discretion of the governing State. Already one of these dependencies is in arms struggling for liberty against us. Read the threats of the imperialists against these people, who dare to rebel against us, and see whether I am misstating or exaggerating the corruption of imperialism on ourselves. The question is once more, whether we are prepared to repudiate the principles which we have been insisting on for one hundred and fifty years, and to embrace those of which Spain is the oldest and most conspicuous representative, or not. (Sumner 1992b, 285)

For Sumner, subjecting conquered peoples to taxation and other forms of exploitation is not the "white man's burden" or the right of the Nordic conqueror that it was for the Roosevelt-styled imperialist. Sumner, who viewed such arguments as plutocratic mystifications, sees exercising such control as yet another instance in which the United States was becoming Spain, this time by forgetting its historical roots in anti-imperialism and fiscal libertarianism and adopting the contrary commitments that characterize Spain's history. History was useful to Sumner's argument in that it may have been difficult for readers accustomed to a world in which the United States was viewed as having far outstripped Spain's preeminence to see that the United States risked becoming Spain; thus, Sumner informs readers that Spain had been a powerful nation when it had embarked upon many of the policies that the United States was taking up. To return to the main point, though, Sumner thought that in a moment of heightened nationalism, an argument that suggested that the United States was compromising its historical pedigree in anticolonial revolution by imitating botched Spanish policies would strike to the heart of conceptions of nation that were being misguided by the superficial glory of territorial aggrandizement. This pride was, for Sumner, a wolf in sheep's garb that would devour the ethos upon which the nation's success had been built.

Although Sumner's racialism does not exhibit Darwinist precision, he certainly appeals to many Anglo-Saxonist narratives regarding Hispanic difference. For instance, in a section in which he excoriates the yellow press for mobilizing militant sentiment, he writes,

> The war with Spain was precipitated upon us headlong, without reflection or deliberation, and without any due formulation of public opinion. Whenever a voice was raised in behalf of deliberation and the recognized maxims of statesmanship, it was howled down in a storm of vituperation and cant. Everything was done to make us throw away sobriety of thought and calmness of judgment and to inflate all expressions with sensational epithets and turgid phrases. It cannot be denied that everything in regard to the war has been treated in an exalted strain of sentiment and rhetoric very unfavorable to the truth. At present the whole periodical press of the country seems to be occupied in tickling the national vanity to the utmost by representations about the war which are extravagant and fantastic. There will be a penalty to be paid for all this. Nervous and sensational newspapers are just as corrupting, especially to young people, as nervous and sensational novels. The habit of expecting that all mental pabulum shall be highly spiced, and the corresponding loathing for whatever is soberly truthful, undermines character as much as any other vice. Patriotism is being prostituted into a nervous intoxication which is fatal to an apprehension of truth. It builds around us a fool's paradise, and it will lead us into errors about our position and relations just like those which we have been ridiculing in the case of Spain. (Sumner 1992b, 274–75)

Sumner here insinuates another US-Spanish substitution. In buying into the yellow press's immoderate rhetoric, US citizens have forsaken their reason for the hotheadedness they ascribe to the Spanish. Sumner assumes that Spaniards are overly passionate and that Anglo-Americans are, or at least would ideally be, rational, an assumption that reflects the Anglo-Saxonist arguments that the United States must guide improvident Hispanophone nations via active expansion that Sumner decried. In this sense, Sumner's appeals to national identity play to the association between US nationality and Anglo-Saxon race. His ideas, thus, were not as far from those of his opponents as it might seem based on his insistence on economic over racial explanations. He shares his culture's basic assumptions about the presence of national and racial US-Hispanic difference.

Although Sumner follows this Anglo-Saxonist narrative, he does so while taking issue with its more virulent strains, particularly its brash, self-assured confidence. The Anglo-Saxonist imperialists with whom Sumner contended argued that in obedience to the nation's duty to protect liberty and encourage prosperity by guiding the world's racially inferior peoples, the nation had to make imperial decisions swiftly and without scruples. Such arguments, perhaps best exemplified by Theodore Roosevelt's "The Strenuous Life" (1902), derided appeals for moderation and respect for negotiation and law as weak-minded, unmanly lack of Anglo-Saxon enterprise and unwillingness to carry out white men's duties in relation to feminine, childlike racial Others (Johnson 1993, 71–155; Kaplan 2002, 225; Michael 2008, 228; Pérez 2008, 65, 81, 84, 134). For Sumner, these arguments constituted an ideological construction of imperial identity that was a smoke screen for plutocratic interests and national vanity. Sumner unmasks the unsavory reality lying behind defenses of imperialism. The truth, for Sumner, is quite far from the notions propagated by moralistic appeals to racial duty. The United States was simply acting from selfish, oppressive motives and was, thus, unwittingly imitating the nation from which it most sought to differentiate itself, Spain.

Indeed, for Sumner, the Anglo-Saxonism that had gained such traction with US whites resonated with a characteristically Spanish quality, as Spanish colonizers had similarly used race to excuse economically unsustainable greed. Sumner's comments to this effect are a curious element of his discussion; on the one hand, they reveal his antireformism, whereas on the other they point to his keen eye for incoherence in US ideologies. It was not racism per se that Sumner contended with. Rather, it was the self-interested deployment of racism and notions of racial responsibility by plutocratic opinion makers. Toward the end of his essay, Sumner writes:

> If I had time to do so, I could go back over the history of negro suffrage and show you how curbstone arguments, exactly analogous to the arguments about expansion, were used to favor it, and how objections were thrust aside in this same blustering and senseless manner in which objections to imperialism are met. . . . The ballot, we were told, was an educator and would solve all difficulties in its own path as by magic. Worse still, Americans cannot assure life, liberty, and the

> pursuit of happiness to negroes inside of the United States. When the negro postmaster's house was set on fire in the night in South Carolina, and not only he, but his wife and children, were murdered as they came out, and when, moreover, this incident passed without legal investigation or punishment, it was a bad omen for the extension of liberty, etc., to Malays and Tagals by simply setting over them the American flag. (Sumner 1992b, 294–95)

The passage reveals his skepticism regarding racial reform, which for Sumner would not necessarily be any more successful in the case of the "white man's burden" in the colonies than it had been in that of Reconstruction black uplift. His cynicism points to a broader attack on inconsistencies in US behavior. How, indeed, can the United States promote racial uplift abroad when it cannot help its own racial minorities at home? At the heart of this incoherence is an irreducible premise: Imperialist plutocrats and policy makers will use any number of oftentimes incompatible tactics to promote their agenda. Identity proves useful because of US society's often contradictory obsession with it. Imperialism could be defended by appeals to racial inferiority and by promises to help the racially inferior access universal rights. Identity thus buttresses a particularly dangerous ideological formation, one that can be used as rhetorical grounds for any number of pernicious policies, much as it had for Spain, which had defended mercantile policies by appealing to the Catholic duty of spreading Christianity among Native Americans. This is one of Sumner's concluding points, which suggests that his distaste for arguments based on the concept of identity was key to his critique of US imperialism.

Rejecting the notion of essential racial responsibilities, Sumner concludes that US identity should be premised on pragmatic criteria. Those he criticized increasingly viewed identity as a transcendental, ontological category, arguing that US imperialism was valid because the United States was a liberal nation; Sumner, by contrast, cautioned that the United States was a liberal nation only to the extent that its actions reflected liberal-democratic procedure. Sumner treated appeals of this nature as mere subterfuge, as they re-termed oppressive, economically unfeasible projects as a special mission of spreading liberal institutions among the less fortunate. They thus reflected Spanish ideology, which had similarly served self-interested policy, not under the guise of liberalism, but, rather, that of religion and royal prerogative. The analogy between liberalism as a rhetorical construct and religion is apt, considering that Sumner viewed universalist theories of political economy as cultural constructs much like religion. Instead of basing its actions on such foundations, Sumner advocated judging actions simply according to whether they promoted economic liberty; imperialism is not a mission or a component of an identity but, rather, an action to be assessed against other options. Only when they condemned imperialism because it compromised economic prosperity, he argued, could US Americans negate their Spanish element and successfully attain the identity they conceived for themselves.

Sumner, Hispanicism, and 1898's Literary Prehistory

Sumner's essay relies on an irreducibly Hispanicist premise. In viewing US national failure as a function of the United States lapsing into Spanish custom, Sumner views self-differentiation from Spain as the measure of the United States' successful fulfillment of its identity as a nation grounded in liberal values. In making his anti-imperialist argument, Sumner—whose writing, despite being work in sociology and political economy, relies on tropes and narrative—plots a tale of national ebbs and flows that has a long history in US literature. That history exhibits the rudiments of the Hispanicism found in Sumner's essay, and the essay's rhetorical effect relies not just on the fact that Spain was the United States' enemy during the conflict but also on how Sumner's audience possessed the literature's assumptions.

To illustrate this point, I briefly reprise this book's arguments. In the first chapter I analyzed Joel Barlow's nationalist epics *The Vision of Columbus* and *The Columbiad*. In these poems, Barlow provides his take on the early national "rising glory of America" poems, premising his sense of the nation's glorious future—particularly in the more doctrinaire second poem—on its capacity to enact Enlightenment ideals of rational, cosmopolitan political institutions and commerce. The poems tell a world-historical story of the nation's fulfillment of these ideals, viewing the nation as the culmination of historical progress and suggesting that it is ushering in a secular millennium. Spain serves as a foil to the United States' role in bringing about progress. Barlow portrays Spain as an antithesis to US ideals by emphasizing its centripetal cultural and economic policies, chiefly as they manifest themselves in its poor treatment of Columbus and its colonial violence against Native Americans. Spain, thus, impeded all that Barlow thought most central to his nation's project. The United States, then, needed to prioritize successfully differentiating itself from the rapacious qualities Spain embodied.

Barlow's narrative evocation of this idea is premised on his poetry's historical imagination. The poems are historical narratives; rather than representing the United States' glories, they focus on placing those triumphs as the endpoint of a series of landmark historical events, particularly important scientific, exploratory, and political accomplishments. These events are always those that are at the vanguard of historical progress, those that transcend the tradition-based limitations that inhibit world-historical growth. The US Revolution is, for Barlow, the latest such event, one promising territorial expansion of liberal institutions that facilitate the cosmopolitan cultural and material commerce Barlow hoped for. Barlow believed the Revolution marked a startling break with history, thus portending the secular millennium toward which his historical vision tended. In this sense, Spain serves not so much as the United States' particular antagonist as, rather, that of the glorious transcendence to which his vision tended. Spain is history itself, in a negative sense. Spain represents traditional limitations that inhibit the millennial break with history's burden.

Sumner follows the pattern set by Barlow, who was a significant literary commentator on issues of nation in the early national United States. The two differed in the conclusions they drew from Hispanicism. The liberal Barlow thought that the United States ought to pursue expansion into the Hispanophone world to spread liberty and prosperity, whereas the more skeptical Sumner believed doing so would morally and economically corrupt the nation. However, like Barlow, Sumner premises the nation's success on its capacity to differentiate itself from the colonial mismanagement and violence Sumner sees in Spanish history. Moreover, historical narrative plays a key role for both; just as Barlow asks his readers to understand the United States' founding by placing the nation in a narrative of world-historical events that transcend the historical limitations Spain represented, so does Sumner point to the nation's assumption of liberal, anti-imperial values that differentiate it from Spain as the foundation of the identity it risks losing by becoming imperial in 1898. Barlow, writing at the nation's inception, had already formulated Sumner's primary premise. Sumner's argument thus appealed to a deeply laid aspect of US national identity formation.

Although James Fenimore Cooper contrasts with Barlow in that he conservatively interrogated excitedly liberal arguments for the United States' providential world-historical role, his *Mercedes of Castile* and *Jack Tier* also provide important precursors to Sumner's argument. Cooper cautioned against the jingoistic nationalism of the pro-US-Mexican War Democratic press, arguing that such rhetoric was inconsistent because it encouraged US Americans not to give credit to accomplished, patriotic Hispanophone peoples with proud histories when those US Americans would give credit to themselves for the same qualities. Cooper's novels thus took issue with the explicitly Hispanophobic elements of Hispanicism. However, Cooper also uses *Jack Tier*'s Mexican patriot Montefalderon to voice Hispanicist arguments for the intrinsic difference between Anglo-American and Hispanophone (here Mexican) populations. Montefalderon cautions that the United

States will not easily conquer the most heavily populated portions of Mexico because these portions will not succumb to being overrun and assimilated into a people so different from themselves. His statements voice Cooper's critique of the All of Mexico movement's bombastic nationalism. Cooper's concerns were premised upon a conservative skepticism regarding not just the possibility that the United States could wholly subdue Mexico but also that the US imposition of abstract liberal political institutions upon Mexicans would successfully reform Mexico. Institutions that were appropriate for US Americans with long histories of possessive individualism and participation in democratic institutions, he warns, may not be appropriate for Mexicans without such histories. Such an imposition would not acknowledge the pull of concrete, persistent, and organic differences between the two peoples. Cooper, in short, questioned incoherent Hispanophobic attitudes but insisted on recognizing national differences. Sumner integrated these views by questioning inconsistencies in imperialist arguments regarding racial uplift and the duties of white imperial nations as part of an anti-imperialist argument based on policing historically inherited differences between Anglo-Americans and Hispanophone peoples.

In "Benito Cereno," Herman Melville offered an even more incisive critique of national identity formation than Cooper, one that not only interrogates elements of Hispanicism but also the discourse per se. Although Sumner certainly does not question Hispanicism on this level, Melville's views present poignant connections to Sumner. Melville's tale can be read as a critique of US national identity formation that deconstructs the United States' prized self-differentiation from Spain and Spanish America. Melville's tale of slave revolt ventriloquizes Hispanicism through its protagonist Amasa Delano. Delano, who views himself as a genial, benevolent man, defines himself against what he views as the ineffectual yet potentially gothic and dangerous Benito Cereno. According to this contrast Delano views himself as a wise, effective manager of men, particularly of the human chattel he believes Cereno leads poorly. Delano, in this sense, hews to Hispanicism's conception of Hispanic-Anglo difference. The reader learns in the tale's climax, though, that this self-differentiation has blinded him to the truth. Cereno's behavior, the disrepair of the ship, and the unruly slaves do not reflect Cereno's Spanish ineptitude but, rather, slave revolt. All that has happened aboard the ship, including behavior on Cereno's part that plays to Delano's Hispanicism, has been cunningly conceived by Babo to deceive the Massachusetts captain. Delano's Hispanicism causes his failure effectively to judge the state of affairs on board the ship. More damningly, in the aftermath of Delano's discovery of the revolt, he shows himself precisely the ruthless, violent man he imagined Cereno to be. "Benito Cereno" thus illustrates that Hispanicism makes it difficult for Anglo-Americans to see human commonality and leads them to convince themselves of their own virtue when that assurance is not warranted. Delano's Hispanicism not only inhibits his ability to understand slave revolt on the high seas but his own moral failures, too. In that Delano seems to embody many qualities Melville more generally sees in the United States at large, the character points to limitations the author sees in those qualities.

"Benito Cereno" is not a direct political intervention like Sumner's essay. Melville uses a Hispanicist-colored free-indirect discourse to explore how stock narratives weigh against the subject's ability to perceive freely and to interpret events accurately—and, importantly in this tale of revolt, safely. Hispanicism, here, provides illustrations of more abstract themes. The tale must be read in terms of the confluence of Melville's literary and epistemological concerns, as opposed to being solely understood as a sociopolitical statement.

However, even if critiquing Hispanicism was not Melville's primary aim, "Benito Cereno" can be read as doing so according to a logic of unintended consequences. Although perhaps most related to other issues, it discusses those issues by critiquing Hispanicism. Therefore, to recognize its more ostensible intentions, its critique of Hispanicism must be ceded. That the effect is secondary does not detract from its significance; indeed, it may not even be unintended, as it is revealing that Melville went to Hispanicism for a powerful example with which to explore how a discursive construct can undermine perception. Melville's literary-philosophical ruminations did not occur in a vacuum. The very discourses that Delano ventriloquizes featured frequently in the pages of the magazine the novella first appeared in, *Putnam's Monthly*, which published material—usually in the form of travelogues set in Spanish America, particularly Cuba—exploring supposed contrasts between US and Hispanic values. In using those discourses to stage his exploration of epistemological failure, Melville engaged cultural constructions pertinent to the magazine and its readership. He takes those constructions to task for their role in blighting the perception of the magazine's readers, whom the tale cannily associates with its protagonist. It is, therefore, difficult to deny that the story functions as a critique.

In these respects, Melville's story exhibits surprising similarities with Sumner's work. Melville differs from Sumner in positing that US national identity formation's problem is not so much that the United States fails to negate Spanish-ness; it is that the national community conceives to do so in the first place. Sumner sees successfully making that differentiation as positive and necessary. Melville is a unique figure in this study in that whereas most of the authors analyzed tacitly agree that US-Hispanophone differences are important regardless of their position on imperialism, Melville takes issue with Hispanicism itself. However, both Melville and Sumner show the dangerous consequences portended by jingoistic positions that obfuscate unfortunate similarities between the United States and its Others.

Mary Peabody Mann provides another important precursor to Sumner. Her novel *Juanita* posits that the United States is led by New England in progressively expanding the nation's liberal protection of its peoples' political and economic autonomy and their access to transparent information about their nation's activities. Therefore, the nation is intrinsically different from and superior to Cuba, where illiberal slavery, despotism, corruption, and a culture of silence that disables rational discussion of such matters are the norm. Yet while depicting her characters pondering whether annexation will enable the United States to tutor Cuba in the development of liberal values or whether it will entail the slave power's expansion, Mann anxiously acknowledges illiberal elements in her own nation, where Southern slaveholding stands in stark contrast to the national identity Mann celebrates. The annexation question thus spurs Mann to agonize over whether the nation is, in fact, the beacon of liberty as her nationalist rhetoric insists. Similarly, when confronted with the question of conquering Spanish colonies, Sumner denounced imperialist arguments for the white man's burden of tutoring Hispanophone peoples in political self-determination and economic liberty. He instead argued that becoming an imperialist nation would enhance illiberal elements in the nation by undermining the interests of the "forgotten man," whose earnings would be taxed to fund imperial interests of no benefit to himself. Both Sumner and Mann, then, worry over the question of whether expansion will enable the United States to maintain its liberal traditions or whether it will bolster illiberal tendencies in the nation, with Sumner deciding more unequivocally on the latter.

My discussion of José Antonio Saco may seem least related to Sumner's concerns given that Saco, as a Cuban author, is the only writer I have analyzed who was not part of a US tradition of discussing differences between Anglo-Americans and Hispanophone peoples. Instead of elaborating this tradition, the chapter on Saco rounds out part II on Cuba by providing a Cuban counterpoint to Mann's dream of benevolent expansion. Yet Saco does engage ideological debates regarding liberalism and conservatism, and in doing so he expresses concerns that are related to those of Sumner. Although representatives of different national intellectual traditions, Sumner and Saco both "conservatively" (again, qualifications must be remembered regarding the term's applicability to Saco) caution against US expansion, which they believe threatens organically unique identities whose traditions are opposed and ought to remain discrete. Along with Cooper, Saco and

Sumner illustrate how this conservative Hispanicist tradition differed from a liberal tradition that also viewed Anglo-American and Hispanophone cultures as distinct but that argued that Hispanophone cultures were ephemeral constraints against Hispanophone peoples' assumption of liberty and social and economic advancement. Whereas the conservatives—especially Cooper and Saco—found organic cultural traditions important and argued that true liberty for Hispanophone peoples would entail balancing protection of these traditions against abstract advancement, the more liberal authors insisted upon a more abstract understanding of liberty that mainly involved adopting liberal-democratic political and economic institutions and that deemphasized and often vociferated against protecting cultural traditions. Taken together, Saco and Sumner exemplify how the conservative view differs from more liberal traditions.

Each author's work can thus be seen as significant interventions into Hispanicism; however, it would be a stretch to argue for their universal influence. Most selectively engaged high-cultural readerships. None were exactly "best sellers," with only Cooper and Melville at times commanding large audiences. Although this is not to say that such works reveal nothing about Hispanicism's presence in the culture—far from it—it is to say that they only speak to its role for a particular portion of the culture. However, there were Hispanicist arguments appearing in other spheres as well. For instance, such narratives had a foundational role in the emergence of working-class reading culture in the later antebellum period. The 1850s saw the rise of the story-paper novelette, an early form of sensation literature that in the 1860s would evolve into the dime novel. These works powerfully impacted the literary marketplace in the postbellum period and well into the twentieth century. Sensation fiction was primarily consumed by working-class readers. It favored shock, terror, and titillation in contrast to the irony and analytical rigor of high culture and the moral suasion of middle-brow sentimentalism (Alemán and Streeby 2007, xvii). To find narrative materials to provoke these reactions, sensation fiction went to empire's borderlands. Tales of Anglo-Mexican violence in Texas, California, and Mexico; filibustering expeditions in Cuba; and the like were very common, oftentimes told with sensational twists such as cross-dressing heroines.

It would be a mistake to ascribe a particular politics to this form; although speaking for and to working-class audiences, the magazines and series expressed a variety of political positions on the time's key issues, being divided, for example, over slavery (Alemán and Streeby 2007, xix). However, it might generally be stated that these fictions promoted an ideology of whiteness. Although they disagree over slavery, for instance, there was never much question regarding the place of African Americans in US racial hierarchies, with antislavery papers being more concerned with how slavery degraded free white labor than with the violence it inflicted upon black bodies. Similarly, even while allegorically probing racial boundaries between Euro- and Hispanic Americans in the imperial borderlands, these fictions tend finally to confirm such divisions as central to US cultural identity when they conclude their plots by setting racial disorder aright (xxv). Similarly, they often equate slavery and its threat to free white labor with the perceived threat to US republican institutions posed by the incorporation of Mexican peonage economies into the nation after the US-Mexican War, thus viewing threats to US values as a Mexicanization of US culture (xxi). These sensation fictions follow the Hispanicist convention—one key to Sumner's essay—of viewing the nation's success in terms of its self-differentiation from Spanish-ness. They do the cultural work of constructing this discourse for working-class audiences.

In their separate ways, all of these works laid the groundwork for Sumner's essay. Each registers particular formulations of the cultural logic through which the United States' greatness was defined according to the nation's ability to distinguish itself from Spain and Spanish America. It might seem that these works contributed little to the public-sphere debate that comprised Sumner's discursive milieu. After all, Sumner's argument is sociopolitical in nature. What do texts produced for varying forms of entertainment and pleasure have to do with such concerns? Quite a bit, as Ezra Tawil suggests: "As far apart as literary and scientific discourse, and the truths they access, appear to us today, in the mid-nineteenth century they were more difficult to distinguish" (Tawil 2006, 14). "If we do not insist," he continues, "on the historicity of 'race' itself, we risk succumbing to the mimetic fallacy that it must have existed prior to, and dwells outside of, its representation in writing." We must entertain "the possibility that fiction itself was an important culture site of racial *formation* as much as racial representation" (8). Tawil's comments pertain to the racial pseudoscience that contributed to the construction of ideas related to African-Anglo difference. Such pseudoscience also informed conceptions of Anglo-Hispanic difference. Tawil's point regarding the role of writing in the construction of race holds for Hispanicism. Ideas related to race do not exist outside of culture; they are just as much if not more so constructed in literature and other cultural forms as they are via more "objective" modes of discourse. Literature, science, history, sociology, and political economy were much less distinct in the early United States than they are today.

The rhetorical coherence of Sumner's opponents relies on Hispanicist assumptions much as did Sumner's own. The two arguments are, of course, diametrically opposed. Sumner argued that in becoming imperial, the United

States was taking on traits that had undermined Spain's empire. Imperialists, though, contended that the US empire, driven by Anglo-Saxon progressivism, was a new and better type of empire that would replace the vicious Spanish one. For these imperialists, the US empire's commitment to free institutions inherent in its Anglo-Saxon character ensured that it would be nothing like the Spanish empire. However, both Sumner and the imperialists rely on the old idea that the measure of the nation's success is its capacity to negate Spanish-ness. Both appealed to culturally prepared thinking with a long history; just as I have shown that Sumner relied on his audience's possession of Hispanicist ideas, Louis A. Pérez Jr. argues that 1898 imperialists relied on their audience's association of the United States' relationship with Cuba and other imperial targets with conventionalized images related to child-parent relationships, with the United States the responsible parent duly correcting the childish errors of its wards (Pérez 2008, 52). The difference between Sumner and his opponents was whether they thought the newly imperial United States was succeeding in the goal of establishing difference from Spain or not.

This plurality of positions responding to what was at core a fundamental concept in US nation-building should not surprise us, as it existed in the early national and antebellum periods as well. As we have seen, a variety of approaches to the issue then existed. For instance, with Barlow, the United States' commitment to free institutions, exemplified in the efforts required to revolt successfully against Britain, signaled its evasion of the historical malaise embodied in the vicious behavior Spain exhibited in its conquest of the West Indies. Barlow used this Hispanicist interpretation to argue that the United States ought to intervene in constrained Spanish economies. Melville, though, shows how Delano fails to distinguish himself from the Spanish captain Cereno over whom he imagines himself to be morally and managerially superior; when read as an embodiment of more general US attitudes, Melville's characterization of Delano can thus be understood to signify the United States' failure to negate the Hispanic Other. What brings these diverging authors together is that both register Hispanicism as a key to national identity. Barlow's text may center a nationalist narrative on Hispanicism, Melville's an opportunity to deconstruct identity construction, but both attest to Hispanicism's centrality to the national narrative.

In short, the US ideas about Hispanophone peoples that characterized 1898 were not exceptional. If they were, the cultural phenomena of the period would appear new and different in historical perspective. However, that is not the case. The major rhetorical moves of "The Conquest of the United States by Spain" were all constructed long before 1898. It was a powerful piece of rhetoric not because it was strikingly original but because it forcefully invoked and attacked ideas long dear to its audience, ideas that had been constructed by and that were present in the culture since the very rise of the nation—if not earlier. It should be seen as part of a tradition of Hispanicist rhetoric, not as an indication of the emergence of that rhetoric in 1898. Understanding 1898 requires recognizing the important strain in US literary history represented by early national and antebellum Hispanicist texts.

1898 and Hispanicism's Maturation

All of that stated, we should not downplay 1898's significance. Although not an exceptional moment, 1898 was important. As a high-tide point for expansion's popularity, the period's views spurred not only the Spanish-American War but also additional expansionist efforts both military and economic, eventually inspiring the emergence of a new form of nonmilitary imperialism. After the turn of the century, the nation continued to pursue military intervention. This policy was highlighted by the Roosevelt administration's gunboat-diplomacy assistance to the Panamanian revolution against Columbia to enable favorable negotiations with newly independent Panama for the Panama Canal contract. It also led to interventions in the Dominican Republic, Haiti, and elsewhere as the nation adopted a liberal interpretation of the Monroe Doctrine. This interpretation stipulated that the United States must occupy nations whose activities were contrary to US interests.

However, territorial intervention became increasingly less popular after the turn of the century, and the United States backed off of military intervention, granted Cuba and other nations under US influence measures of sovereignty, and encouraged economic expansion into rather than military control of these areas. The US government thus modeled what would eventually become its dominant mode of exerting influence in Latin America in the twentieth century—economic imperialism. This is not to say that the nation became unwilling to use force. After the beginning of the Cold War, for instance, it committed itself to halting Soviet influence by all means possible. But this would not be the United States' chief tendency. By creating economic dependencies through capital investment and negotiating favorable import-export policies, US interests reaped the benefits of imperialism, while the nation did not have to deal with the expense of maintaining a colonial empire or the domestic and international turmoil prompted by interventionism. The most clearly articulated version of this approach was Franklin Roosevelt's Good Neighbor Policy, which sought to expand US business interests in Latin America through promises of nonintervention and reciprocity. Yet this model's emergence does not exactly suggest that 1898 was exceptional. The means were new, but the conditions for the emergence of this mode of interacting with the Hispanophone world are to be found earlier, in Hispanicism. Without this discourse, the rationale for viewing Latin America as an economic dependent would not have existed.

The year 1898 thus had profound material and geopolitical consequences. Moreover, although 1898 Hispanicism was not unique per se, it was uniquely mature and predominant and was increasingly interpreted to offer warrant for imperialism. It was, after all, very popular and powerful in a way that had formerly not been the case. It had become the dominant epistemology by which US Americans understood their place in the world. There is a certainty and confidence to 1898 Hispanicism that was lacking in earlier periods. Differentiation from Spanish-ness had always been key to how the nation understood itself, but there were always loudly voiced questions about the Hispanicist narrative. Had the United States truly differentiated itself from Spanish-ness through the establishment of liberal institutions, or was there still ground to make up? If it had, was it capable of incorporating the Hispanophone peoples of Mexico and the Caribbean without corrupting its Anglo-Saxon institutions? Such qualms remained in 1898, but they had become less of an object. The aftermath of the Civil War lent credence to the idea that the nation had dealt with its demons, that it had established internal coherence and a sense of national mission by eliminating the element, slavery, that undermined its claims to success in its national project. The increased prominence of racial science, rudimentarily formulated in the antebellum period but more widely accepted in the postbellum years, cemented the idea of hierarchical difference between Anglo-Americans and Hispanophone peoples. The idea of the "white man's burden"—the sense that it was the responsibility of the northern European nations to command and by doing so to alleviate the sufferings of the darker-skinned peoples of the world—had by this time become much more popular. The confluence of these factors contributed to the United States' self-construction as an imperial nation with a special mission of spreading its beneficial liberal values throughout the world—a nation whose status would not be compromised by imperialism but, rather, could only be fulfilled by tutoring illiberal Hispanophone nations in the establishment of liberal principles. Although there remained those, like Sumner, who opposed the Spanish-American War, theirs was not the dominant view. Sumner's critique was characteristic, though, in that he was unable to challenge 1898 imperialism on any but Hispanicist grounds. His view relies on the same cultural logic as that of his opponents, which illustrates the centrality of the Hispanicist worldview to the 1898 moment.

Although 1898 Hispanicism was mature, it was not coherent. Although more powerfully serving as a center of gravity at this time, the discourse, just as it had been in the early national and antebellum periods, remained fractured. This should not be surprising. Identity formation via difference in 1898 was then, as before and after, an untenable mode of discursive mystification. In violently dividing the world according to US and Hispanic types, it denied the essential commonality shared by Spain and the United States as nations that sought mastery under the guise of protestations to benevolence. Although his writing reflected this identity-focused logic by insisting that the nation distinguish itself from Spain, Sumner registered the incoherence of Hispanicism in its imperialist guise as the false consciousness of expansionist racial pseudotheories. We certainly ought to condemn undesirable elements in his thought such as his Social Darwinism, but we would do well to heed a basic lesson of his writing: that exploitative US policies that are defended by reference to assumptions of superiority to Hispanophone peoples ought to be questioned rather than blindly followed.

Notes

Introduction

1. I use the term "US literature" (and the adjective "US" in general) instead of the more conventional "American literature" here because the United States is only one of many nations that lay claim to being "American." Referring to the United States and its people as "American" while referring to those other nations as "Latin American," "Luso-American," and such, perpetuates the pernicious exceptionalist notion that the United States is the "true" America. Using "US" as an adjective is somewhat awkward because "United States literature" is not grammatical. However, this seems to me the best, most concise option. The fact that there are no grammatically perfect alternatives to "American" may indicate the extent to which language and power are interrelated.

2. I adopt the term "US Americans" (Rodríguez 2010, 8–9) as opposed to "Americans" for reasons similar to those for which I use "US literature." The term will particularly be used in the place of "American" when referring to Anglo-Americans, remembering that for a dominant strain of US exceptionalists, US nationality is racialized as white. As an adjective, "US" will not always have the same racialized import. Use of "US" can signify in many ways, including to US diversity.

3. I use "Hispanophone world" to refer to Spain and Spanish America. I am regretfully unable to address Hispanophone Africa in this study.

4. As DeGuzmán (2005, xvi, xxi) explains, US Americans used terms such as "Spanish" and "Spanish American" to homogenize heterogeneous peoples and places into a single category that they opposed to the United States. Johnson (1993, 13) explains how Anglo-Americans level differences among Latin American types to play up cherished self-conceptions. As Horsman (1981, 4) explains, the term "Anglo-Saxon" was used in a similarly imprecise manner to describe vaguely Aryan peoples who may or may not have been Saxon in descent.

5. For more about the Black Legend, consult DeGuzmán 2005; Fernández Retamar 1989; Gibson 1971; Greer, Mignolo, and Quilligan 2007; Johnson 1993, 10–11.

6. This is true also of US representations of other Mediterranean peoples; Hispanophone peoples, though, are more "present" in the US cultural imaginary for reasons I will discuss.

7. Other contrasts are similarly telling. For instance, the Swiss John Coustos's popular 1746 account of his struggles with the Portuguese Inquisition reflects pre-racialist views regarding Iberian depravity, while antebellum anti-Catholic sentiment took on more racial overtones, as seen in George Lippard's *'Bel of Prairie Eden*. Educational nations-of-the-world chapbooks also reflect this pattern. The 1819 *People of All Nations* exhibits incipient racial thinking in its description of Spaniards (Anonymous 1819, 21), whereas the 1848 *Book of Nations, for Children* does even more so (Werden 1848, 2).

8. Similarly, Gruesz writes that Spanish America is that "'other America' [that] was always present as a repressed national memory" (Gruesz 2002, 210); this repression constitutes a vexed discourse of identity construction. For more about such relationships between the United States, Spain, and Spanish America, consult Brickhouse 2004; Cabañas 2008; Goudie 2006.

9. For more about New Formalism, also consult Castiglia and Castronovo 2004; Levine 2008; Otter 2008.

10. I contrast Delany's views on Hispanicism to those of Mann in a 2016 essay that appeared in *College Literature*.

11. I hope that reframing the antebellum period in these terms will spur additional consideration of ways to better understand antebellum phenomena in transnational lights. For instance, my opening consideration of Agassiz and Shaler suggests that the Civil War might be rethought in such terms. The fracturing of self-conceptions of nation that occurred during the Civil War might seem an internal issue, but that issue was refracted along Hispanicism's transnational lines.

12. This interest in looking for hope in the uncertainty with which historical writers engaged their presents and the fact that our present is one of many possible futures at which our society could have historically arrived has become increasingly prominent in literary studies. Coronado (2013, 34) provides another example.

Chapter 1

1. Gilroy (1993) and Posnock (1998) similarly celebrate cosmopolitan, anti-identity traditions.

2. Bernstein 1985; Ford 1971; Woodress 1958; Zunder 1969 provide biographies of Barlow.

3. As DeGuzmán (2005, xix) explains, Columbus represents a distinctly US American figure in the poem, whereas Ferdinand represents a typical Spaniard who betrays Columbus.

4. Scholars discussing crises of national identity in the early national period include Bailyn 1968; Buell 1992; Davidson 1986; Fliegelman 1982; Kierner 2007; Gordon Wood 1972.

5. Translations from French are my own.

6. As McWilliams writes, by the time Barlow wrote *The Columbiad*, he believed that *The Vision of Columbus* formed the basis for a "wholly new heroic code for the epic" (McWilliams 1989, 54). Barlow, McWilliams continues, believed not

that epic was antiquated but that it needed a new core narrative that deemphasized machinery, war, and individual renown (55–56).

7. I disagree with McWilliams's claim that Barlow was not "a chauvinist waving a literary flag for thirteen United States" but an "international republican" (McWilliams 1989, 43). Although McWilliams rightly insists that we recognize Barlow's cosmopolitanism, Barlow sees that cosmopolitanism as the United States' provenance.

8. This shift toward a more confident exceptionalism characterizes much of Barlow's later work, such as the 1809, esp. 4–5, Fourth of July oration he delivered in Washington, DC.

Chapter 2

1. The passage coheres with what Iglesias (2011, 185) describes as Cooper's suspicion of the underlying motivations for the calls to national honor that characterized the Democratic press's war rhetoric.

2. Ironically, whereas Cooper had turned to realism by this period and sought to demystify Mexico for his readers, soldiers, as Johannsen (1985, 149) explains, viewed Mexico through the romantic depictions of times past that Cooper cultivated in his earlier fiction.

Chapter 3

1. Emery (1984, 50); Sundquist (1993, 136) note, in varying manners, the interrelationships between Hispanicism and Africanism in "Benito Cereno."

2. Américo Paredes's novel *George Washington Gómez* illustrates this usage. In it Anglo-Texans and white Tejanos refer to white Tejanos as "Spanish" and darker-skinned Tejanos as "Mexicans" (e.g., Paredes 1990, 173).

3. Robbins (1997, esp. 547, 548–51, 551–52, 555) views Melville's choice to publish in *Putnam's* as tacit approval of its hard-nosed, ironic antislavery rhetoric. Post-Lauria (1995, esp. 5) further argues that Melville joined forces with *Putnam's* on both its critique of slavery and imperialism. However, *Putnam's* regularly published pro-imperialist work, as seen with "Annexation." I would argue that he parted with the magazine's frequently nationalist, imperialist stance.

4. This focus on frames was a long-standing one for Melville. For instance, Herbert (1980, 21) explains that *Typee* emphasizes how Americans experience encounter with Marquesans more so than anything concrete about Marquesans themselves.

Chapter 4

1. Ard (2000, xvi); Marshall (2005, 527) discuss the novel's composition and publication history. Mann outlined the work while in Cuba in the 1830s, completed a draft by 1858, and made final revisions in the 1880s. An undated letter from Mann to Eleanor Lewis, likely written in May 1886, reveals that Mann had begun compos-

ing the novel while in Cuba (Mann 1886). Early portions of the work had been published in 1858 in *The Bee*, a newspaper published as an educational exercise by Mann's son George (Mann 1858). As such, it is likely that significant portions of the novel had been completed by that date. An 1860 letter from Mann to her sister Sophia, in which she asks whether Hawthorne would have any interest in writing an abolitionist novel based on her narrative of her experiences in Cuba, suggests both the novel's original purpose as an abolitionist work and that by 1860 Mann had an incomplete version of the story sketched out (Mann 1860).

For more about Mann's biography, consult Ard 2000; Luiggi 1965; Marshall 2005; Velleman 2001.

2. Noting its antebellum resonances, Windell (2014, 306) describes how the patterns of racialization in the novel, such as the depiction of Juanita as a tragic mulatta, are drawn from the sentimental abolitionist tradition. Ard (2000, xii) also notes the novel's contrasting antebellum and postbellum sensibilities.

3. Michaela B. Cooper (2006, esp. 146–47, 152) argues that Mann critiques a cult of domesticity embodied by Isabella's reticence to challenge her husband, with Helen representing a threshold figure pointing toward later models for independent female agency; it may be the case that the novel does not so much critique domesticity per se as it does corrupt Cuban domestic conventions.

4. Women's duty to voice concerns that men would not due to men's corruptive participation in the public sphere was a favorite theme of Mann's. In a January 18, 1852, letter to Mary Messer discussing congressional disputations regarding the Fugitive Slave Law and related controversies, Mann wrote that "it will be a good opportunity to say a great many things that ought to be said. If I were a Rep. or a Senator, this would be my [unreadable—may be 'course'], but I am sadly afraid the gentlemen will not be so patriotic or persevering as I should be. I almost wish myself a man for the time being" (Mann 1852).

5. For more about the historical and literary contexts of Cuban annexationism, consult Chaffin 1996; Cruz-Taura 1997; Lazo 2005; Opatrný 1993; Pérez 1990; Schoultz 2009, esp. 13–33.

6. As Kaplan (1998, 589) writes in her study of "manifest domesticity," domestic writers often discussed empire in terms of domesticating the foreign but also expressed anxiety about the introduction of foreignness into the home.

Chapter 5

1. All translations from Spanish are my own.
2. Saco (1928c, 8) echoes this view in an 1837 letter to José Alfonso.

Epilogue

1. The claim has long been popular with imperial apologists who reject the idea that the United States has a conventionally imperial history, e.g., Schwabe 1986, 12. The year 1898 is not only unique for imperial apologists, however. In the tellingly

titled *The Spanish-Cuban-American War and the Birth of American Imperialism*, Foner (1972, esp. vii, ix, x) argues that 1898 is the exceptional starting point in his twentieth-century history of US imperialist economic interventionism as an intrinsic aspect of the era. LaFeber (1998, xxxii, 60, 101) echoes these views. As Kaplan (1993b, esp. 11–19) points out, literary critics have often echoed these historians. For instance, Chase (1957, 12) described US literature according to metaphors of anti-imperiousness. According to this logic, Schwabe's idea that 1898 is an aberration is an easy leap.

2. As this general description suggests, Sumner's theories entailed many tensions. As Bannister (1992, x, xvii) describes, he was both conservative and liberal, both committed to individual liberty and to history and tradition as a check on individual excess. Sumner was, moreover, both Darwinist and a proponent of a relativist, antiprogressivist understanding of history. Sumner's work also contains misrecognitions. As Notestein (1955, 394, 399) explains, Sumner opposed plutocratic influence on governance but failed to perceive that the corporate interests he celebrated wielded exactly the sort of influence he feared. He never resolved these tensions.

3. As Dennis (1995, 244) notes, Sumner could put his Darwinist thinking to racialist purposes, for instance, arguing that slavery had benefited society by allowing advanced peoples the leisure to develop refined cultures. As Dennis (245) continues, Sumner was indeed more racist than his contemporary Herbert Spencer. However, he was not as zealously racist as the eugenicist Anglo-Saxonists of the era and did not contribute to their movements.

Works Cited

Primary Sources

Abbott, John S. C. 1860. *South and North; or, Impressions Received during a Trip to Cuba and the South*. New York: Abbey and Abbott.

Agassiz, Louis, and Elizabeth Cabot Cary Agassiz. 1868. *A Journey in Brazil*. Boston: Ticknor and Fields.

Anonymous. 1809. "Spain: An Account of the Public Festival Given by the Citizens of Boston, at the Exchange Coffee House, January 24, 1809, in Honor of Spanish Valour and Patriotism. With the Regular and Volunteer Toasts, and All the Original Songs and Odes Sung on the Occasion. In Which Is Also Introduced a Brief Sketch of Spain, Geographical, Historical and Political." Boston: Russell and Cutler.

Anonymous. 1819. *The People of All Nations: Being a Miniature Description of the Manners and Customs of the Inhabitants of the Different Nations of the World. Designed for the Improvement of Youth. Ornamented with Sixty-Two Elegant Engravings*. Auburn, NY: D. Rumsey.

Anonymous. 1831. *A Peep at the Various Nations of the World: With a Concise Description of the Inhabitants*. Concord, NH: Hoag and Atwood.

Anonymous. 1840. Review of *Mercedes of Castile*. *Athenaeum* 686: 1005.

Anonymous. 1841. Review of *Mercedes of Castile*. *Iris or Literary Messenger* 3: 137.

Anonymous. 1853a. "Cuba." *Putnam's Monthly Magazine of American Literature, Science, and Art* 1 (1): 3–16.

Anonymous. 1853b. "A Glance at Havana." *Putnam's Monthly Magazine of American Literature, Science, and Art* 1 (2): 185–94.

Anonymous. 1853c. "How They Live in Havana." *Putnam's Monthly Magazine of American Literature, Science, and Art* 1 (3): 288–99.

Anonymous. 1854. "Annexation." *Putnam's Monthly Magazine of American Literature, Science, and Art* 3 (14): 183–94.

Barlow, Joel. 1809. "Oration Delivered at Washington, July Fourth, 1809: At the Request of the Democratic Citizens of the District of Columbia." Washington, DC: R. C. Weightman.

——. 1896. "Plan proposé pour faire une revolution dans la Louisiane." *Annual Report of the American Historical Association* 1: 945–53.

——. 1970a. *The Columbiad: A Poem, with the Last Corrections of the Author*. 1807. *The Works of Joel Barlow, Volume II: Poetry*. Gainesville, FL: Scholars' Facsimiles and Reprints, 371–852.

——. 1970b. *The Vision of Columbus*. 1787. *The Works of Joel Barlow, Volume II: Poetry*. Gainesville, FL: Scholars' Facsimiles and Reprints, 101–370.

——. 1995. "Advice to a Raven in Russia, December 1812." 1812. In *The Columbia Anthology of American Poetry*, edited by Jay Parini, 68–70. New York: Columbia University Press.

Benzoni, Girolamo. 1962. *La historia del mondo nuovo*. 1565. Graz: Akademische Druck-u. Verlagsanstalt.

Bonicelli, Paul. 2016. "Obama's Cuba Visit Aims to Knock America Down a Peg." *Federalist*. FDRLST Media, February 29. Accessed July 1, 2016, http://thefederalist.com/2016/02/29/obamas-cuba-visit-aims-to-knock-america-down-a-peg/.

Brooks, Van Wyck. 1918. "On Creating a Usable Past." *The Dial* 54 (765): 337–41.

Bryant, William Cullen. 1852. "Discourse on the Life, Character, and Genius of James Fenimore Cooper." *Memorial of James Fenimore Cooper*, 39–73. New York: G. P. Putnam.

Burke, Edmund. 2009. *Reflections on the Revolution in France*. 1790. Edited by L. G. Mitchell. Oxford: Oxford University Press.

Casas, Bartolomé de las. 1974. *Brevísima relación de la destrucción de las Indias*. 1552. Barcelona: Fontomara.

——. 1977. *The Spanish Colonie; or, a Briefe Chronicle of the Acts and Gestes of the Spaniards in the West Indies*. 1583. Ann Arbor: University of Michigan Microfilms.

Cisneros, Gaspar Betancourt. 1928. Letter to José Antonio Saco, August 7, 1849. In *Contra la anexión*, edited by Fernando Ortiz, 2: 49–52. Havana: Imprenta de cultural.

Cooper, James Fenimore. 1840. *Mercedes of Castile; or, the Voyage to Cathay*. 2 vols. Philadelphia: Lea and Blanchard.

——. 1848. *Jack Tier; or, the Florida Reef*. 2 vols. New York: Burgess, Stringer.

——. 1983. *The Last of the Mohicans: A Narrative of 1757*. 1826. Edited by James Franklin Beard, James A. Sappenfield, and E. N. Feltskog. Albany: State University of New York Press.

——. 2000a. *The American Democrat*. 1838. In *The American Democrat and Other Political Writings*, edited by Bradley J. Birzer and John Willson, 361–494. Washington, DC: Regnery.

——. 2000b. "A Letter to His Countrymen." 1834. In *The American Democrat and Other Political Writings*, edited by Bradley J. Birzer and John Willson, 267–359. Washington, DC: Regnery.

Coustos, John, and Antonio Gavin. 1821. *The Mysteries of Popery Unveiled, in the Unparalleled Sufferings of John Coustos, at the Inquisition of Lisbon [1746]: To Which Is Added, the Origin of the Inquisition, and Its Establishment in Various Countries; and, A Master-Key to Popery [1773]*. Hartford, CT: P. Reynolds and Thompson.

Delano, Amasa. 1970. *A Narrative of Voyages and Travels in the Northern and Southern Hemispheres: Comprising Three Voyages Round the World: Together with a Voyage of Survey and Discovery, in the Pacific Ocean and Oriental Islands*. 1817. Edited by C. Hartley Grattan. New York: Praeger.

Emerson, Ralph Waldo. 1983a. "Self-Reliance." 1841. In *Essays and Lectures*, 257–82. New York: Library of America.

———. 1983b. "The Young American." 1844. In *Essays and Lectures*, 213–30. New York: Library of America.

Henry, O. 1904. *Cabbages and Kings*. Garden City, NY: Doubleday, Page.

Hobbes, Thomas. 1997. *Leviathan: Authoritative Text, Backgrounds, Interpretations*. 1651. Edited by Richard E. Flathman and David Johnston. New York: Norton.

Irving, Washington. 1991. *The Alhambra*. 1832. In *Bracebridge Hall, Tales of a Traveller, The Alhambra*, 719–1050. New York: Library of America

Lee, Michelle Ye Hee. 2015. "Donald Trump's False Comments Connecting Mexican Immigrants and Crime." *Washington Post*, July 8. Accessed July 26, 2015, https://www.washingtonpost.com/news/fact-checker/wp/2015/07/08/donald-trumps-false-comments-connecting-mexican-immigrants-and-crime/?utm_term=.548b855604dc.

Lippard, George. 1848. *'Bel of Prairie Eden*. New York: R. M. De Witt.

Mann, Mary Peabody. 1834a. Letter to Horace Mann. March 30. TS 516–18, Robert L. Straker Collection of Mann Letters. Antiochiana, Antioch College.

———. 1834b. Letter to Rawlins Pickman. August 6. TS 836, Robert L. Straker Collection of Peabody Letters. Antiochiana, Antioch College.

———. 1835. Letter to Horace Mann. January 15. TS 615, Robert L. Straker Collection of Mann Letters. Antiochiana, Antioch College.

———. 1852. Letter to Mary Messer. January 18. Mann-Messer Family Letters. Massachusetts Historical Society.

———. 1858. "Slavery in Cuba." *The Bee* 1 (2, 4). Antiochiana, Antioch College.

———. 1860?. Letter to Sophia Hawthorne. Undated. TS 2149–50, Robert L. Straker Collection of Peabody Letters. Antiochiana, Antioch College.

———. 1868. Preface. In *Life in the Argentine Republic in the Days of the Tyrants; or, Civilization and Barbarism*, by Domingo Faustino Sarmiento, iii–xxviii. New York: Hurd and Houghton.

———. 1874. Essay Three. In *Sex and Education: A Reply to Dr. E. H. Clarke's "Sex in Education"*, edited by Julia Ward Howe, 52–71. Boston: Roberts Brothers.

———. 1886?. Letter to Eleanor Lewis. Undated. TS 3424, Robert L. Straker Collection of Peabody Letters. Antiochiana, Antioch College.

———. 2000. *Juanita: A Romance of Real Life in Cuba Fifty Years Ago*. 1887. Edited by Patricia M. Ard. Charlottesville: University Press of Virginia.

———. 2001. *"My Dear Sir": Mary Mann's Letters to Sarmiento (1865–1881)*. Edited by Barry L. Velleman. Buenos Aires: ICANA.

Mann, Mary Peabody, and Elizabeth Palmer Peabody. 1870. *Moral Culture of Infancy, and Kindergarten Guide, with Music for the Plays*. 1863. 4th ed. New York: J. W. Schemerhorn.

Melville, Herman. 1987. "Benito Cereno." 1855. In *The Piazza Tales and Other Prose Pieces, 1839–1860*, edited by Harrison Hayford, Alma A. MacDougall, G. Thomas Tanselle, et al., 46–117. Evanston: Northwestern University Press; Chicago: Newberry Library.

Morse, Jedidiah. 1789. *The American Geography; or, A View of the Present Situation of the United States of America*. Elizabethtown, NJ: Shepard Kollock.

O'Reilly, Bill. 2004. "Back of the Book." *O'Reilly Factor*. FOX, February 11.

O'Sullivan, John L. 1839. "The Great Nation of Futurity." *United States Magazine, and Democratic Review* 6 (23): 426–30.

——. 1845. "Annexation." *United States Magazine, and Democratic Review* 17 (85): 5–10.

——. 1847. "The War." *United States Magazine, and Democratic Review* 20 (104): 99–102.

Paine, Thomas. 1945. *Rights of Man*. 1791. In *Complete Writings*. Vol. 1. Edited by Philip S. Foner. New York: Citadel Press.

——. 1989. *Common Sense*. 1776. In *Political Writings*, edited by Bruce Kuklick, 1–38. Cambridge: Cambridge University Press.

Paredes, Américo. 1990. *George Washington Gómez: A Mexicotexan Novel*. Houston: Arte Público Press.

Peabody, Elizabeth Palmer. 1984. Letter to Harriet Mulford Stone Lothrop. 1887. In *Letters of Elizabeth Palmer Peabody: American Renaissance Woman*, edited by Bruce A. Ronda, 447–48. Middletown, CT: Wesleyan University Press.

——. 2000. Explanatory Note. In *Juanita: A Romance of Real Life in Cuba Fifty Years Ago*, by Mary Peabody Mann, 223. Charlottesville: University Press of Virginia.

Perry, John A. 1853. *Thrilling Adventures of a New Englander: Travels, Scenes, and Sufferings in Cuba, Mexico, and California*. Boston: Redding.

Poe, Edgar Allan. 1841. Review of *Mercedes of Castile*, by James Fenimore Cooper. *Graham's Monthly Magazine of Literature, Art, and Fashion* 18 (1): 47–48.

Prescott, William H. 1957. *History of the Conquest of Mexico, and History of the Conquest of Peru*. 1843 and 1847. New York: Modern Library.

Quenqua, Douglas. 2013. "Unsettling News on Knee Surgery, and a Striking Neanderthal Gene." *New York Times*, December 30. Accessed January 9, 2014, http://www.nytimes.com/2013/12/31/science/unsettling-news-on-knee-surgery-and-a-striking-neanderthal-gene.html.

Robertson, William. 1829. *The History of the Discovery and Settlement of America*. 1777. New York: Harper.

Roosevelt, Theodore. 1902. "The Strenuous Life." In *The Strenuous Life: Essays and Addresses*, 1–24. New York: Century.

Saco, José Antonio. 1928a. "Ideas sobre la incorporación de Cuba en los Estados Unidos." 1848. In *Contra la anexión*, edited by Fernando Ortiz, 1: 33–68. Havana: Imprenta de cultural.

——. 1928b. Letter to Gaspar Betancourt Cisneros. March 19, 1848. In *Contra la anexión*, edited by Fernando Ortiz, 2: 8–15. Havana: Imprenta de cultural.

——. 1928c. Letter to José Alfonso. January 21, 1837. In *Contra la anexión*, edited by Fernando Ortiz, 2: 6–8. Havana: Imprenta de cultural.

———. 1928d. "Origen del movimiento anexionista en Cuba: Ideas de Saco acerca de la anexión; Motivos de su oposición a ella." In *Contra la anexión*, edited by Fernando Ortiz, 1: 20–31. Havana: Imprenta de cultural.

———. 1928e. "Paralelo entre la Isla de Cuba y algunas colonias inglesas." 1837. In *Contra la anexión*, edited by Fernando Ortiz, 1: 3–6. Havana: Imprenta de cultural.

———. 1928f. "Réplica a V. Vázquez Queipo en la polémica con J. A. Saco sobre el incremento de la población blanca en Cuba." 1847. In *Contra la anexión*, edited by Fernando Ortiz, 1: 7–17. Havana: Imprenta de cultural.

———. 1928g. "Réplica de don José Antonio Saco a los anexionistas que han impugnado sus 'Ideas sobre la incorporación de Cuba en los Estados Unidos.'" 1849. In *Contra la anexión*, edited by Fernando Ortiz, 1: 69–239. Havana: Imprenta de cultural.

Shaler, Nathaniel Southgate. 1909. *The Autobiography of Nathaniel Southgate Shaler, with a Supplementary Memoir by His Wife*. Boston: Houghton Mifflin.

Smiley, Thomas T. 1839. *The Encyclopædia of Geography: Comprising a Description of the Earth, Exhibiting Its Relation to the Heavenly Bodies, Its Physical Structure, the Natural History of Each Country, and the Industry, Commerce, Political Institutions, and Civil and Social State of All Nations; Illustrated by Numerous Engravings, Representing the Most Remarkable Objects of Nature and Art in Every Region of the Globe; On the Plan of Murray's Encyclopædia of Geography*. Philadelphia: Hogan and Thompson.

Stowe, Harriet Beecher. 2010. *Uncle Tom's Cabin; or, Life among the Lowly*. 1852. Edited by Elizabeth Ammons. 2nd ed. New York: Norton.

Sumner, William Graham. 1913. "The Boon of Nature." 1887. In *Earth-Hunger, and Other Essays*, edited by Albert Galloway Keller, 233–38. New Haven, CT: Yale University Press.

———. 1992a. "The Absurd Effort to Make the World Over." 1894. In *On Liberty, Society, and Politics: The Essential Essays of William Graham Sumner*, edited by Robert C. Bannister, 251–61. Indianapolis: Liberty Fund.

———. 1992b. "The Conquest of the United States by Spain." 1898. In *On Liberty, Society, and Politics: The Essential Essays of William Graham Sumner*, edited by Robert C. Bannister, 272–97. Indianapolis: Liberty Fund.

———. 1992c. "The Fallacy of Territorial Extension." 1896. In *On Liberty, Society, and Politics: The Essential Essays of William Graham Sumner*, edited by Robert C. Bannister, 265–71. Indianapolis: Liberty Fund.

———. 1992d. "The Forgotten Man." 1883. In *On Liberty, Society, and Politics: The Essential Essays of William Graham Sumner*, edited by Robert C. Bannister, 201–22. Indianapolis: Liberty Fund.

Ura, Alexa, and Morgan Smith. 2014. "'Invasion' Remarks Fuel a Heated Debate in a G.O.P. Race." *New York Times*, February 6. Accessed April 1, 2014, http://www.nytimes.com/2014/02/07/us/invasion-remarks-fuel-a-heated-debate-in-a-gop-race.html?_r=0.

Valdes, Alisa. 2014. "The New York Times and NPR Are Still Clueless about Latinos." *Alisa Valdes: Official Website for Writer and Producer Alisa Valdes*, January 6. Accessed January 9, 2014, http://alisavaldes.com/new-york-times-npr-still-clueless-latinos/.

Vega, Garcilaso de la, el Inca. 1688. *The Royal Commentaries of Peru*. 1607. Translated by Paul Rycault. London: Miles Flesher.

Volney, Constantin-François. 1991. *The Ruins; or, Meditations on the Revolutions of Empires; and, The Law of Nature*. 1802. Translated by Joel Barlow and Thomas Jefferson. Baltimore: Black Classics Press.

Werden, Elias Irish. 1848. *Book of Nations, for Children*. Pittsfield, MA: E. Werden.

White, Trumbull. 1898. *Pictorial History of Our War with Spain for Cuba's Freedom: A Thrilling Account of the Land and Naval Operations of American Soldiers and Sailors in Our War with Spain, and the Heroic Struggles of Cuban Patriots against Spanish Tyranny; Including a Description and History of Cuba, Spain, Philippine Islands, Our Army and Navy, Fighting Strength, Coast Defenses, and Our Relations with Other Nations, etc., etc.* Vancouver: J. M. MacGregor; Freedom Publishing.

Wood, Edmond. 1901. "Can Cubans Govern Cuba?" *Forum* 32: 66–73.

Secondary Sources

Alemán, Jesse, and Shelley Streeby, eds. 2007. Introduction to *Empire and the Literature of Sensation: An Anthology of Nineteenth-Century Popular Fiction*, xiii–xxx. New Brunswick, NJ: Rutgers University Press.

Anderson, Benedict. 1991. *Imagined Communities: Reflections on the Origin and Spread of Nationalism*. Rev. ed. New York: Verso.

Ard, Patricia M. 2000. Introduction to *Juanita*, by Mary Peabody Mann, xi–xxxviii. Charlottesville: University Press of Virginia.

Arsić, Branka. 2007. *Passive Constitutions; or, 7 1/2 Times Bartleby*. Stanford, CA: Stanford University Press.

Bailyn, Bernard. 1968. *The Origins of American Politics*. New York: Knopf.

Bannister, Robert C. 1992. Introduction to *On Liberty, Society, and Politics: The Essential Essays of William Graham Sumner*, by William Graham Sumner, ix–xxxvi. Indianapolis: Liberty Fund.

Bauer, Ralph. 1995. "Colonial Discourse and Early American Literary History: Ercilla, the Inca Garcilaso, and Joel Barlow's Conception of a New World Epic." *Early American Literature* 30 (3): 203–32.

Bercovitch, Sacvan. 2012. Preface to *The American Jeremiad*, xi–xl. 1978. Anniversary ed. Madison: University of Wisconsin Press.

Bernstein, Samuel. 1985. *Joel Barlow: A Connecticut Yankee in an Age of Revolution*. Cliff Island, ME: Ultima Thule Press.

Bhabha, Homi. 2004. "DissemiNation: Time, Narrative, and the Margins of the Modern Nation." In *The Location of Culture*, 199–244. New York: Routledge.

Birzer, Bradley, and John Willson. 2000. Introduction to *The American Democrat and Other Political Writings*, by James Fenimore Cooper, vii–xxiv. Washington, DC: Regnery.

Blackmon, Douglas A. 2008. *Slavery by Another Name: The Re-Enslavement of Black Americans from the Civil War to World War II*. New York: Doubleday.

Bloch, Ruth H. 1985. *Visionary Republic: Millennial Themes in American Thought, 1756–1800*. Cambridge: Cambridge University Press.

Boggs, Colleen Glenney. 2007. *Transnationalism and American Literature: Literary Translation, 1773–1892*. New York: Routledge.

Bowra, C. M. 1948. *From Virgil to Milton*. London: Macmillan.

———. 1952. *Heroic Poetry*. London: Macmillan.

Bradley, James. 2010. *The Imperial Cruise: A Secret History of Empire and War*. New York: Little, Brown.

Brickhouse, Anna. 2004. *Transamerican Literary Relations and the Nineteenth-Century Public Sphere*. Cambridge: Cambridge University Press.

Bryant, John. 1984. "'Nowhere a Stranger': Melville and Cosmopolitanism." *Nineteenth-Century Fiction* 39 (3): 275–91.

———. 1987. "Citizens of a World to Come: Melville and the Millennial Cosmopolite." *American Literature* 59 (1): 20–36.

———. 2009. "Melville Cosmopolite: The Future of the Melville Text." *Leviathan: A Journal of Melville Studies* 11: 119–32.

Buell, Lawrence. 1992. "American Literary Emergence as a Postcolonial Phenomenon." *American Literary History* 4 (3): 411–42.

Cabañas, Miguel A. 2008. *The Cultural "Other" in Nineteenth-Century Travel Narratives: How the United States and Latin America Described Each Other*. Lewiston, NY: Edwin Mellen Press.

Camacho, Jorge. 2007. "El indígena en la literatura cubana del siglo XIX: José Martí, José Antonio Saco y Francisco Sellen." *Latin American Indian Literatures Journal* 23 (1): 27–42.

Castiglia, Christopher, and Russ Castronovo. 2004. "A 'Hive of Subtlety': Aesthetics and the End(s) of Cultural Studies." *American Literature* 76 (3): 423–35.

Chaffin, Tom. 1996. *Fatal Glory: Narciso López and the First Clandestine U.S. War against Cuba*. Charlottesville: University Press of Virginia.

Chase, Richard. 1957. *The American Novel and Its Tradition*. Garden City, NY: Doubleday Anchor.

Cheng, Eileen Ka-May. 2008. *The Plain and Noble Garb of Truth: Nationalism and Impartiality in American Historical Writing, 1784–1860*. Athens: University of Georgia Press.

Codina Carreira, Pablo. 1967. "Ensayo para una biografía de José Antonio Saco." *Revista de Indias* 27 (107–8): 89–135.

Cooper, Michaela B. 2006. "Should Not These Things Be Known? Mary Mann's *Juanita* and the Limits of Domesticity." In *Reinventing the Peabody Sisters*, edited by Monika M. Elbert, Julie E. Hall, and Katharine Rodier, 146–62. Iowa City: University of Iowa Press.

Coronado, Raúl. 2013. *A World Not to Come: A History of Latino Writing and Print Culture*. Cambridge, MA: Harvard University Press.

"cosmopolitan, adj. and n." 2013. OED online, December 15.

Cruz-Taura, Graciela. 1997. "Annexation and National Identity: The Issues of Cuba's Mid-Nineteenth Century Debate." *Cuban Studies* 27: 90–109.

Culler, Jonathan. 2007. *The Literary in Theory*. Stanford, CA: Stanford University Press.

Darda, Joseph. 2014. "Introduction: Narratives of Exception in the Warfare State." *Literature Interpretation Theory* 25: 80–87.

Davidson, Cathy. 1986. *Revolution and the Word: The Rise of the Novel in America*. Oxford: Oxford University Press.

DeGuzmán, María. 2005. *Spain's Long Shadow: The Black Legend, Off-Whiteness, and Anglo-American Empire*. Minneapolis: University of Minnesota Press.

Delbanco, Andrew. 2005. *Melville: His World and His Work*. New York: Alfred A. Knopf.

Dennis, Rutledge M. 1995. "Social Darwinism, Scientific Racism, and the Metaphysics of Race." *Journal of Negro Education* 64 (3): 243–52.

Dowling, William C. 1990. *Poetry and Ideology in Revolutionary Connecticut*. Athens: University of Georgia Press.

Doyle, Laura. 2008. *Freedom's Empire: Race and the Rise of the Novel in Atlantic Modernity, 1640–1940*. Durham, NC: Duke University Press.

Duno Gottberg, Luis. 2003. *Solventando las diferencias: La ideología del mestizaje en Cuba*. Madrid: Iberoamericana; Frankfurt am Main: Vervuert.

Elbert, Monika. 2013. "The Paradox of Catholicism in New England Women's Gothic." In *Transnational Gothic: Literary and Social Exchanges in the Long Nineteenth Century*, edited by Monika Elbert and Bridget M. Marshall, 113–36. Burlington, VT: Ashgate.

Elbert, Monika M., Julie E. Hall, and Katharine Rodier, eds. 2006. Introduction to *Reinventing the Peabody Sisters*, vii–xxi. Iowa City: University of Iowa Press.

Emery, Allan Moore. 1984. "'Benito Cereno' and Manifest Destiny." *Nineteenth-Century Literature* 39 (1): 48–68.

Ewart, Mike. 1977. "Cooper and the American Revolution: The Non-Fiction." *Journal of American Studies* 11 (1): 61–79.

Fanuzzi, Robert. 2012. "Lincoln's Hemispheric Relations." In *The Cambridge Companion to Abraham Lincoln*, edited by Shirley Samuels, 183–94. Cambridge: Cambridge University Press.

Fernández Retamar, Roberto. 1989. "Against the Black Legend." In *Caliban and Other Essays*, 56–73. Minneapolis: University of Minnesota Press.

Fiedler, Leslie. 1997. *Love and Death in the American Novel*. Normal, IL: Dalkey.

Fishkin, Shelley Fisher. 2005. "Crossroads of Cultures: The Transnational Turn in American Studies." *American Quarterly* 57 (1): 17–57.

Fitz, Earl E. 1991. *Rediscovering the New World: Inter-American Literature in a Comparative Context*. Iowa City: University of Iowa Press.

Fliegelman, Jay. 1982. *Prodigals and Pilgrims: The American Revolution against Patriarchal Authority, 1750–1800*. Cambridge: Cambridge University Press.

Foner, Philip S. 1972. *The Spanish-Cuban-American War and the Birth of American Imperialism, 1895–1902*. 2 vols. New York: Monthly Review Press.

Ford, Arthur L. 1971. *Joel Barlow*. New York: Twayne.

Fredericksson, George M. 1987. *The Black Image in the White Mind: The Debate on*

Afro-American Character and Destiny, 1817–1914. 1971. Middletown, CT: Wesleyan University Press.

Gibson, Charles, ed. 1971. Introduction to *The Black Legend: Anti-Spanish Attitudes in the Old World and the New*, 3–27. New York: Knopf.

Gilroy, Paul. 1993. *The Black Atlantic: Modernity and Double-Consciousness*. Cambridge, MA: Harvard University Press.

———. 2000. *Against Race: Imagining Political Culture beyond the Color Line*. Cambridge, MA: Belknap Press of Harvard University Press.

Goodfellow, Donald M. 1940. "The Sources of *Mercedes of Castile*." *American Literature* 12: 318–28.

Goudie, Sean X. 2006. *Creole America: The West Indies and the Formation of Literature and Culture in the New Republic*. Philadelphia: University of Pennsylvania Press.

Greer, Margaret, Walter D. Mignolo, and Maureen Quilligan, eds. 2007. Introduction to *Rereading the Black Legend: The Discourses of Religious and Racial Difference in the Renaissance Empires*. Chicago: University of Chicago Press.

Grejda, Edward S. 1974. *The Common Continent of Men: Racial Equality in the Writing of Herman Melville*. Port Washington, NY: Kennikat Press.

Gruesz, Kirsten Silva. 2002. *Ambassadors of Culture: The Transamerican Origins of Latino Writing*. Princeton, NJ: Princeton University Press.

Guterl, Matthew Pratt. 2006. "'I Went to the West Indies': Race, Place, and the Antebellum South." *American Literary History* 18 (3): 446–67.

Gutiérrez de la Solana, Alberto. 1988. "Literatura y destierro: Una carta inédita de José Antonio Saco." *Círculo* 17: 97–105.

Halpern, Faye. 2008. "In Defense of Reading Badly: The Politics of Identification in 'Benito Cereno,' *Uncle Tom's Cabin*, and Our Classrooms." *College English* 70 (6): 551–77.

Hanrahan, Heidi. 2013. "'Worthy the imitation of the whites': Sarah Winnemucca and Mary Peabody Mann's Collaboration." *MELUS* 38 (1): 119–36.

Harthorn, Steven P. 2004. "Truth and Consequences: James Fenimore Cooper on Scott, Columbus, Bumppo, and Professional Authorship." *James Fenimore Cooper Society Miscellaneous Papers* 20: 1–10.

Havard, John C. 2015. "John Rollin Ridge's *Joaquín Murieta*: Sensation, Hispanicism, and Cosmopolitanism." *Western American Literature* 49 (4): 321–49.

———. 2016. "Mary Peabody Mann's *Juanita* and Martin R. Delany's *Blake*: Cuba, Urban Slavery, and the Construction of Nation." *College Literature* 43 (3): 509–41.

Herbert, T. Walter, Jr. 1980. *Marquesan Encounters: Melville and the Meaning of Civilization*. Cambridge, MA: Harvard University Press.

Hofstadter, Richard. 1941. "William Graham Sumner, Social Darwinist." *New England Quarterly* 14 (93): 457–77.

Holmes, Stephen. 1993. *The Anatomy of Antiliberalism*. Cambridge, MA: Harvard University Press.

Horsman, Reginald. 1981. *Race and Manifest Destiny: The Origins of American Racial Anglo-Saxonism*. Cambridge, MA: Harvard University Press.

Iglesias, Luis. 2011. "Pirates, Patriots, and the Mexican War: *Jack Tier* and Cooper's Argument with the Nation." *Literature in the Early American Republic: Annual Studies on Cooper and His Contemporaries* 3: 173–96.

Ignatiev, Noel. 1995. *How the Irish Became White*. New York: Routledge.

Jakšić, Iván. 2007. *The Hispanic World and American Intellectual Life, 1820–1880*. New York: Palgrave Macmillan.

Johannsen, Robert W. 1985. *To the Halls of the Montezumas: The Mexican War in the American Imagination*. Oxford: Oxford University Press.

Johnson, John J. 1993. *Latin America in Caricature*. Austin: University of Texas Press.

Jones, Robert F. 1992. *"The King of the Alley": William Duer, Politician, Entrepreneur, and Speculator, 1768–1799*. Philadelphia: American Philosophical Society.

Juderías, Julián. 1926. *La leyenda negra: Estudios acerca del concepto de España en el extranjero*. 1914. 7th ed. Barcelona: Araluce.

Kaplan, Amy. 1993a. "Black and Blue on San Juan Hill." In *Cultures of United States Imperialism*, edited by Amy Kaplan and Donald E. Pease, 219–36. Durham, NC: Duke University Press.

———. 1993b. "'Left Alone with America': The Absence of Empire in the Study of American Culture." In *Cultures of United States Imperialism*, edited by Amy Kaplan and Donald E. Pease, 3–21. Durham, NC: Duke University Press.

———. 1998. "Manifest Domesticity." *American Literature* 70 (3): 581–606.

———. 2002. *The Anarchy of Empire in the Making of U.S. Culture*. Cambridge, MA: Harvard University Press.

Karcher, Carolyn L. 1980. *Shadow over the Promised Land: Slavery, Race, and Violence in Melville's America*. Baton Rouge: Louisiana State University Press.

Kavanagh, James H. 1986. "That Hive of Subtlety: 'Benito Cereno' and the Liberal Hero." In *Ideology and Classic American Literature*, edited by Sacvan Bercovitch and Myra Jehlen, 352–84. Cambridge: Cambridge University Press.

Kierner, Cynthia. 2007. Introduction to *The Contrast*, by Royall Tyler. New York: New York University Press.

Kirk, Russell. 1982. Introduction to *The Portable Conservative Reader*, edited by Russell Kirk. New York: Viking Press.

———. 2001. *The Conservative Mind: From Burke to Eliot*. 1953. 7th rev. ed. Washington, DC: Regnery.

LaFeber, Walter. 1998. *The New Empire: An Interpretation of American Expansion, 1860–1898*. 1963. Ithaca, NY: Cornell University Press.

Larkin, Jack. 2013. "What He Did for Love." *Common-Place* 13 (3). Accessed January 28, 2014, http://www.common-place-archives.org/vol-13/no-03/larkin/.

Lazo, Rodrigo. 2005. *Writing to Cuba: Filibustering and Cuban Exiles in the United States*. Chapel Hill: University of North Carolina Press.

———. 2006. "Against the Cuba Guide: The 'Cuba Journal,' *Juanita*, and Travel Writing." In *Reinventing the Peabody Sisters*, edited by Monika M. Elbert, Julie E. Hall, and Katharine Rodier, 180–95. Iowa City: University of Iowa Press.

Levander, Caroline F., and Robert S. Levine. 2008. "Introduction: Essays beyond the Nation." In *Hemispheric American Studies*, edited by Caroline F. Levander and Robert S. Levine, 1–17. New Brunswick, NJ: Rutgers University Press.

Levine, Robert S. 1989. *Conspiracy and Romance: Studies in Brockden Brown, Cooper, Hawthorne, and Melville*. Cambridge: Cambridge University Press.

———. 2008. *Dislocating Race and Nation: Episodes in Nineteenth-Century American Literary Nationalism*. Chapel Hill: University of North Carolina Press.

Levinson, Marjorie. 2007. "What Is New Formalism?" *PMLA* 122 (2): 558–69.

Locke, John. 1980. *Second Treatise of Government*. 1689. Indianapolis: Hackett.

Lounsbury, Thomas R. 1882. *James Fenimore Cooper*. Boston: Houghton, Mifflin.

Luiggi, Alice Houston. 1965. *The 65 Valiants*. Gainesville: University of Florida Press.

Macpherson, C. B. 1980. *Burke*. New York: Hill and Wang.

Madison, Robert D. 1985. "Cooper's Columbus." *James Fenimore Cooper: His Country and His Art* 5: 75–85.

Mann, Barbara. 2007. "Race Traitor: Cooper, His Critics, and Nineteenth-Century Literary Politics." In *A Historical Guide to James Fenimore Cooper*, edited by Leland S. Person, 155–86. Oxford: Oxford University Press.

Marshall, Megan. 2005. *The Peabody Sisters: Three Women Who Ignited American Romanticism*. Boston: Houghton Mifflin.

McWilliams, John P., Jr. 1989. *The American Epic: Transforming a Genre, 1770–1860*. Cambridge: Cambridge University Press.

Menand, Louis. 2000. *The Metaphysical Club*. New York: Farrar, Strauss, and Giroux.

Michael, John. 2008. *Identity and the Failure of America: From Thomas Jefferson to the War on Terror*. Minneapolis: University of Minnesota Press.

Morrison, Toni. 1989. "Unspeakable Things Unspoken: The Afro-American Presence in American Literature." *Michigan Quarterly Review* 28 (1): 1–34.

———. 1993. *Playing in the Dark: Whiteness and the Literary Imagination*. New York: Vintage.

Mukherjee, Sahana, Ludwin E. Molina, and Glenn Adams. 2013. "'Reasonable Suspicion' about Tough Immigration Legislation: Enforcing Laws or Ethnocentric Exclusion?" *Cultural Diversity and Ethnic Minority Psychology* 19 (3): 320–31.

Naranjo Orovio, Consuelo. 2001–3. "La otra Cuba: Colonización blanca y diversificación agrícola." *Contrastes: Revista de historia* 12: 5–20.

Navarro García, Luis. 1994. "Patriotismo y autonomismo en José Antonio Saco." *Anuario de estudios americanos* 51 (2): 135–54.

Nelson, Dana D. 1993. *The Word in Black and White: Reading Race in American Literature, 1638–1867*. New York: Oxford University Press.

———. 1998. *National Manhood: Capitalist Citizenship and the Imagined Fraternity of White Men*. Durham, NC: Duke University Press.

Newman, Lea Bertani Vozar. 1986. *A Reader's Guide to the Short Stories of Herman Melville*. Boston: G. K. Hall.

Norton, Anne. 1988. *Reflections on Political Identity*. Baltimore: Johns Hopkins University Press.

Notestein, Robert B. 1955. "The Moralist Rigorism of W. G. Sumner." *Journal of the History of Ideas* 16 (3): 389–400.

Oberholtzer, Ellis Paxson. 1906. *The Literary History of Philadelphia*, 273. Philadelphia: George W. Jacobs.

Opatrný, Josef. 1993. *U.S. Expansionism and Cuban Annexationism in the 1850s*. Lewiston, NY: Edwin Mellen Press.

———. 1994. "José Antonio Saco's Path toward the Idea of *Cubanidad*." *Cuban Studies* 24: 39–56.

Ortiz, Fernando. 1928. Prologue. In *Contra la anexión*, by José Antonio Saco. Edited by Fernando Ortiz. Vol. 1. Havana: Imprenta de cultural.

Otter, Samuel. 2008. "An Aesthetics in All Things." *Representations* 104: 116–25.

Pearce, Roy Harvey. 1959. "Toward an American Epic." *Hudson Review* 12 (3): 362–77.

———. 1965. *The Savages of America: A Study of the Indian and the Idea of Civilization*. Rev. ed. Baltimore: Johns Hopkins University Press.

Pease, Donald E. 2009. "Re-thinking 'American Studies after US Exceptionalism.'" *American Literary History* 21 (1): 19–27.

Person, Leland S., ed. 2007. Introduction to *A Historical Guide to James Fenimore Cooper*, 3–26. Oxford: Oxford University Press.

Pérez, Louis A., Jr. 1990. *Cuba and the United States: Ties of Singular Intimacy*. Athens: University of Georgia Press.

———. 2008. *Cuba in the American Imagination: Metaphor and the Imperial Ethos*. Chapel Hill: University of North Carolina Press.

Philbrick, Nathaniel T. 1961. *James Fenimore Cooper and the Development of American Sea Fiction*. Cambridge, MA: Harvard University Press.

Pike, Fredrick B. 1992. *The United States and Latin America: Myths and Stereotypes of Civilization and Nature*. Austin: University of Texas Press.

Pitt, Leonard. 1966. *The Decline of the Californios: A Social History of the Spanish-Speaking Californians, 1846–1890*. Berkeley: University of California Press.

Pocock, J. G. A. 2003. *The Machiavellian Moment: Florentine Political Thought and the Atlantic Republican Tradition*. 1975. Princeton, NJ: Princeton University Press.

Posnock, Ross. 1998. *Color and Culture: Black Writers and the Making of the Modern Intellectual*. Cambridge, MA: Harvard University Press.

Post-Lauria, Sheila. 1995. "Editorial Politics in Herman Melville's 'Benito Cereno.'" *American Periodicals* 5: 1–13.

Quinton, Anthony. 1978. *The Politics of Imperfection: The Religious and Secular Traditions of Conservative Thought in England from Hooker to Oakeshott*. London: Faber and Faber.

Railton, Stephen. 1978. *Fenimore Cooper: A Study of His Life and Imagination*. Princeton, NJ: Princeton University Press.

Ringe, Donald. 1962. *James Fenimore Cooper*. New York: Twayne.

Riss, Arthur. 2006. *Race, Slavery, and Liberalism in Nineteenth-Century American Literature*. Cambridge: Cambridge University Press.

Robbins, Sarah. 1997. "Gendering the History of the Antislavery Narrative: Juxtaposing *Uncle Tom's Cabin* and 'Benito Cereno,' *Beloved* and *Middle Passage*." *American Quarterly* 49 (3): 531–73.

Rodríguez, Jaime Javier. 2010. *The Literatures of the U.S.-Mexican War: Narrative, Time, and Identity*. Austin: University of Texas Press.

Rosenthal, Debra J. 2004. "Race Mixture and the Representation of Indians in the

Andes: *Cumandá, Aves sin nido, The Last of the Mohicans*, and *Ramona*." In *Mixing Race, Mixing Culture: Inter-American Literary Dialogues*, edited by Monika Kaup and Debra J. Rosenthal, 122–40. Austin: University of Texas Press.

Rowe, John Carlos. 2000. *Literary Culture and U.S. Imperialism: From the Revolution to World War II*. Oxford: Oxford University Press.

Ruttenberg, Nancy. 1998. *Democratic Personality: Popular Voice and the Trial of American Authorship*. Stanford, CA: Stanford University Press.

Said, Edward. 1979. *Orientalism*. New York: Vintage.

Saldívar, José David. 2000. "Looking Awry at 1898: Roosevelt, Montejo, Paredes, and Mariscal." *American Literary History* 12 (3): 386–406.

Sbriglia, Russell. 2013. "Dissensus Communis: Conservatism, Skepticism, and Sympathy in the American Renaissance." PhD diss., University of Rochester.

Schmidt-Nowara, Christopher. 2001. "The Specter of Las Casas: José Antonio Saco and the Persistence of Spanish Colonialism in Cuba." *Itinerario* 25 (2): 93–109.

Schoultz, Lars. 2009. *That Infernal Little Cuban Republic: The United States and the Cuban Revolution*. Chapel Hill: University of North Carolina Press.

Schultz, Dieter. 1991. "Cooper's Knight of Columbus; *Mercedes of Castile* as Chivalric Romance." *Letterature d'America* 44: 31–46.

Schwabe, Klaus. 1986. "The Global Role of the United States and Its Imperial Consequences, 1898–1973." In *Imperialism and After: Continuities and Discontinuities*, edited by Wolfgang J. Mommsen and Jürgen Osterhammel, 12–33. London: Allen and Unwin.

Shepherd, William R. 1918. "Bolivar and the United States." *Hispanic American Historical Review* 1 (3): 270–98.

Shields, David S. 1990. *Oracles of Empire: Poetry, Politics, and Commerce in British America, 1690–1750*. Chicago: University of Chicago Press.

———. 2006. "'We declare you independent whether you wish it or not': The Print Culture of Early Filibusterism." *Proceedings of the American Antiquarian Society* 116 (2): 233–59.

Sioli, Marco. 2003. "Liberty and Nature: Joel Barlow's Diplomatic Mission in Algiers." In *America and the Mediterranean*, edited by M. Bacigalupo and P. Castagneto, 551–57. Turin: Otto Editore.

Spiller, Robert E. 1965. *James Fenimore Cooper*. Minneapolis: University of Minnesota Press.

Streeby, Shelley. 2002. *American Sensations: Class, Empire, and the Production of Popular Culture*. Berkeley: University of California Press.

Sundquist, Eric J. 1993. *To Wake the Nations: Race in the Making of American Literature*. Cambridge, MA: Harvard University Press.

Sutton, Walter. 1980. "Apocalyptic History and the American Epic: Cotton Mather and Joel Barlow." In *Toward a New American Literary History*, edited by Louis J. Budd, Edwin H. Cady, and Carl L. Anderson, 69–83. Durham, NC: Duke University Press.

Tawil, Ezra. 2006. *The Making of Racial Sentiment: Slavery and the Birth of the Frontier Romance*. Cambridge: Cambridge University Press.

Van Wagenen, Michael Scott. 2012. *Remembering the Forgotten War: The Enduring Legacies of the U.S.-Mexican War*. Amherst: University of Massachusetts Press.

Velleman, Barry L. 2001. Introduction to *"My Dear Sir": Mary Mann's Letters to Sarmiento (1865–1881)*, 1–33. Buenos Aires: Instituto Cultural Argentino Norte-americano.

Walker, Jeffrey. 2010. "Reading Rose Budd; or, Tough Sledding in *Jack Tier*." *James Fenimore Cooper Society Miscellaneous Papers* 27: 11–14.

Wallace, James D. 1995. "Race and Captivity in *The Wept of Wish-ton-Wish*." *American Literary History* 7 (2): 189–209.

Wardrop, Stephanie. 1997. "Last of the Red-Hot Mohicans: Miscegenation in the Popular American Romance." *MELUS* 22 (2): 61–74.

Wertheimer, Eric. 1999. *Imagined Empires: Incas, Aztecs, and the New World of American Literature, 1771–1876*. Cambridge: Cambridge University Press.

White, Ed. 2004. "Early American Nations as Imagined Communities." *American Quarterly* 56 (1): 49–81.

Williams, Amy L., et al. 2014. "Sequence Variants in SLC16A11 Are a Common Risk Factor for Type 2 Diabetes in Mexico." *Nature* 506 (7486): 97–101.

Windell, Maria. 2014. "Moor, *Mulata*, Mulatta: Sentimentalism, Racialization, and Benevolent Imperialism in Mary Peabody Mann's *Juanita*." *J19: The Journal of Nineteenth-Century Americanists* 2 (2): 301–29.

Wood, Gordon S. 1972. *Creation of the American Republic, 1776–1787*. New York: Norton.

Woodress, James Leslie. 1958. *Yankee's Odyssey: Life of Joel Barlow*. London: Greenwood.

Yellin, Jean Fagan. 1970. "Black Masks: Melville's 'Benito Cereno.'" *American Quarterly* 22 (3): 678–89.

Zunder, Theodore Albert. 1969. *The Early Days of Joel Barlow: A Connecticut Wit—Yale Graduate, Editor, Lawyer, and Poet Chaplain during the Revolution War*. New Haven, CT: Yale University Press.

Index